ISBN 978-1-334-06322-0
PIBN 10581549

This book is a reproduction of an important historical work. Forgotten Books uses
state-of-the-art technology to digitally reconstruct the work, preserving the original format
whilst repairing imperfections present in the aged copy. In rare cases, an imperfection in
the original, such as a blemish or missing page, may be replicated in our edition. We do,
however, repair the vast majority of imperfections successfully; any imperfections that
remain are intentionally left to preserve the state of such historical works.

1 MONTH OF
FREE
READING

at
www.ForgottenBooks.com

By purchasing this book you are
eligible for one month membership to
ForgottenBooks.com, giving you
unlimited access to our entire
collection of over 700,000 titles via
our web site and mobile apps.

To claim your free month visit:

www.forgottenbooks.com/free581549

English
Français
Deutsche
Italiano
Español
Português

www.forgottenbooks.com

Mythology Photography **Fiction**
Fishing Christianity **Art** Cooking
Essays Buddhism Freemasonry
Medicine **Biology** Music **Ancient**
Egypt Evolution Carpentry Physics
Dance Geology **Mathematics** Fitness
Shakespeare **Folklore** Yoga Marketing
Confidence Immortality Biographies
Poetry **Psychology** Witchcraft
Electronics Chemistry History **Law**
Accounting **Philosophy** Anthropology
Alchemy Drama Quantum Mechanics
Atheism Sexual Health **Ancient History**
Entrepreneurship Languages Sport
Paleontology Needlework Islam
Metaphysics Investment Archaeology
Parenting Statistics Criminology
Motivational

THE STONOR LETTERS
AND PAPERS

1290-1483

EDITED, FOR THE ROYAL HISTORICAL SOCIETY, FROM THE
ORIGINAL DOCUMENTS IN THE PUBLIC RECORD OFFICE

BY

CHARLES LETHBRIDGE KINGSFORD

M.A., F.S.A.

VOL. I.

CAMDEN THIRD SERIES
VOL. XXIX.

LONDON
OFFICES OF THE SOCIETY
22 RUSSELL SQUARE, W.C. 1
1919

CONTENTS OF VOL. I.

GENEALOGICAL TABLES.

THE S[TONO]R FAMILY.

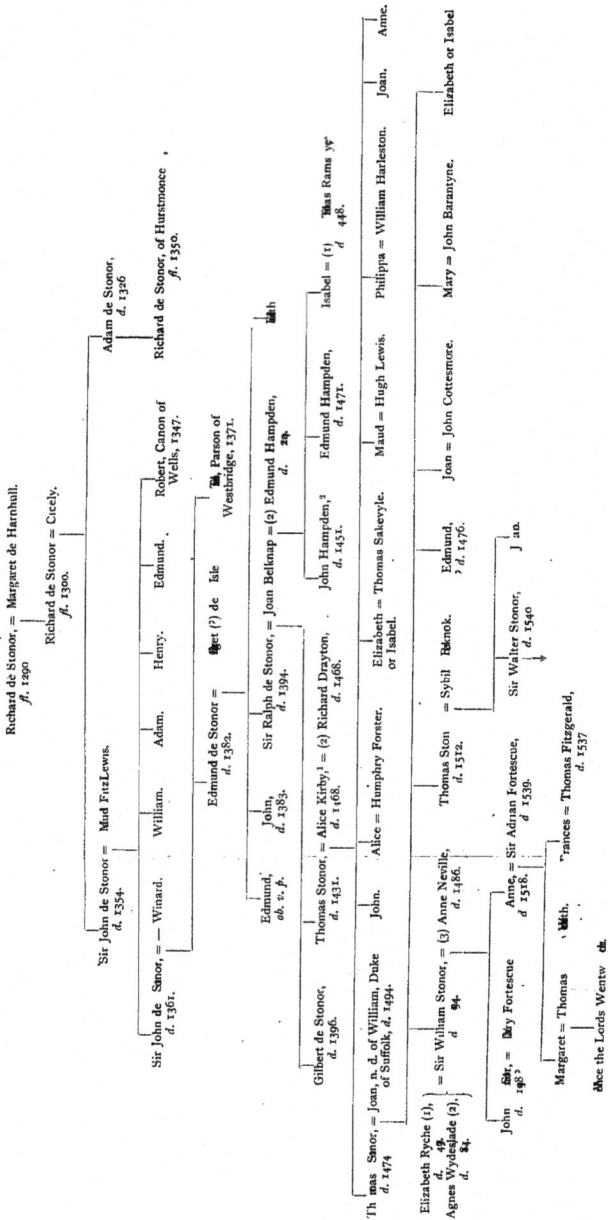

Richard de Stonor, = Margaret de Harnhull. *fl.* 1290.

Richard de Stonor = Cicely. *fl.* 1300.

Adam de Stonor, *d.* 1326.

Richard de Stonor, of Hurstmonceux, *fl.* 1350.

Sir John de Stonor = Maud FitzLewis. *d.* 1354.

William.   Adam.   Henry.   Edmund.   Robert, Canon of Wells, 1347.

Sir John de Stonor, = —— Winard. *d.* 1361.

Edmund de Stonor = *d.* 1382.

..., Parson of Westbridge, 1371.

...(?) de Isle

John, *d.* 1385.

Sir Ralph de Stonor, = Joan Belknap = (2) Edmund Hampden, *d.* 1394.   *d.* 14..

Edmund, *ob. v. p.*

Thomas Stonor, = Alice Kirby,[1] = (2) Richard Drayton, *d.* 1431.   *d.* 1468.

John Hampden,[2] *d.* 1451.

Edmund Hampden, *d.* 1471.

Isabel = (1) ... Thomas Ramsey yᵉ *d* 448.

Gilbert de Stonor, *d.* 1396.

John.   Alice = Humphry Forster.

Elizabeth = Thomas Sakevyle. or Isabel.

Maud = Hugh Lewis.

Philippa = William Harleston.   Joan.   Anne.

Thomas Ston..., = Joan, n. d. of William, Duke of Suffolk, *d.* 1494. *d.* 1474.

Thomas Ston... = Sybil Babok. *d.* 1512.

Edmund, *d.* 1476.

Joan = John Cottesmore.

Mary = John Barantyne.

Elizabeth or Isabel.

Elizabeth Ryche (1), *d.* ... = Sir William Stonor, (3) Anne Neville, *d.* 1486.

Agnes Wydeslade (2), *d.* ...

Sir Walter Stonor, *d.* 1540.

John, = Mary Fortescue, *d.* 148..?

Anne, = Sir Adrian Fortescue, *d.* 1539. *d.* 1518.

Frances = Thomas Fitzgerald, *d.* 1537.

Joan

Margaret = Thomas ...

Alice the Lords Wentw...

---

[1] Alice Kirby probably had daughters by Richard Drayton. p. xxii.

[2] Father of Thomas Hampden. See No...

[3] Father of Tho[ma]s Ramsey (*d.* 1509). See Nos. 144, 57, 177, 179.

INTRODUCTION.

THE Stonor Family was certainly established at Stonor in Oxfordshire about five miles north of Henley early in the reign of Edward I, and no doubt derived its name from the place at which it has now had its home for over six centuries. The history of the family begins with Richard de Stonor, who about 1290 granted to Richard, his son and heir, and to Cicely, his son's wife, a half virgate of land in Bixbrand,[1] a manor which was then and long afterwards connected with Stonor. Richard the elder married Margaret, daughter and heiress of Sir John de Harnhull.[2] Of Richard the younger we know no more than the name of his wife, by whom he had two sons, John and Adam, and the bald fact that in 1291 he acquired some land at Goldore near Watlington.[3]

The elder son of Richard the younger was Sir John de Stonor, who was, with two intervals, Chief Justice of the Common Pleas for five and twenty years. He was the founder of the fortunes of his family and the most notable name in its history. Since he must have been of full age when he purchased the wardship of Thomas de la Hay at Henbury in 1307,[4] and was a serjeant-at-law in 1313, he was probably born not later than 1285; and since he did not resign his office as Chief Justice till shortly before his death in 1354, it is not likely that the date of his birth was more than a few years earlier.

During the early part of the reign of Edward II, John de Stonor occurs frequently as an advocate in the Year Books, and in 1313 he

[1] No. 1.
[2] Pedigree *ap.* NASH, *Worcestershire*, i, 2; the pedigree is not quite accurate, but John de Harnhull lived in the reign of Edward I, and his daughter no doubt married Richard de Stonor.
[3] *Ancient Deeds*, C. 294: see vol. ii, p. 171.
[4] *Id.*, C. 1185: see vol. ii, p. 171.

was summoned to attend in Parliament as one of the Serjeants-at-law. On 24th September, 1314, he was appointed on a commission to inquire into allegations against the sheriffs in the counties of Gloucester, Hereford, and Worcester.[1]   From 1316 onwards, he was employed on a variety of commissions relating to the ordinary administration of justice.[2] A more important service was his appointment on 26th June, 1319, as one of the justices to inquire into the alleged misgovernment of the Channel Islands under Otho de Grandison ; this inquiry was of long duration and of great importance for the constitutional history of the Islands.[3]   It marked the conclusion of Stonor's judicial apprenticeship, and had not been long completed when on 16th October, 1320, he was appointed one of the Justices of the Common Pleas.[4]

John de Stonor was no doubt a trusted official, who served without any political opinions of his own.   No special significance can, therefore, be attached to his employment to pass judgment on the two Roger Mortimers in July, 1322, or to hold an inquiry concerning persons who had aided the King's rebels in the West Midlands in December, 1323.[5] Nevertheless he must have been in the confidence of Edward II and his minister, Hugh le Despencer, for on 8th July, 1324 (before which date he had been knighted), he was one of those appointed to treat with the French King for a meeting, and for the surrender of the Castle of Mompezat in Gascony.[6]   He did not, however, leave England at this time, and his name appears in various commissions between July, 1324, and January, 1325.   On 6th February, 1325, he was appointed with Arnold Guhlelmi de Byarn, William de Weston, and Peter de Galiciano to treat for marriages between the King's son and Eleanor, sister of Alfonso, King of Castile, and between Alfonso himself and the English princess, Eleanor, eldest daughter of Edward II.[7]   Stonor and his colleagues left England on 15th February, and were at Valladolid in Easter-week (7th-14th April), when he wrote home with news of their progress.[8] Stonor's allowance for his expenses from 15th February to 27th August, on which day he returned to England, was at the rate of 6s. 8d. for each day at sea, and 13s. 4d. for each day on land.[9]

During the last year of the reign of Edward II, Stonor continued in

[1] *Cal. Pat. Rolls*, Edw. II, ii, 244.   [2] *Id.*, ii, 580, 598, 678, 686, etc.
[3] *Trans. Royal Hist. Soc.*, 3rd series, iii, 166-67.
[4] *Cal. Pat. Rolls*, Edw. II, iii, 508.
[5] *Id.*, iv, 249, 385.   [6] *Id.*, v, 1 ; *Foedera*, ii, 559.
[7] *Id.*, ii, 587; *Cal. Pat. Rolls*, v, 84, 103 ; *Cal. Close Rolls*, iv, 344, 350.   •
[8] No. 2.   [9] *Cal. Close Rolls*, iv, 417.

favour; he was employed in the summer of 1326 on inquisitions in Staffordshire as to unlawful assemblies against the King's peace, and on 7th October, 1326, was appointed Keeper of the Castle of Wallingford.[1] That his action was purely official is shewn by his reappointment as Justice of the Common Pleas, after the deposition of Edward II, on 31st January, 1327.[2] In the autumn of that year, he was one of the Justices sent to try the rioters at Bury St. Edmund's,[3] and in January, 1328, had similar employment as to the disturbances at Abingdon Abbey. On 22nd February, 1329, Stonor was appointed Chief Baron of the Exchequer, but on 3rd September following, returned to the Common Pleas as Chief Justice.[4] In 1330 he was employed on the trial of the adherents of the Earl of Kent.[5] In spite of his close association with the government under Isabella and Mortimer, he continued in office as Chief Justice till 2nd March, 1331.[6] His removal on that date can hardly have been political, for on 1st April he was appointed Second Justice.[7] That he was not in disfavour is further shewn by the pardon granted to him on 25th June, 1331, in consideration of his services and expenses for the late and present king, of the yearly farm of 45l. in respect of the Manor of Ermington.[8] On 16th July, 1334, he vacated his office as Justice of the Bench, but was still employed on various commissions till his reappointment on 7th July, 1335, as Chief Justice of the Common Pleas.[9] It was whilst he was out of office that the Prior of Christchurch, Canterbury, suggested that Stonor should be asked to accept the post of Seneschal of the Monastery, as one who was "prudent, well-known, and beloved amongst the great". In June, 1335, the archbishop informed the Prior that Sir John de Stonor, whilst expressing his goodwill, had for many reasons begged to be excused.[10]

The only important event of Stonor's later years was his implication in the ministerial crisis of 1340, when he was one of those who, on the King's sudden return from Flanders in November, were removed from office and committed to the Tower.[11] But after a short imprisonment he was restored to his office on 9th May, 1342.[12] He then held it without interruption till shortly before his death. On 22nd February,

[1] Cal. Close Rolls, iv, 456, 652; Cal. Pat. Rolls, v, 331.
[2] Id., Edw. III, i, 2.
[3] Memorials of St. Edmund's Abbey, ii, 348, 353; iii, 302.
[4] Cal. Pat. Rolls, i, 355, 439.   [5] Id., i, 556.
[6] Id., ii, 78.   [7] Id., ii, 102.
[8] Id., ii, 146.   [9] Id., iii, 39, 136, 351.
[10] Litterae Cantuarienses, ii, 84. 87, 98.
[11] Murimuth, Chron., p. 117.   [12] Cal. Pat. Rolls, v, 427.

1354, Stonor was directed to deliver the rolls of the Common Pleas to Roger Hillary; he was thanked for his many services, and, since weakness of body excused him from further travail in the office of justice, was discharged from the cares of the Court; but the King desired that he should still remain on the Privy Council.[1] Stonor died about six months later at the end of August,[2] and was buried in the choir of Dorchester Abbey in Oxfordshire.[3]

The dullness of the record of Sir John de Stonor's career is perhaps the best indication we can obtain as to the excellence of his good qualities. He was no doubt a prudent, trustworthy, and competent judge, who not concerning himself in politics was able to serve on the bench for over thirty years. It seems to have been sufficient for him that the prizes of his profession enabled him to amass great wealth.

Amongst the Stonor Letters there are three which were addressed to Sir John de Stonor, all of a formal character.[4] The letter which he wrote from Valladolid in 1325[5] is more interesting, but throws no light on his personality. In the *Litterae Cantuarienses*[6] there is a letter in which John de Stonor recommends a suitable person for the post of Seneschal, which he had himself declined.

From John de Stonor's career, we may turn with more interest to his family and to the means whereby he established its fortunes. He had one brother, Adam, who is styled Master Adam de Stonor on 2nd January, 1321.[7] Sir John de Stonor and Adam, his brother, had a grant of the Manors of Werpesgrave and Esyndon on 6th August, 1324.[8] On 12th July, 1326, Sir John de Stonor and Henry de Langebergh, parson of Werpesgrave, were acting as executors of Master Adam de Stonor.[9] Adam de Stonor was apparently the father of Richard de Stonor of Hurstmonceux,[10] on complaint of the breaking of whose park a commission of oyer et terminer was issued in May, 1340, at the instance of John de Stonor.[11] Richard de Stonor held one-sixth of a knight's fee at Westden, Sussex, in 1341,[12] and there is a reference to him as late as 1365, when

---

[1] *Cal. Close Rolls*, x, 4.

[2] The date of his death is given variously in the Inquisitions as 12, 24 or 31 August.

[3] Leland, *Itinerary*, i, 117: "there lyeth one Stoner, sumtyme a juge, as it apperithe by his habits".

[4] See Nos. 3 and 4.

[5] No. 2.

[6] *Litterae Cantuarienses*, ii, 108.

[7] *Cal. Pat. Rolls*, Edw. II, iii, 553.

[8] See vol. ii, p. 172.

[9] *Cal. Close Rolls*, Edw. II, iv, 632.

[10] See vol. ii, p. 166.

[11] *Cal. Pat. Rolls*, Edw. III, iv, 557.

[12] *Cal. Close Rolls*, Edw. III, vi, 150.

he acknowledges the receipt of muniments which had been in the charge of John de Stonor.[1] There does not seem to be any trace of descendants.

Sir John de Stonor married, before 1317, Maud FitzLewis,[2] who survived him. They had five or six sons; John, William, and Adam, sons of John de Stonor, are mentioned in 1354;[3] Henry and Edmund were parties with their father to a suit about messuages at Brightwell and Sotwell, Berks, in 1342;[4] Robert de Stonor, who was a canon of Wells in 1347[5] and Rector of Stanton Harcourt, Oxfordshire, in 1354,[6] was possibly another son. Of the second, John de Stonor, some account will be given in due course. Of the others, Henry is perhaps the Henry de "Stonnord," who held lands at "Stonnord," Oxfordshire, in 1361.[7] A James de Stonore was on the commission of peace in Cornwall in 1330,[8] and a Henry Stonard of Cornwall occurs in 1371.[9] But if they belonged to the same family their place in the pedigree is uncertain.

Some account of the family estates is necessary for the understanding of the documents here printed. Since the greater part of them were either inherited or acquired by Sir John de Stonor this is the most convenient place wherein to deal with them.

Stonor in OXFORDSHIRE was the original home of the family and has always been its principal seat; it is now in Pishill parish, but was anciently in Pyrton. With Stonor went Bix, including Bixbrand and Bixgebwyn. Watcombe was also a Stonor manor, and there were other lands in Oxfordshire at Watlington, and elsewhere.[10] At the Inquisition for Sir John de Stonor in 1362, the manor of Stonor and Bix was said to be held in demesne as of fee.[11] At the Inquisition after the death of Ralph de Stonor in 1394, it was found that Stonor was held of the Duke of Gloucester by service unknown, Bixgebwyn was held of the Earl of Oxford, Bixbraund and Brounesdon of the

---

[1] See vol. ii, p. 166 below. See also Brantingham, *Issue Rolls*, p. 188.

[2] *Ancient Deeds*, C. 3598, see vol. ii, p. 171 below; Nash, *Worcestershire*, i, 2. In the next century, Philip FitzLewis called Sir William Stonor his cousin. See No. 326. The *Visitation of Oxfordshire* (Harleian Society), p. 143, describes Sir John's wife as a daughter of the Lord Lisle; but this pedigree is very untrustworthy, and there seems to be a confusion with the wife of Edmund de Stonor.

[3] *Cal. Close Rolls*, x, 127.   [4] *Year Book*, 16 Edward III, i, 7-10; ii, 58.

[5] *Cal. Close Rolls*, viii, 264.   [6] *Cal. Pat. Rolls*, x, 67.

[7] *Id.*, Edw. III, xii, 102.   [8] *Id*, i, 567.   [9] *Id.*, xv, 171.

[10] See No. 137 giving the Oxfordshire lands of the second Thomas Stonor.

[11] *Ch. Inq. p.m.*, Edw. III, File 164.

Honour of Wallingford by knight service, and the Manor of Hoo, Watlington, of the King as of the Honour of Wallingford.[1]

Sir John de Stonor seems to have done something to consolidate his Oxfordshire estates by exchanging lands in Bixbraund, Bixgebwyn, Nettlebed, and Warberge or Warborough, with the Abbot of Dorchester for lands in Puryton or Pyrton.[2] He also acquired the Manor of Pushull (or Pishill) Venables from Peter de Werberton before 1335.[3]

Of Stonor House itself, in Sir John de Stonor's time, we know only that in 1349 he had licence for the alienation in mortmain of a suitable place within his manor of Stonor for the habitation of six chaplains, regular or secular, to celebrate divine service in the chapel founded within the manor in honour of the Holy Trinity, together with land not held in chief to the yearly value of 20l.[4] This is no doubt the chapel in the house at Stonor, to which there are several references in the next century.[5] At the Inquisition for the second John de Stonor in 1362 the house is described as a messuage with divers buildings and dovecotes.[6] It must have been of considerable size, for Edmund de Stonor was able to entertain Robert Tresilian and two other justices with their trains.[7] Edmund's grandson, the first Thomas Stonor, seems to have done much building in 1416-17, when Flemish workmen were employed "pro opere de Stonore," and 200,000 bricks were procured from Crockernend at a cost of 40l. together with 15l. for the expense of carriage to Stonor.[8] The Inventory of Heirlooms at Stonor in 1474[9] mentions the Hall, with its hangings of black say, the Little Chamber adjoining the Parlour, hanged with paled cloth of purple and green, three Chambers hanged with paled say of red and green, the Chamber at the nether end of the Hall, and the Parlour Chamber, which from the description of the furniture was perhaps the principal bedroom. There is also mention of the Buttery, Kitchen, and Bakehouse. In Elizabeth Stonor's letters [10] there are various references to chambers in the house. Richard Germyn refers to Sir William Stonor's "stode" at Stonor.[11] Sir William seems to have added to the house and improved the gardens.[12] The park was from an early time well-stocked with deer and game.[13] Leland writes of Stonor: "Ther is a fayre parke, and a

[1] Ch. Inq. p.m., Richard II, File 85.   [2] Cal. Pat. Rolls, Edw. II, ii, 569, 663.
[3] Cal. Close Rolls, Edw. III, iii, 499.   [4] Cal. Pat. Rolls, Edw. III, viii, 290.
[5] Nos. 140 and 157.   [6] Ch. Inq. p.m., Edw. III, File 164.
[7] See No. 19.   [8] See No. 41.   [9] See No. 140.
[10] See Nos. 172, 233.   [11] No. 285.
[12] See No. 260.   [13] See No. 255.

waren of connes, and fayre woods. The mansion place standithe clyminge on an hille, and ha:he two courtes buylded with tymber, brike and flynte. Syr Walter Stonor now pocessor of it bathe augmentyd and strengthed the howse." [1]

Stonor is so close to the county boundary that lands in BERKSHIRE were probably held at an early date. Sir John de Stonor acquired the Manor of Didcot in 1317 from Hugh de Blund.[2] In the same year he acquired land at Tilehurst.[3] His son held of the Abbot of Reading lands at Reading with the Manor of Bensheves and land at Tilehurst. He held Sotwell of the Bishop of Winchester as of the Manor of Brightwell, and the Manor of Didcot of the Honour of Wallingford.[4] Other lands were probably acquired later. Sir Ralph de Stonor in 1394 held lands at Arle (Erley), Burfield, Mapledurham, Shilele and Englefield.[5] The first Thomas Stonor purchased the reversion of the Manor of Burwardescote or Buscot,[6] which was bequeathed in 1474 to Edmund Stonor, but through his death shortly returned to his brother, Sir William.[7]

In BEDFORDSHIRE Sir John de Stonor, the judge, had land at Wylden,[8] which his descendants parted with at any early date.

In BUCKINGHAMSHIRE he had lands at Wendover, and at Bourton or Bierton near Aylesbury. The land at Wendover does not appear again. Bierton, with which went Stoke and Stokehallyng, seems to have been acquired in 1324 and 1329.[9] Ralph de Stonor had also lands at Stoke Mandeville and Walcote.[10] The first Thomas Stonor apparently sold Stoke.[11] His son sold Bierton to Sir Ralph Verney in 1469. The second Thomas Stonor at his death held no land in Buckinghamshire except for a tenement called Mosholes at Fawley.[12]

In DEVONSHIRE Sir John de Stonor acquired the Manor and Hundred of Ermington. In the reign of Edward I, this property belonged

[1] Leland, *Itinerary*, v, 72.
[2] *Cal. Pat. Rolls*, Edw. II, iii, 47; *Ancient Deeds*, C. 3598.
[3] *Id.*, C. 1710, see vol. ii, p. 171 below.
[4] *Ch. Inq. p.m.*, Edw. III, File 164.   [5] *Id.*, Richard II, File 85.
[6] Apparently in 1417, see No. 41.
[7] See Nos. 54, 137, and 228. No. 137 gives the lands of the second Thomas Stonor in Berkshire.
[8] *Ch. Inq. p.m.*, Edw. III, File 128.
[9] *Cal. Pat. Rolls*, Edw. II, ii, 434; *Ancient Deeds*, C. 231, see also vol. ii, p. 172 below.
[10] *Ch. Inq. p.m.*, Richard II, File 85.   [11] See No. 54.
[12] *Ch. Inq. p.m.*, Edw. IV, File 82.

to John Peverel.[1] Then it came into the possession of John de Benstead, who was a prominent official under Edward II. John de Stonor
obtained the custody of the lands of Benstead's heir at a farm of 45l.,
which was remitted to him in 1331.[2] Afterwards by some means he
obtained possession of the manor in his own right, and held it jointly
with his eldest son. In 1344 the Abbot of Buckfastleigh and others
encroached on the fishery of John de Stonor and John, his son, at
Ermington. Walter de Screcchesle, the steward, and Robert de
Cundicote, the bailiff of the manor, raised a hue and cry against them ;
then came Richard Giffard, bailiff of the Hundred, with his white wand
to attach the Abbot, who took away his wand, which was a trespass
against the franchise. In a suit two years later, Stonor recovered 30l.
against the Abbot.[3] In November, 1351, John de Stonor, the elder,
chivaler, and John de Stonor, the younger, chivaler, made complaint
that Robert de Ferers and others at " Ermyngham " had broken their
close, houses, chests and park, carried away horses, cattle, and sheep
worth 800l., killed stock worth 100 marks, carried away geese, etc.,
worth 100s., injured their crops and assaulted their servants.[4] In the
next century the Stonors had prolonged disputes with the Fortescues at
Ermington, and also as to the fishery.[5] Ermington was held by Sir John
de Stonor jointly with his son John, and Maud his wife, of Hugh de
Courtenay, Earl of Devon, by the service of one-third of a knight's fee
as of the Castle of Plympton.[6] It was valued in 1430 at 80 marks,[7]
and was one of the most important of the Stonor estates. The property
included the advowson of Ermington and of the free chapel in the
cemetery.[8] In the reign of Edward IV, Sir William Stonor held other
extensive lands in Devonshire in right of his second wife, Agnes Wydeslade, and retained part of them after her death.[9]

In GLOUCESTERSHIRE Sir John de Stonor held land at Condicote of
Matthew Fitzherbert, and at Henbury of the bishop of Worcester.[10]
Possibly these lands may have been the dower of Margaret de Harn-
hull. The other Gloucestershire estates, which were acquired by the

---

[1] *Ancient Deeds*, C. 4688, see vol. ii, p. 171 below. See also No. 45, and *Feudal
Aids*, i, 399.
[2] *Cal. Pat. Rolls*, Edw. III, ii, 146.   [3] *Year Book* 20, Edw. III, i, 236-56.
[4] *Cal. Pat. Rolls*, Edw. III, ix, 205-6.
[5] See Nos. 42, 45, 46, 63, 64, 71, 72, 79-82, 126, 127, and 184.
[6] *Feudal Aids*, i, 399 ; see also Nos. 38, 79, and 81.   [7] See No. 54.
[8] See Nos. 137, 279 284, 286, 291.   [9] See Nos. 272, 313, and p. xxxii below.
[10] *Ch. Inq. p.m.*, 28 Edw. III, File 128 ; cf. *Cal. Close Rolls*, Edw. III, x, 127,
and *Feudal Aids*, ii, 291.

Stonors somewhat later, were certainly part of her inheritance. Edmund de Stonor held Harnhull of the Earl of Buckingham as in right of his wife, Bourton of Edward le Despenser, Doughton of the King in chief, and Henbury of the bishop of Worcester.[1]

The chief estate in HAMPSHIRE was the Manor of Penyton Meysy or Penton Mewsy which Robert de Harnhull settled in 1323 with remainder to the heirs of John de Stonor.[2] Penton Mewsey and Foxcott only came into possession in the time of Edmund de Stonor. But Sir John de Stonor had held Asshe as of the Manor of Hampstead Marshal;[3] Edmund de Stonor sold it in 1370 to William of Wykeham.[4] Penton Mewsey was held of the Seymours, and Foxcott of the Pophams.[5] Sir William Stonor, about 1479, bought other Hampshire property at Nurseling.[6]

In KENT Sir John de Stonor held a small amount of land of the Abbot of Lesnes;[7] it does not seem to have been retained by his descendants. The more important estate of Horton Kirby came to the Stonors by the marriage of Thomas Stonor to Alice Kirby in the reign of Henry V. Thomas Stonor acquired other property in the same county.[8]

In LINCOLNSHIRE Sir John de Stonor held the Manor of Repinghale of Sir Thomas Roos as of the Manor of Dowsby, the Manor of Walcote as of the Abbot of Peterborough, with other lands in Hacomby and Kirkby.[9] He had acquired this property before 1327[10] from John, son of Adam, son of John de Repinghale, with whom he was engaged in a law-suit about it in 1333.[11] Repinghale and all the Lincolnshire lands were sold by the first Thomas Stonor in 1425.[12]

In the City of LONDON Sir John de Stonor acquired before 1348 from Margery, late wife of Sir William Lovel, a messuage in the Lane of St. Peter the Little. At his death it was valued at 50s. 8d.[13] This is probably the hostel which Edmund de Stonor was asked to lend to Henry le Scrope.[14] At Sir Ralph de Stonor's death it was valued at 100s., and

---

[1] Ch. Inq. p.m., 5 Richard II, File 21.   [2] V.C.H., Hampshire, iv, 382.
[3] Feudal Aids, ii, 329; Ch. Inq. p.m., Edw. III, File 164.
[4] Cal. Close Rolls, Edw. III, xiii, 195-99.
[5] Ch. Inq. p.m., Richard II, Files 21, 61, 85.   [6] See Nos. 304, 305, 323, 325.
[7] Ch. Inq. p.m., Edw. III, File 128.   [8] See No. 54.
[9] Feudal Aids, iii, 203.   [10] See vol. ii, p. 177 below.
[11] Cal. Close Rolls, Edw. III, iii, 163.
[12] Ancient Deeds, C. 1223, see vol. ii, p. 173 below.
[13] Ch. Inq. p.m., Edw. III, File 128.   [14] See No. 33.

in 1395 his widow had a writ of livery of dower in respect of it.[1]   It was sold shortly before the death of the first Thomas Stonor.[2]

Sir John de Stonor had another London residence at Westminster, which was afterwards ca led "La Mote". He acquired it on 29th September, 1334, from William, son of William, son of Sir Edward Charles.[3] Joan, the widow of the elder William Charles, held in 1305 a messuage and 32 acres of land of the Abbot of Westminster rendering 10s. to him, 5s. to the Church of St. Margaret, and 10d. to Master William de Wauden.[4] At Stonor's death in 1354 he was found to have held a messuage and sixty acres of land with their appurtenances in Westminster, rendering 10s. to the Abbot. In 1334 the property was described as situate in the vills of Westminster and Eye; so it probably lay between the Abbey and Ebury. In 1382 Edmund de Stonor had 20s. annual rent from four shops in Westminster held of the Abbot. In 1390 Edmund's son, John, was found to have held a tenement with its appurtenances, called "La Mote," in Westminster, yielding 46s. 8d. in rents, and a barn and 60 acres of land of the Abbot. In 1394, at the death of Ralph de Stonor, "Le Mot" with three cottages was valued at 33s. 4d.[5] Thomas de Stonor in 1431 left "La Mote" in Westminster to his widow in dower.[6] Sir William Stonor sold "The Moote" on 18th February, 1478, to the Abbot of Abingdon.[7]

In addition to the lands which formed the estates of his descendants, Sir John de Stonor held various other property from time to time. In 1314 he had a grant from Robert de Maundevill jointly with Hugh de Courtenay of lands in Estcoker and Suthcoker;[8] this may, however, have been held in trust. In 1339 he acquired the reversion of the lands of Sir Edward Charles in Silham and Ryngeshale, Suffolk.[9] In 1340 he held a knight's fee in Churcocle, Hants.[10] He also held at one time the Manor of Peckham, with lands in Camberwell and Dulwich, which he sold in 1353 to Thomas Dolseley of London for 200l.[11]

We may now return to the history of the family. The eldest son of the Chief Justice, the second John de Stonor, was returned as over forty years of age at his father's death; in two of the Inquisitions his age was given as over 44 or 45. Probably therefore he was born about 1310. He must have been married about 1340, and is described as a

[1] Ch. Inq. p.m., Richard II, File 85.   [2] See No. 54.
[3] Cal. Close Rolls, Edw. III, iii, 339.   [4] Cal. Inq., iv, 299.
[5] Ch. Inq. p.m., Richard II, Files 21, 61, and 85.   [6] No. 54.
[7] No. 202.   [8] Cal. Close Rolls, Edw. II, ii, 235.
[9] Id., Edw. III, v, 327.   [10] Id., ix, 20.   [11] Id., ix, 582, 584.

knight in 1351.[1]   There are a few references to him after his father's death, but the only one of interest is his pardon in 1355 for having received William Mayhew, who had been indicted for stealing a cup of mazer at Exeter and a load of fish at Ermington, though he knew well that these felonies had been committed.[2]   He is said to have married a daughter of John Wenard of Oxfordshire,[3] and died on 10th July, 1361.   Edmund, his son and heir, was then fifteen years old.   Thomas Stonor, who was parson of Westbrigge, Norfolk, in 1371,[4] may have been a younger son.

Edmund de Stonor was made a ward of Isabella, Countess of Bedford, the King's daughter, on 28th August, 1361.[5]   On 12th September, 1365, having given proof of his age and done homage and fealty, it was directed that he should have seisin of his lands.[6]   He must, therefore, have been somewhat older than was alleged in 1361.   He served as Sheriff of Oxfordshire and Berks in 1377-78, and was a knight of the shire for the former county in the Parliament of January, 1380, receiving an allowance of 10l. for fifty days in March.[7]   In February, 1380, he was on a commission to inquire as to the lands of St. Frideswide's Priory at Oxford [8] which had fallen into poverty.   He was on the commission of peace for Oxfordshire in May, 1380,[9] and in December, 1381, he was a commissioner against unlawful assemblies.[10]   He had himself been a sufferer by the Peasant's Revolt, when his charters, tallies, and muniments had been burnt by the rebels in Hertfordshire.[11]   His career was simply that of a country gentleman living on his estates and discharging such public duties as fell to his lot.

Edmund de Stonor is the first of the family whose private papers other than Deeds and Accounts have been preserved in any quantity. The larger part of these papers consist of letters addressed to him as Sheriff, with writs and mandates issued to or by him in that office.[12] The series is one which for its size and early date has much value as illustrating the work of the Sheriff.   But some of the private letters,

---

[1] *Cal. Pat. Rolls*, Edw. III, ix, 205.   [2] *Id.*, x, 221.

[3] Nash, *Worcestershire*, i, 2. Is there a possible error of Wenard Oxon. for Wenard Exon. ? In Burke's *Commoners*, ii, 440, he is described as Wenard of Cornwall. For the later connexion of the Devonshire Wennards with the Stonors, see p. xxxix.

[4] *Cal. Pat. Rolls*, Edw. III, xv, 93.

[5] *Id.*, xii, 57; see Nos. 6 and 7 below.   [6] *Cal. Pat. Rolls*, xii, 82.

[7] *Cal. Close Rolls*, Richard II, i, 356.

[8] *Cal. Pat. Rolls*, Richard II, i, 466.   [9] *Id.*, i, 513.

[10] *Id.*, ii, 84.   [11] *Id.*, 87.   [12] See Nos. 9 to 23 below.

though they throw little light on Edmund's personality, are of greater interest.   The letter in which Brother Edmund sends a report to his patron on his son's welfare and progress is probably a unique description of a preparatory school (kept by a married master) in the fourteenth century.[1]   The begging letter from an Oxford scholar, John Halonton,[2] is almost as delightful in another way.   An Account of Household Expenses[3] is of interest as including the payment for the *jentaculum* or entertainment, which as sheriff he gave to the justices.

Edmund de Stonor died on 25th April, 1382.[4]   His wife seems to have been a sister of Waryn de l'Isle.[5]   By her he had three sons, Edmund, who died before him, John and Ralph, and one daughter Elizabeth.

Immediately after Edmund de Stonor's death the custody of his lands was granted on 12th May, 1382 to Queen Anne.[6]   John de Stonor was then only thirteen years of age.   His marriage was granted to John Holt, one of the serjeants-at-law and afterwards a justice of the Common Pleas.   Holt soon parted with his rights to Sir Robert Belknap, the Chief Justice.   In November, 1382, Thomas Seyvill, serjeant-at-arms, was ordered to bring Ralph, brother of John de Stonor, and his sister Elizabeth to London, and to deliver them to Sir Robert Belknap, who was to maintain them suitably.   Belknap had acquired their marriage in the event of their brother's death, and there was crafty design on the part of certain persons to marry Ralph and Elizabeth, by reason of the weak health of their brother.[7]

The little John de Stonor died two months later on 6th January, 1383. At an Inquisition held in 1390 it was stated that his brother Ralph, was then between 21 and 22 years of age ;[8] consequently John must have been rather more than thirteen in 1382, unless the two brothers were twins.   Ralph de Stonor had received a grant in November, 1389 of 40 marks a year out of his inheritance for his maintenance.[9]   After the usual custom his guardian married him to his own daughter Joan. Of Ralph's history we know only that he was a knight when he accompanied Richard II on his expedition to Ireland in September, 1394,[10]

---

[1] No. 30.   [2] No. 31.   [3] No. 19.
[4] *Ch. Inq. p.m.*, Richard II, File 21.
[5] See No. 17.   She is possibly the Dame Margaret of No. 29.
[6] *Cal. Pat. Rolls*, Richard II, ii, 117.   [7] *Id.*, ii, 202, 204.
[8] *Ch. Inq. p.m.*, Richard II, File 61.   The Inquisitions were held at various dates between January and June ; that for Southampton was held on 27 June and gives Ralph's age as 21 and a half and more.
[9] *Cal. Pat. Rolls*, Richard II, iv, 174.   [10] *Id.*, v, 476, 482.

and that he died, presumably in Ireland, on 13th November of that year.[1]
He left two sons, of whom Gilbert the elder was born on 19th January,
1393, and died in 1396. Ralph de Stonor's widow married, before
3rd October, 1395, as her second husband, Edmund Hampden of Hampden.[2] Edmund Hampden, by his will dated 25th November, 1419,
directed that he should be buried in the chancel of the church of
Great Hampden, and that a small white stone should be placed over
him and his wife Joan within one year after his decease with the in-
scription : " ȝe þat þys see, pray ȝe for charyte for Edmundes soule and
Janes a pater noster and an aue ".[3] This may perhaps indicate that
Jane or Joan Hampden died before her husband; in any case she died
before 1425.[4] By her second husband she had two sons, John[5] (d.
1451), whose son Thomas was the writer of two letters here printed,[6]
and Edmund, who was knighted and died before 1471. She had also
a daughter Isabel, who married (1) Thomas Ramsey of Hitcham,
Bucks, and (2) Sir John Wroughton. Ramsey died in 1448.[7] His
son and namesake was during many years the confidential adviser of
the second Thomas Stonor, and of Sir William Stonor.[8]

Sir Ralph de Stonor's second son Thomas was born on 26th April, presumably in 1394. The custody of his lands was granted on 15th February,
1395, to William Wilcotes and Thomas Barantyn,[9] who a little later
transferred the charge of Harnhull and Doughton to Nicholas Monketon.
On 30th November, 1403, Thomas Chaucer had a grant of the marriage
of Thomas de Stonor, and soon afterwards for a payment of 200l. also
obtained custody of the lands.[10] According to a sixteenth century
pedigree [11] Chaucer, who was probably the son of the poet, had married
a daughter (Maud) of Sir John Boroughwashe or Burghersh. The
mother of Maud Burghersh had first married Sir John Rayle of Cornwall, and was by him mother of Joan, wife of John Whalesburgh.
Whalesburgh's daughter Elizabeth married John Hampden, half-brother

[1] Ch. Inq. p.m., Richard II, File 85.   [2] Cal. Pat. Rolls, Richard II, v, 621.
[3] P.C.C., 21 Marche. Proved 20 April, 1420. The expenses of his funeral,
other than alms to the poor, were not to exceed 20s. Two of his executors were
Thomas Joye, rector of Penyngton (Penton Mewsey) and John Starlyng, rector of
Hampden.
[4] See note to No. 47 below.   [5] See Nos. 54 and 56 and ii, 173, 175.
[6] Nos. 75 and 187.
[7] Ch. Inq. p.m., Henry VI, File 132. See also vol. i, 50 and vol. ii, 181.
[8] See Nos. 144, 157, 177, 179, and ii, 187. He married Anne, daughter of William
Norris; see pedigree, ap. Harley MS., 1533, f. 57, and p. 118 below.
[9] Cal. Pat. Rolls, Richard II, v, 564.   [10] Id., Henry IV, ii, 335, 455.
[11] Ap. Harley MS., 1391, f. 19.

of the first Thomas Stonor. From this pedigree it would appear that Chaucer acquired the wardship of the young Thomas Stonor as a friend of the family. His own home was at Ewelme within a few miles of Stonor. He and his daughter Alice, who married William de la Pole, Duke of Suffolk, were in friendly relationship with the Stonor family for over seventy years.

Thomas Stonor married before 1416,[1] Alice, daughter and heiress of Thomas Kirby,[2] with whom he acquired a good estate at Horton in Kent. It is possible that he served in the French war during 1419 and 1420; for in the former year the rents of part of the estates were paid to the lady of Stonor,[3] and in 1420 it would seem likely that he was absent from England.[4] But otherwise his career was that of a well-to-do country gentleman, though, perhaps through the influence of Thomas Chaucer, he occupied a position of somewhat greater importance than his age warranted. He represented the county of Oxford in the Parliaments of 1416, 1419, 1425, 1427, 1429, and 1431, and twice served as sheriff in 1423-24 and 1427-28. But he only appears on the commission of peace for Oxfordshire in 1423, though he was acting as a justice in 1425, and was one of the commissioners for a loan to the King in 1430.[5]

It is, however, with Thomas Stonor that the real interest of the Stonor Papers begins. Out of fourteen documents belonging to his time here printed[6] six only are letters. Of these only one was written (or dictated) by Stonor,[7] though the others seem to show that he was a man of affairs and judgment. Of the other documents the Account of Funeral Expenses at Rippinghale[8] appears to have been kept by Stonor himself. The most interesting matters relate to Ermington,[9] where the rights of the Stonors were in dispute as they had been seventy years before and were again fifty years later.

It will be convenient to notice here and on similar occasions the most prominent persons who come into the history. Sir John Fortescue, the father of the Chief Justice, had an estate near Ermington. His famous son appears as on friendly terms with Thomas Stonor at the be-

---

[1] See p. 30 below.
[2] For her descent, see Wrottesley, *Pedigrees from the Plea Rolls*, p. 323. She and Thomas Stonor sued John Isaak for lands in Hopelond, Chistlet and Stury as heirs of Ralph de St. Lawrence, *temp.* Edw. I.
[3] *Ancient Deeds*, C. 5558.   [4] No. 42.
[5] *Cal. Pat. Rolls*, Henry VI, i, 303, 568; ii, 51.   [6] Nos. 41-54.
[7] No. 46.   [8] No. 47.   [9] Nos. 42, 45 and 46.

ginning of his legal career.[1]   Two other sons, Henry and Richard, seem
to have had an ill-name for lawless conduct.   In 1422 Henry Fortescue
and other evil-doers were said to have broken the house of Thomas
Gylle at Dodbrook, to have pursued him into the market with drawn
swords and assaulted and wounded him there.   In 1434 William
Rytte of Devonshire filed a petition in Chancery against[2] "Richard
Fortescue that is a grete meyntenour and oppressour in the countrey".[3]
This Richard Fortescue was father of the Richard Fortescue, who between 1460 and 1468 so vexed the second Thomas Stonor and his
bailiffs at Ermington.[4]   The feud was in a sense settled by the marriage
of the children of Sir John Fortescue of Punsborne to the children of
Sir William Stonor.[5]   Sir John Fortescue of Punsborne was a son of
the first Richard Fortescue, and is the John Fortescue the younger,
cf. No. 154.   His sister Elizabeth was married to John Crocker of
Lyneham, the writer of No. 92.

The first Thomas Stonor died on 2nd March, 1431.[6]   He left two
sons, Thomas and John, and mentioned in his will five unmarried
daughters, Elizabeth (or Isabel), Maud, Philippa, Joan, and Anne.[7]
Probably his eldest daughter Alice, who was wife of Humphrey Forster[8]
the elder, of Harpeden or Harpsdon near Henley, was already married.
Elizabeth or Isabel married Thomas Sackville of Fawley.[9]   Of the others,
Maud was wife of Hugh Lewis of Essex, and Philippa, wife of William
Harleston[10] of Denham, Suffolk, and another was wife of H—— S——
of Stockbridge,[11] Hampshire.   The second son John may possibly be
the John Stonor, who had married Anne, sister of Margaret, wife of Sir
Robert Harcourt, and co-heiress of Cookham and Bray:[12] otherwise
there is no mention of him after 1432.[13]

Alice Kirby or Kirkby after her first husband's death married, before
1st December, 1432,[14] Richard Drayton, an Oxfordshire squire.   Alice
and Richard Drayton were apparently living at Stonor in 1432-33 and
in 1436,[15] but in their later years resided at Horton, where they died
within two days of one another in October, 1468.[16]   There is nowhere
any definite reference to children of theirs, but Thomas Mull, who was

---

[1] See No. 46.   [2] Cal. Pat. Rolls, Henry V, ii, 447.
[3] Early Chancery Proceedings, 75/77 (P.R.O.).
[4] See Nos. 63, 64, 71, 72, 79-82, and 91.   [5] See p. xxxv below.
[6] Ch. Inq. p.m., Henry VI, File 48.   [7] No. 54.   [8] Nos. 87, 115.
[9] Nos. 60 and 87-88.   [10] Burke, Commoners, ii, 440; cf. Nos. 135, 260.
[11] Nos. 98 and 99.   [12] Cal. Pat. Rolls, Edw. IV, iii, 487.
[13] No. 56.   [14] Id.
[15] Nos. 55 and 56, see also vol. ii, p. 181.   [16] No. 91.

Drayton's executor, addresses the second Thomas Stonor as brother,[1] and was probably married to a daughter of Richard and Alice Drayton.[2] Thomas Rokes is another person, who addresses the second Thomas Stonor as brother.[3] Since his wife's name was Alice,[4] it may be conjectured that she also was a daughter of Drayton.[5]

Alice Stonor or Drayton, in addition to her own lands at Horton, had the manors of Ermington, Harnhull and Bierton and La Mote at Westminster in dower, and Penton Mewsey and all lands in Kent, which had been newly acquired, for the sustenance of his daughters.[6] Her eldest son writes with obvious affection of his mother and step-father.[7] Richard Drayton in 1465 sold Rotherfield Peppard to his step-son;[8] but otherwise apart from occasional references in connexion with Ermington,[9] he and his wife do not figure in the Stonor Letters. Drayton's own property was near Dorchester in Oxfordshire. By his will,[10] made at Horton on 27th April, 1464, he directed that he should be buried in Dorchester Abbey before the image of St. Mary de Gravenyng between the tomb of Sir William Drayton and the wall of the church on the south side. He made bequests of 3s. 4d. to the high altar of Horton, and of 6s. 8d. for tithes forgot and of 3s. 4d. for repairs to Pyrton church near Stonor.

The second Thomas Stonor was barely seven years old when his father died, having been born on 22nd March, 1424.[11] By his father's will[12] Thomas Chaucer was appointed his guardian. But Chaucer died in 1434, and the care of the estates was apparently in the hands of John Warfeld, the Receiver and one of the feoffees of the elder Thomas Stonor, and of Humphrey Forster. Warfeld was succeeded as receiver

---

[1] Nos. 69, 90, 100.   [2] Cf. No. 111, where he calls Drayton his father.
[3] No. 89.   [4] No. 182.
[5] The keeper of the Accounts in No. 96 seems also to be a son or son-in-law of Alice Drayton; he refers to "my brother Mull". The reference in the Account to the "dethe of my modyr" may be a note by Thomas Stonor.
[6] See No. 54. The Devonshire Inquisition at Alice Drayton's death (*Ch. Inq. p.m.*, Edward IV, File 29) recites that her first husband being sused of the manor of Ermington and hundred of Ermington, forty acres in Bukford Walles, the water of Erme and its fishery, the "hundredespeny," view of frank pledge of Great Modbury, "et de tremura de Kilbury," with the advowson of Ermington and of the free chapel in the cemetery, enfeoffed Thomas Chaucer and others, who on 2nd May, 1432 demised all except the fishery to Alice for life. The feoffers in 1468 were John Hampden, John Wroughton, John Butteller, William Bekyngham, John Lydyard, Richard Bedford, and Henry Dogett.
[7] No. 91.   [8] See No. 77 and *Ancient Deeds*, C. 6944, vol. ii, p. 174 below.
[9] Cf. Nos. 64 and 92   [10] *P.C.C.*, 26 Godyn.
[11] *Ch. Inq. p.m.*, Henry VI, File 48.   [12] No. 54.

about 1443 by Henry Dogett, who retained the position for nearly forty years.[1] After Chaucer's death the Stonor family remained on friendly terms with his daughter Alice, who married successively Thomas Montagu, Earl of Salisbury, and William de la Pole, Duke of Suffolk. In the Visitation of Oxfordshire [2] Thomas Stonor is said to have married a natural daughter of William de la Pole. The association of the families makes this not unlikely, and the story receives some confirmation from the fact that on 11th May, 1453, Joan, wife of Thomas Stonor, born in Normandy and dwelling in England from the time of her marriage, had letters of denization.[3]

The second Thomas Stonor, like his father, followed the ordinary life of a country gentleman. He represented Oxfordshire in the Parliaments of 1447 and 1449, was sheriff of Oxford and Berks in 1453-54 and again in 1465-66. But he does not appear on any commissions during the reign of Henry VI, and only occasionally in that of Edward IV. There is nothing to show that he took any decided part in the troubled politics of his time. He preserved amongst his papers the official Yorkist account of the first Battle of St. Albans,[4] and was summoned by Edward IV for military service in 1463 and again in 1470.[5] But if he had any political leaning it was probably on the side of the Nevilles, for he was certainly on friendly terms with George Neville, the archbishop of York, and is described as one of his servants.[6] He appears on three commissions during the Lancastrian Restoration in October, 1470.[7] But on the other hand, he was appointed a commissioner of array for Oxfordshire after the Battle of Barnet on 28th April, 1471, and again in March, 1472.[8] He was on the commission of peace continuously from 1466 till his death in 1474,[9] and this is perhaps evidence that he had never committed himself decidedly on either side.

[1] See vol. ii, p. 181. Dogett appears frequently in the Letters. He died in 1491, and by his will directed that he should be buried in the church of Pusey in the chapel of St. Nicholas. *P.C.C.*, 1 Dogett. Cf. No. 256.
[2] *Visitation of Oxfordshire*, p. 123, Harleian Society. In the pedigree *ap*. Nash, *Worcestershire*, i, 2, Thomas Stonor's wife is called a daughter of John de la Pole; this is of course absurd, as John de la Pole was not born till 1445. William de la Pole was serving in France from 1417 to 1430, and may well have had a daughter of suitable age "born in Normandy".
[3] *Cal. Pat. Rolls*, Henry VI, vi, 70.   [4] No. 59.
[5] Nos. 70 and 112.   [6] See Nos. 82 and 97.
[7] *Cal. Pat. Rolls*, Edward IV, ii, 248-9; he only appears on one commission of earlier date.
[8] *Id.*, ii, 285, 350.
[9] *Id.*, i, 570; ii, 625; he held a session with William Marmion at Henley in January, 1465—see K. B., *Ancient Indictments*, 315/18 (P.R.O.).

Of his private life there is little more to be said. We find him visit-
ing his estates in Kent and Devonshire, and in London on business.[1]
He was often enough away from home to draw a gentle rebuke from
his wife.[2]   The Letters give just a hint at his personality, an affectionate son and husband,[3] perhaps a strict parent.   William Stonor was
clearly somewhat in awe of him, and Thomas Mull discreetly suggested
that his brother should call his son to walk with him, give him words
of comfort, and be a good father unto him.[4]   There was so much inter-
change of service between country squires, that one cannot attach
special weight to the letters addressed to Thomas Stonor by his neigh-
bours; but Thomas Hampton of Kimble at all events regarded him as
a valuable counsellor.[5]   The most considerable topic in his correspondence is the renewal of disputes at Ermington, first with the son of his
father's old adversary, Richard Fortescue, who molested his bailiffs and
tenants,[6] and afterwards as to the rights of fishery.[7]   The settlement
of his mother's affairs,[8] and a projected match for his son [9] gives us an
interesting series of letters from a Kentish brother-in-law, Thomas Mull,
who was also one of his legal advisers.[10]   Less frequent correspondents
were his cousin, Thomas Hampden of Hampden,[11] Humphrey Forster,[12]
Thomas Rokes,[13] Richard Quatermayns [14] and Sir Richard Harcourt.[15]

The second Thomas Stonor died on 23rd April, 1474,[16] and was buried
with much pomp and feasting at Pyrton Church.[17]   That a sum of no
less than 74*l.* 2*s.* 5½*d.* [18] should have been spent on his funeral is perhaps more convincing than the meagre history of his life, as proof of
the importance of his social position.

In his will[19] the second Thomas Stonor made provision for three
daughters; Jane, who was already married to John Cottesmore,[20] a
ward of her father, Mary, who afterwards married John Barantyne of
Haseley,[21] and Elizabeth.   He had three sons, William, Thomas, and
Edmund.   William, the eldest, is the principle figure in the Stonor
Letters.   Thomas, the second, was betrothed to Sybil, daughter of John
Breknok, in 1471,[22] but was apparently still unmarried in 1475.[23]   They

---

[1] Nos. 71, 86, 92, 96, 98, 106.
[2] No. 106.   [3] No 91.   [4] No. 124.
[5] Nos. 65, 67, and 76.
[6] Nos. 63, 64, 71, 72, 79-82, and 91.
[7] Nos. 126, 127.
[8] Nos. 100, 111.   [9] Nos. 121-24.
[10] Nos. 69, 100.
[11] No. 75.   [12] Nos. 87, 115, 197.
[13] Nos. 89, 179, and 182.
[14] Nos. 94, 116.   [15] No. 110.
[16] *Ch. Inq. p.m.*, Edw. IV, File 82.
[17] No. 138.   [18] No. 157.
[19] No. 137.
[20] Nos. 109, 110, 128, 136.
[21] No. 294.
[22] No. 114.   [23] No. 153.

were, however, married before 1477[1] and had at least two children,
Walter, who eventually succeeded to the family estates[2] and was
ancestor of the later Stonors, and Joan, who is mentioned in her grandmother's will.[3] Thomas Stonor, the third, was given the manor of
Rotherfield Peppard by his father.   There are three letters[4] written by
him to his brother William, two of which have the curious signature
"Thomas Staunton". He shows himself as a sportsman, fond of a
joke, and apt to get into scrapes, who took part with zest in the French
expedition of 1475, but able to give his brother shrewd advice.   He
survived to claim Stonor as heir male and died in 1512.[5]   Edmund,
the third brother, was given an estate at Burwardescote or Buscot in
Berkshire; like Thomas he went on the expedition to France in 1475;
he is the writer of three letters,[6] from one of which he would seem to
have lived for a time at Stonor and helped to manage the family
estates; he probably died young, for Burwardescote had reverted to
William Stonor before 1473.[7] Neither Thomas nor Edmund appear
in the family papers after 1475, save that Thomas seems to have expressed himself too openly on Dame Elizabeth Stonor's social ambitions.[8]

Of Jane Stonor we have two letters addressed to her husband, one
to a daughter, and one to her eldest son.[9]   Her curious spelling (she
wrote "thesyryd" for desired, "sendyd" for sent it, and " wonto" for
wont to) may possibly suggest her foreign education.   Like her husband
she seems to have been a strict parent.   There was some friction with
her eldest son after her husband's death,[10] and a few years later there
was a more serious dispute, when she shewed herself possessed of a
sharp tongue.[11]   However, the quarrel was made up before her death,
and in her will,[12] dated 13th April, 1493, her son Sir William Stonor and
Thomas Ramsey were named her executors.   Jane Stonor had rights of
dower at Penton Mewsey where at one time she seems to have lived.
But in 1493 she was living at Henley and directed that she should be
buried at the entry of the west door of the church there, without the
church door. She made bequests of 6s. 8d. each to the churches of
Stowell[13] St. John, Stowell Stonor, Didcot and Penton Mewsey; to

[1] *Early Chancery Proceedings*, 64/910 (P.R.O.).   [2] See p. xxxvi below.
[3] See p. xxvi below.   [4] Nos. 142, 151, and 153.
[5] See p. xxxv below.   [6] Nos. 152, 155, and 156.
[7] See Nos. 228 and 232; perhaps he died of smallpox in 1476, see No. 169.
[8] Nos. 175 and 180.   [9] Nos. 70, 106, 120, and 158.
[10] Nos. 157 and 158.   [11] Nos. 301 and 320
[12] *P.C.C.*, Vox 16.   Proved 16th November, 1494.
[13] Sotwell St. John, and Sotwell Stonor.

thirty-one priests at her burial saying the trental of St. Gregory with
mass of requiem, 12d. each ; to every priest at the month-mind saying
dirige and mass, 12d.'; to every poor man holding torches at her burial
and month-mind, 6d. ; and to the poorest men of Henley and six of
her poorest tenants, 8d. with gowns and hoods.   Her feoffees were
directed "to make estate of the house I dwell in to Jane Stonor,
youngest daughter of my son Thomas Stonor, and the heirs of her body,"
with remainders to Walter, son of Thomas Stonor and to Sir William
Stonor.   " Also I give to the seid Syr Wylyam Stonar vj bellys of sylver
of a sute with a coveryng."

William Stonor was returned as 24 years of age at his father's death,
and was therefore probably born in 1449.[1]   He may have been a god-
son of his mother's father the Duke of Suffolk.   There are some references to him as a boy ; he accompanied his father on a visit to
Ermington in 1466,[2] and got into disfavour with his uncle, Humphrey
Forster, for riotous conduct in 1471.[3]   Still he seems to have been
trusted by his father with a share in the management of the family
estates,[4] though Thomas Mull wrote that he was disposed to be a
muser and a studier.[5]   In April, 1473, he was at Ermington in order to
deal with a difficult dispute there ; his report shows that it was not his
first errand of this kind.[6]   He was already showing the sharp eye for business and the matrimonial ambitions, which were his chief characteristics
in later years.   On the death of William Marmyon he wrote to his
father suggesting that he might secure him the succession to valuable
stewardships.[7]   Whilst on a visit to Kent in 1472 he met with a wealthy
heiress, daughter of Sir Thomas Etchingham, and widow of William
Blount, son of the first Lord Mountjoy.[8]   Encouraged by Thomas
Mull he paid suit to her, but the match failed over money matters,
whether the lady was too grasping, or Thomas Stonor not liberal
enough in his offers of a settlement.

After his succession to the estates, William Stonor looked about once
more for a wife.   His brother Thomas wrote to him from London
marvelling at his absence, " remembering how greatly in conceit ye
stand with a gentlewoman in London," and warning him of dangerous
rivals and mischief-makers.[9]   This may perhaps have reference to
William Stonor's first wife, Elizabeth.   Elizabeth Stonor fills so large a

[1] See Note to No. 139. A Berkshire Inquisition held in October, 1482 (Ch. Inq.
p.m., Edw. IV, File 82) gives William Stonor's age as 33.
[2] No. 86.   [3] No. 115.   [4] Nos. 97, 118, 127, 128.   [5] No. 124.
[6] No. 127.   [7] No. 136.   [8] Nos. 121-4.   [9] No. 142.

place in the correspondence between 1475 and 1479 that a full account of her is necessary. She was not a lady of rank like Lord Mountjoy's daughter-in-law, but her wealth may have been an even greater attraction to the young Oxfordshire squire. Her father, John Croke, was a London alderman, and her mother Margaret was daughter of William Gregory, a well-known mayor. Her sister Margaret was wife of Sir William Stocker, who had been mayor in 1471-72 and is often mentioned in the Letters.[1] Her brother John was the writer of No. 183. Elizabeth had married before 1465[2] Thomas Ryche, the son of a wealthy mercer. Richard Ryche, who died in 1464, left, besides much other property, 500*l.* to his wife, and 200*l.* with lands in Islington and Ratcliffe to his son Thomas;[3] his daughters had married well in the city, one was wife of William Marowe, who was mayor in 1455-56, a second was wife of John Walden, an alderman, and a third was wife of Thomas Ursewyk, who was Recorder of London from 1454 to 1471, and Chief Baron of the Exchequer from 1471 to 1479. Thomas Ryche, the son, made his will on 2nd July, 1471, apparently rather over three years before his death.[4] His father had provided for a sumptuous funeral, but Thomas directed that no month-mind should be kept and that the money saved should be given to the poor by the advice of his father-in-law John Croke. Only forty marks were left for an honest tomb on his sepulture in the chapel of the Guildhall. He bequeathed his wife the customary third of his residue, which she was to choose by the advice of her father, and to his children, including one unborn, the second third.[5] By Ryche, Elizabeth had three daughters, Katherine, god-daughter of her great-grandfather William Gregory, Jane,[6] and Anne,[7] who married Richard Thornell; and, one son, John, who was perhaps the youngest of the family. Katherine Ryche married in 1478 Thomas Betson, of whom more hereafter.

Elizabeth Ryche was probably a few years older than William Stonor, whom she took for her second husband in the summer of 1475. To him the attractions were probably in part her wealth and the opening

[1] See Nos. 168, 183.

[2] *Collections of a London Citizen*, p. xlvi, where Gregory in his will dated 6th November, 1465, mentions his god-daughter Kateryn, daughter of Thomas Ryche.

[3] *P.C.C.*, 4 Godyn.

[4] See No. 168, which suggests that Ryche died in August, 1474.

[5] *P.C.C.*, 20 Wattys. It was not proved till 4th October, 1475. But Ryche certainly died before 1st July, 1475 (*Letter Book*, L., p. 131), and Elizabeth had probably remarried before that date.

[6] See Nos. 248-50.   [7] See Nos. 222, 224-5.

3333

which an alliance with merchants interested in the wool-trade offered to a great sheep-grazier with a desire to make money. To Elizabeth one attraction was no doubt the prospect of social distinction. There are hints that her new relatives looked on her as something of a parvenue, who had involved her husband in extravagance;[1] and she herself supplies us with a glimpse at the citizen's daughter who had become a great lady and gone to Court.[2] She was much in London, partly perhaps on pleasure, but not forgetting to combine business therewith: for she was a masterful woman, who took an active interest in her husband's affairs. Yet she wrote often to him with a manifest affection, and if Thomas Betson sometimes addressed her a mild remonstrance on her too lavish expenditure, he did so as a warm and devoted friend.[3]

Thomas Betson himself is perhaps the most individual and attractive personality in the whole correspondence.[4] The playful letter[5] which he wrote to his future wife, as a child of twelve or thirteen, is amongst the most charming of all private letters of the time that have survived. He had been factor and servant to John Fenn, who died in 1474,[6] and became a partner of William Stonor in the wool-trade in 1475. He was already or very soon afterwards betrothed to Katherine Ryche. The business association seems to have been broken by Elizabeth Stonor's death about the end of 1479, but whilst it lasted his letters show him as a trusty man of business and loyal adviser. He was a welcome visitor at Stonor, where he had his own chamber in the mansion.[7] When he lay sick in 1479, Sir William Stonor seems to have been as much concerned for Betson's recovery as for the safety of his own money.[8] It is therefore the more surprising that in later years the old friendship was so completely broken as the occasional references to his debts to Stonor would seem to imply.[9] The sincerity and honesty of Betson's character as revealed in his letters, forbids one to suppose that he was to blame. Affection, prudence, and a genuine piety are shown both in his correspondence and his will. He died in the spring of 1486, having made a will[10] three years previously on 12th May, 1483. He described himself therein as stockfishmonger and merchant of the Staple at Calais, and gave direction for " the costes of my burying to

[1] Nos. 175, 180. [2] No. 172.
[3] For her Letters, see Nos. 168-70, 172-3, 175-6, 180, 204, 208, 226, 229, 237.
[4] For his Letters see Nos. 161-2, 166, 185, 205, 207, 211, 212, 216-18, 224.
[5] No. 166. [6] Fenn's Will, *P.C.C.*, 17 Wattys.
[7] Nos. 172, 217-18. [8] Nos. 249-51. [9] Nos. 264, 282.
[10] *P.C.C.*, 24 Logge. There is a codicil dated 30th September, 1485. The will was proved on 12th May, 1486.

be don not outrageously, but sobrely and discretly and in a meane maner, that it may be unto the worship and laude of Almyghty God" Forty marks were left for the repair of the rood-loft in his parish church of Allhallows, Barking, and thirty pounds to the garnishing of the Staple Chapel in Our Lady Church at Calais to buy some jewel. There were legacies to Hugh and Margaret Fenn, two cousins of whom we hear often in the Stonor Letters, and one of 40s. to Thomas Henham, his old colleague in the service of Sir William Stonor.[1]   He left 20l. to the Stockfishmongers to buy plate, and appointed the Warden and Fellowship to be guardians of his children's goods, and "to be chargyed with the fyndyng of my said children according as the maner is after ther poor haveours". The feoffees of his house in Holborn were to give an estate to Thomas, his elder son, and by a codicil dated 30th September, 1485, he left his wife the place lately purchased of Sir John Scott, and also his house in Holborn for life, with remainders to his sons Thomas and John; in default the houses were to be sold and the proceeds divided amongst his daughters, Elizabeth, Agnes, and Alice. Katherine Betson married as her second husband William Welbek, haberdasher, by whom she had another son, William. She died early in 1510, and directed that she should be buried by her first husband at Allhallows, Barking, where she was "to be brought to the ertbe sumwhat honestly after the discrecion of my executors".[2]

Another association which William Stonor owed to his marriage with Elizabeth Ryche, was the wardship of the Fenns. John Fenn, a stockfishmonger and apparently a kinsman of Ryche and Betson, left at his death in the autumn of 1474[3] four children, John, Hugh, Elizabeth, and Margaret. On 6th December, 1475, Richard Quatermayns and Richard Fowler, fishmongers,[4] and Thomas Harward and Thomas Unton, drapers, became sureties for the payment of 758l. 19s. 0½d. by Quatermayns to the Chamber of London to the use of Hugh and Margaret Fenn when they came of age or married.[5] On the same date Lawrence Fyncham[6] was one of the sureties for the payment of a like sum on behalf of John and Elizabeth. Elizabeth married in 1479, and John came of age in 1482. Hugh and Margaret were much younger. They were in the charge of Elizabeth Stonor as early as March, 1477.[7]

---

[1] Nos. 163, 222, 251.   [2] *P.C.C.*, 25 Bennett.

[3] *P.C.C.*, 17 Wattys. Elizabeth Stonor bought wax for his mind in September 1477, see No. 227. Henry Fenn and Lawrence Fyncham were his executors.

[4] As well as country gentlemen: see Nos. 94 and 116.

[5] *Calendar of Letter Book*, L., p. 136.

[6] See Nos. 185, 208.   [7] No. 180.

After Quatermayns' death in the autumn of that year some fresh arrangement for the care of their property must have been necessary. But it was not till 15th February, 1479, that Sir William Stonor assumed the responsibility.[1] In the Stonor Letters there is reference to some questions as to the apprenticeship of John Fenn, the younger, in September, 1479, which involved business with Lawrence Fyncham.[2] John Fenn, the father, had a house at Stepney, which William Stonor purchased in 1477.[3] After the death of Elizabeth Stonor her husband's interest in the Fenn children ceased, and in January, 1481, he was negotiating through Walter Elmes for a transfer of the wardship.[4] Ultimately the bond was taken over by John Picton on 7th April, 1481, Thomas Bradbury being one of the sureties.[5] John Fenn must have been a man of considerable wealth, for he bequeathed 400*l.* for the use of the children of Thomas Ryche; for this bequest Sir William Stocker and John Stocker were two of the sureties in July, 1475;[6] the account which Thomas Betson rendered in 1479 to Lady Stonor[7] may possibly have had reference to this bequest.

During the five years after his father's death William Stonor, whether through or in spite of the commercial enterprise which chiefly interested him at this time, had certainly much improved his position. A quarrel with his cousin, Thomas Rokes, had caused him some trouble in 1477,[8] and may perhaps account for the few letters that belong to that year. But the cloud was only a passing one. He represented Oxfordshire in the Parliament of 1478, and on 18th January in that year was made a Knight of the Bath, on the occasion of the marriage of the King's second son Richard, Duke of York.[9] Thus his knighthood was more than the formal honour of a country gentleman of good estate; and not long afterwards he was further appointed one of the knights of the King's body.[10] He may have owed his promotion at Court to the favour of the Duke of Suffolk. But neither he nor his wife were slow to push their own advantage, and they both had a keen eye for profitable wards and stewardships. In 1479 he secured the stewardship of Thame from Thomas Rotherham, then bishop of Lincoln.[11] Rotherham became archbishop of York in 1480, but his successor at Lincoln, John Russell,

[1] *Calendar of Letter Book*, L., p. 162.   [2] No. 249.   [3] No. 183.
[4] Nos. 282, 287, 288.   [5] No. 287. See *Calendar of Letter Book*, L., p. 177.
[6] *Id.*, p. 131.   [7] No. 248.   [8] Nos. 179, 182.
[9] Shaw, *Knights of England*, i, 137-8.
[10] He seems to have been made a knight of the body between July, 1478, and September, 1479; compare Nos. 220 and 247.
[11] No. 255; see also No. 278.

was also an important political personage,[1] association with whom must have been greatly to Stonor's advantage.[2] It was probably not without thought of future interest that Stonor and his wife made a grant of an annuity to William Hatteclyff, the King's secretary.[3]

Social ambitions have always been costly. William Harleston's warning to his nephew, "that ye will not over-wish you, nor over-purchase you, nor over-build you," coupled with the hope that after the death of his wife he would take the opportunity to stablish his household more sadly and wisely with a convenient fellowship and keep within his livelihood,[4] tells its own tale. This warning gives point to Thomas Stonor's gibe at Dame Elizabeth's " meyny of boys,"[5] and to Thomas Betson's gentle remonstrance against debt.[6]

Harleston hoped to find his nephew the worshipfulest of Stonors that ever he saw. Sir William so far took his uncle's advice to heart that he seems to have abandoned his association with his first wife's citizen relatives, and in his next alliance aimed at an improvement in his worldly position. Within a short time he paid his court to Agnes Wydeslade,[7] widow of the son of a Devonshire squire, and in her own right a great heiress. Her grandfather, William Winnard or Wynard, had been a rich citizen of Exeter and sometime Recorder, with large estates in Devon and Cornwall. He was the founder of an almshouse at Exeter, which still survives as Wynard's Almshouse,[8] and was a generous benefactor to the Friars Minors at Exeter. At his death in 1442 he left the Friars 100 marks for a new cloister, and directed that he should be buried in the chapel which he had built in their church.[9] His son, John Winnard, died in 1468, and by his will, dated 1st May, 1459, appointed Richard Wydeslade to be guardian of his daughter, Annes or Agnes.[10] Agnes Winnard married her guardian's son, but in 1479 was a widow without children. Her grandfather's estates included the manors of Wonford, Clist Barnevile, and Hode in Devonshire, with lands in other places, several thousand acres in extent, and the manor of Wolveston in Cornwall.[11] Her marriage with Sir William Stonor

---

[1] For other stewardships see Nos. 237, 239, 244.
[2] Cf. No. 312.   [3] No. 238.   [4] No. 260.
[5] No. 180. See also No. 179 where in 1477 Thomas Ramsey advises Stonor to keep " grete sadde rewle ".
[6] No. 211 ; see the references to debts in Nos. 222, 224, and 229.
[7] Nos. 261-2.   [8] Oliver, *Monasticon Exoniense*, pp. 404-6.
[9] *P.C.C.*, 14 Rous.   [10] *Id.*, 25 Godyn.
[11] The Devonshire Inquisition on Agnes Stonor's death deals with lands at Wonefordhill, South Woneford, East Woneford, Hode, Lowvale, Wyllemorlegh, Chollewylle, South Wympell, Brode Clyst, Cavykestrete, Wodelegh, Ayshe Hodewyle,

must have taken place early in 1480, and certainly before May of that year.[1]

The management of Agnes Stonor's inheritance and disputes with regard to it furnish the chief subject of the Stonor Letters during her lifetime.   Her own heir was her cousin, John Speke[2] of Bamford, son of Sir John Speke and grandson of Sybil, sister of William Winnard. Thomas Worthe, who was probably another kinsman, had some sort of claim on Wolveston, which involved Stonor in a legal dispute that seems to have lasted two years.[3]   Stonor retained Clist Barnevile, Hode, and Wolveston after Agnes' death; he claimed to hold them under a Fine levied in February, 1481, which secured a remainder to him and the heirs of his body.[4]   Another matter of dispute was the patronage of the Exeter Almshouse, the administration of which was in the hands of Richard Germyn.[5]   Germyn, who was an Exeter merchant of some wealth, seems also during 1480 and 1481 to have had charge of all the Devonshire estates.[6]   The Manor of Clist Barnevile was held of the Marquis of Dorset, in right of his wife. Possibly this may have been the beginning of a political connexion between Sir William Stonor and the Woodville interests.   There are indications that Stonor was regarded with disfavour by Richard, Duke of Gloucester,[7] and Germyn wrote to Stonor "ye be the greatest man with my lord [Dorset] and in his conceit; his servants report of you that ye be the most courteous knight that ever was."[8]   On the other hand Jane Stonor, who was at variance with her son during 1481-82,[9] seems to have been able to command the interest of the Queen, and her brother, Lionel Woodville, bishop of Salisbury.[10] Agnes Stonor was in ill-health during the whole of her married life, which lasted little over a year.   If she had a child, it must have died young.   By her death on 4th May, 1481, Sir William Stonor, found himself for the second time a widower without children.

If Sir William's second marriage had been a step upwards, he did still better on his third venture.   His first two wives were wealthy

Bukyngton, Manston, Sydbury, Kyngswere, Hatherleigh, Pynne, Sterton, Dawlish Kenton, and Exeter. *Ch. Inq. p.m.*, Edw. IV, File 42.
[1] See Nos. 267-8.   [2] See Nos. 268.   [3] See Nos. 266-8.
[4] *Ch. Inq. p.m.*, Edw. IV, File 80; they were forfeited in 1483 (see p. xxxiv), but recovered and held by Stonor at his death, *Cal. Inq.*, Henry VII, i, 977.
[5] Nos. 268, 272, 284, 285, 289.   [6] Cf. No. 285.
[7] Cf. Nos. 230, 287, 288.   [8] No. 285.   [9] Nos. 301.
[10] No. 320.   Sir William Stonor had a dispute of his own with the Queen: see Nos. 313, 319.

widows, a little older than himself.   His third wife, whom he married
in the autumn of 1481,[1] was a young girl of the noblest blood in England, Anne Neville, eldest daughter of John, Marquis of Montagu, the
brother of the Kingmaker, and a cousin of the royal house.   Anne was
staying with the Marquis of Dorset at Taunton in the spring of 1482,[2]
and in August of that year presented her husband with a son.[3]   The
death of her only brother, George, in the following summer made her a
great heiress.[4]   Though she had apparently been a ward of Richard of
Gloucester, the marriage had strengthened the connexion between her
husband and Dorset.   This had probably its bearing on the greatest
crisis in Stonor's career.   The letters from Simon Stallworth[5] in June,
1483, show that Stonor followed events in London with interest.   Still
he accepted the assumption of the throne by Richard of Gloucester and
was present at the King's coronation.[6]   His eventual attitude was, however, probably determined by his association with Dorset.   His own
position was of sufficient importance to make Francis Lovell anxious to
secure his support for King Richard.   The letter which Lovell wrote
for this purpose on 11th October, 1483,[7] is the latest document in the
collection.   Stonor disregarded the summons, joined in Buckingham's
rebellion and was attainted.   It is at least possible that a consequent
seizure of his papers accounts for their preservation amongst the Public
Records.

   During the lifetime of Stonor's first wife the interest of the correspondence had turned chiefly on his commercial speculation as a
merchant in the wool-trade.   During the three or four years that
followed, the interest centres—as so often in other private correspondence of the time—chiefly round legal business.   His two principal
correspondents, besides Richard Germyn, during this time were Walter
Elmes and Richard Page.   Elmes, who was a cousin, was perhaps his
Steward, or may possibly have succeeded Dogett as Receiver.   Page
was a London lawyer, apparently a member of the Temple.[8]   He had
an estate in Kent, and resided at Horton, possibly as a tenant of Sir
William Stonor at the manor house of the Kirby family.   He may
perhaps have been connected with Stonor by marriage, for Philip Fitz

---

[1] See Nos. 305-6.   [2] Nos. 306, 314.   [3] Cf. Nos. 321, 322.   [4] No. 328.
[5] Nos. 330, 331.   [6] *Excerpta Historica*, p. 384.   [7] No. 333.
[8] In his will—*P.C.C.*, Vox. 12—dated 22nd August, 1483, and proved 20th October,
1493, he makes bequests to the high altars of the church within the Temple and at
Horton.   He refers to Beterys his late wife, and left his son Edmond his lands in
Kent, with remainder to his grandson Richard, son of his son Henry.

Lewis, who called himself Stonor's cousin, wrote of Page as his brother.[1] The letters of Walter Elmes relate chiefly to the Devonshire estates,[2] but also to money matters and the business arising out of the wardship of the Fenns.[3]   Page was chiefly concerned with affairs at Horton, with the mismanagement by the farmer there,[4] and with an obscure controversy with Fitz Lewis.[5]   But he was the chief, though not the only legal adviser of his employer.   Stonor was clearly an impetuous client, who acted without thinking, and Page had to intervene to protect him from the consequences.[6]   Other legal advisers were Thomas Moleyns,[7] and Hugh Unton who apparently acted also as a general agent for his employer in London.[8]   Mention may also be made of John Shynner, the parson at Penton Mewsey and a Modbury man, who wrote with a quaint humour:[9] of Henry Makney, a petty Berkshire squire, who had sold his estate to the Stonors and became apparently their local steward;[10] and Thomas Banke, an Oxford don, who in an interesting letter gives us a glimpse at University life and shows that Sir William Stonor had at least enough intellectual interest to be a generous patron of needy scholars.[11]

After Sir William Stonor's attainder his estates were forfeited, probably in October or November, 1483.[12]   His lands are mentioned as being in the King's hands through his treason in February, 1484.   On 24th May, 1484, John, Lord Cobham, had a grant of the manor and hundred of Ermington, and of the manors of Hode in Dertington, Devon, and Wolston or Wolveston, Cornwall, late the property of Sir William Stonor, knight and rebel.   On 28th July, Clist Barnefeld, Devon, late of William Stonor, was granted to Richard Taillour.[13] Hode, Wolveston, and Clist Barneville were part of the inheritance of Agnes Stonor, which he held after her death by a special remainder.[14]   Horton was granted to William Mistelbroke on 27th January, 1485.   Stonor itself, with tenements in Watlington and the reversion of "Barowyscotte" after the death of Anne Kedwell, was granted to Francis Lovell.[15]   Other lands were apparently promised to

---

[1] No. 326. [2] Nos. 263, 282, 287-8. [3] Nos. 282, 287, 288.
[4] Nos. 247, 276, 309, 310, 321. [5] Nos. 322, 324, 326-7.
[6] Nos. 220, 221. [7] Nos. 291, 311. [8] Nos. 313, 317.
[9] Nos. 299-301. [10] Nos. 190-2, 275, 304. [11] No. 303.
[12] Cf. Harley MS. 433, f. 121, for estates in Bucks. and Beds. on 2nd Nov., 1483.
[13] Cal. Pat. Rolls, 1476-85, pp. 378, 433, 481.
[14] See p. xxxii above.
[15] Harley MS. 433, f. 286. For Anne Kedwell and Barowyscotte or Buscot see No. 228.

John Kendale, the King's secretary, who was granted an annuity of 80*l.* during the life of Jane Stonor,[1] whose life interest was untouched by the attainder of her son.

Sir William Stonor's friendship with the Marquis of Dorset makes it likely that he accompanied him in his flight to Brittany. After the accession of Henry VII, Dorset's influence and his own services secured the restoration of the estates. Stonor was replaced on the commission of peace in January, 1486, and regained his position as a Knight of the body.[2] He was sheriff of Oxon. and Berks. in 1485, and of Devon in 1490-91. In February, 1486, he had the reversion of the profitable office of Constable of Wallingford Castle.[3] He fought for Henry VII at Stoke on 16th June, 1487, when he was made a knight banneret on the field.[4] In 1492 he became Steward of the University of Oxford; though his position in the county must have made his name familiar, his local importance was hardly sufficient to have secured him the post if he had not possessed an additional recommendation as a favoured courtier. Anne Stonor died before 5th November, 1486;[5] she left two children, John, who was born in August 1482,[6] and Anne. The long feud of Stonor and Fortescue at Ermington was composed by a double marriage, when Sir William's son was betrothed to Mary, daughter of Sir John Fortescue of Punsborne, and his daughter married to Fortescue's son Adrian.

Sir William Stonor died on 21st May, 1494. By his will,[7] dated 11th April, 1489, he appointed Thomas Ramsey and Walter Elmes to be his executors. His daughter was to have 1000 marks for her marriage; if she predeceased her brother, the money was to be applied for the souls of Anne, his wife, his other wives, his father, mother, and ancestors.

On 15th February, 1495, custody of the lands and marriage of John Stonor were granted during his minority to Sir John Fortescue.[8] John Stonor did not long survive his father, and on his death his sister Anne became her father's heir.[9] But her inheritance was disputed by her uncle Thomas Stonor. Many actions ensued which continued all the life of Thomas Stonor to the great expense and impoverishing of both parties. Thomas Stonor died in 1512 and his niece six years later. There then arose new strife between Sir Adrian Fortescue, claiming by

---

[1] Harley MS. 433, f. 59, and *Cal. Pat. Rolls*, p. 454.
[2] *Cal. Pat. Rolls*, Henry VII, i, 205.   [3] *Id. ib.*
[4] *Paston Letters*, vi, 187.   [5] *Cal. Inq.*, Henry VII, i, 161.
[6] Cf. Nos. 321-2; he was returned as 4 years old at his mother's death.
[7] *Cal. Inq.*, Henry VII, i, 077; for his will see *P.C.C.*, 20 Vox.
[8] *Cal Pat. Rolls*, Henry VII, iii, 21.   [9] In 1499, cf. *Cal. Inq.*, ii, 118.

the curtesy of England, and his daughters Margaret and Frances, and their husbands, Thomas Wentworth and Thomas Fitzgerald, of the one part, and Sir Walter Stonor, son of Thomas Stonor, of the other part. By reason hereof there were great expenses and divers and sundry riots, assaults and affrays, until after a general inquiry an award was made by assent. Sir Walter was to have the manors of Stonor, Pushull Venables, Pushull Napp, Warnescombe and Bixgybyn with other lands in Oxfordshire, and ultimately the manor of Ermington also. By an Act of Parliament in 1537 these estates were entailed on the heirs male of the body of Thomas Stonor, grandfather of Sir Walter, and in default to his right heirs.[1] By virtue of this Act, the descendants of Sir Walter Stonor have held their ancestral home till this day.[2] Sir Adrian Fortescue, less happy, was executed for treason in 1539. Thomas Wentworth, husband of his daughter Margaret, had by her a numerous family, and was created Lord Wentworth, a title now held by the Earl of Lovelace. Thomas Fitzgerald, the husband of Frances, succeeded his father as 10th Earl of Kildare, was executed for treason in 1537 and left no descendants.

From the history of the Stonor Family we must now turn to give some account of their early papers which are here printed. It seems most probable that the family papers were confiscated on the occasion of the attainder of Sir William Stonor in 1483. With one possible exception[3] there are no papers of Sir William Stonor's of later date than 1483, and it is not likely (seeing how carefully he preserved his correspondence) that the collection should have stopped short at this point if the papers had remained in the possession of the family. There are it is true in the Record Office a number of formal documents (chiefly Accounts) relating to the Stonor estates, which belong to the time of Sir Adrian Fortescue. These later papers have, however, nothing of the interest which attaches to the early ones, and although it is possible that all may have been confiscated at the same time, it seems probable that the papers of Sir William Stonor and of his son-in-law found their way into Chancery on two separate occasions. Sir Adrian Fortescue's own troubles might account for the presence of the later papers. It is, however, a possible alternative that the whole of the papers came into

---

[1] *Statutes of the Realm*, iii, 690-93, ed. 1807, 28 Henry VIII, cap. 36.
[2] The John Stonor who died on 29th August, 1512, and was buried at Wyrardisbury, seems to have been a son of Walter Stonor. *Coll. Top et Gen.*, viii, 400.
[3] See vol. ii, p. 184.

Court as an exhibit at some stage of the proceedings between Thomas and Walter Stonor and Sir Adrian Fortescue. But such a solution leaves the absence of any but formal documents of a later date than 1483 unexplained.[1]

As part of the Chancery Records the Stonor Papers were preserved in the Tower. In 1805 Samuel Lysons printed No. 112, and in 1822 John Bayley, the keeper of the Records, printed the account of the Battle of St. Albans in *Archæologia*.[2] A few years later several letters were printed in *Excerpta Historica*.[3] In spite of some occasional references in more recent times, the value of the collection as a whole has not received adequate recognition. Originally no doubt the Stonor Papers, including Letters, Deeds, Accounts, Court Rolls and other family muniments, were preserved together. It is unfortunate that at some time in the last century the Collection was broken up and its contents distributed amongst various classes of records, as Ancient Correspondence, Ancient Deeds, and Ministers Accounts. Owing to this unhappy dispersal it has become difficult to restore the collection in its entirety. Of the Letters the greater part were placed in vol. xlvi of *Ancient Correspondence;* but in the same volume were included other letters, some of which it is safe to reject as forming no part of the original collection, whilst in some other cases there is room for doubt. Moreover, some few letters which certainly formed part of the Stonor Papers have been placed in other volumes of *Ancient Correspondence*, where also there may be others which it is no longer possible to identify. The Deeds are to be found scattered through the printed volumes of the *Catalogue of Ancient Deeds*, whilst a few may still be buried in the vast mass of Deeds which remain uncatalogued.[4] A number of documents were for some reason not assigned to any class, and some of these appear for a time to have been mislaid.[5] Recently all these remaining documents have been brought together and arranged as part of the *Chancery Miscellanea*.[6] In these two volumes an attempt has been made to restore the whole collection. All the Letters, with some trifling exceptions,[7] have been

---

[1] There are no papers at all between 1483 and 1492.   [2] No. 59.
[3] Nos. 148, 151, 204, 229, 330, 331.   [4] See No. 54.
[5] E.g. Nos. 134 and 298 only came to light in 1916. No. 59 was reprinted in the *Paston Letters* from *Archæologia*, the original not then being forthcoming.
[6] *Chancery Miscellanea*, 37. See the list in vol. ii, pp. 165-70. They include all the documents relating to the office of sheriff, household accounts, inventories, and other miscellaneous papers such as the Funeral Accounts in Nos. 47 and 138.
[7] The omitted Letters are all too fragmentary to be worth printing; some of those which are printed are slight in themselves, but any omissions would have been open

printed, together with full copies or abstracts of all such Deeds as are
of special interest in themselves or for the family history; the most
valuable of the documents in the *Chancery Miscellanea* are also given
in their proper place.   In an Appendix, Calendars are given of the
Deeds, Ministers Accounts etc., and of the various documents now in
Chancery Miscellanea.   A few documents, which do not properly
belong to the collection but are important for its illustration, have been
added from other quarters.[1]   The original source of every document
is given in the prefatory note.[2]   The Calendars in the Appendix[3] and
the List of Letters in *Ancient Correspondence*[4] will supply convenient
cross-references.

The history of the Stonor family has served the purpose of a general
review of the letters and of the persons by whom or to whom they were
written.   Some further comment of a more particular character (though
unavoidably brief) seems, however, to be required.

The Stonor Letters are next to the Paston Letters by far the most
considerable collection of private correspondence of the fifteenth century
which has yet come to light.[5]   Though they lack the political interest
which is so marked a characteristic of the more celebrated collection,
in all that is of value for the social life of the time they do not fall short.
They cover a somewhat longer period (though with two considerable
gaps), and they have in some respects a more varied range.   The fortunes of both the Paston and Stonor families were laid by a successful
lawyer.   But whilst the Pastons during the greater part of the time
covered by their correspondence had to struggle to maintain their newly-
won rank, Sir William Stonor and his ancestors during four generations
were country gentlemen of established position.   Though no member
of the family since the Chief Justice had a public career of any importance, yet they had maintained their wealth and made good marriages.
They had substantial estates in six counties, and took an active share in
such public work as fell normally to country gentlemen of rank and
fortune.   Edmund de Stonor, Thomas Stonor, the elder, and Thomas

to exception; English letters of this early date are seldom devoid of interest of
some kind, and even the slightest have generally some value for the illustration of
other Letters or Documents.

[1] Nos. 80, 82 (the greater part), and 182.

A. C. = Ancient Correspondence; *Ch. Misc.* = Chancery Miscellanea.

[3] See vol. ii, pp. 165-84.   [4] Vol. ii, pp. 185-8.

[5] There are 256 letters (not counting fragments), and upwards of 600 documents
all told; see vol. ii, pp. 165-88.

Stonor, the younger, all served their turn as sheriff, and all represented their native county in Parliament. Sir William Stonor was the first who showed any higher ambition, and with the exception of the young Sir Ralph de Stonor was the first of his family to receive knighthood after the death of the Chief Justice. It is curious that in a family of such fortune there was hardly one who did any real military service. Sir Ralph died during the expedition to Ireland in 1394, and his son Thomas may possibly have served for a short time in France. But no member of the family took an active part in the Wars of the Roses till Sir William fought for Henry VII at Stoke. His father was twice summoned by Edward IV,[1] but seems successfully to have evaded compliance. The service of Thomas and Edmund Stonor in the brief French campaign of 1475 [2] hardly constituted an exception to the stay-at-home lives of the family. In this we have a sufficient explanation of the almost complete absence of material for political history. Thomas Stonor preserved a valuable narrative of the first Battle of St. Albans, which has unwarrantably found its way into the Paston Letters.[3] His papers also include the Proclamation of the Truce in 1464,[4] and letters of Privy Seal summoning him to the support of the King in 1470.[5] Unfortunately but few of his earlier papers have been preserved, or we might have expected to find some reference to the tragic fall of his father-in-law the Duke of Suffolk. The papers of Sir William Stonor contain some scattered allusions to the King's movements and to Councils,[6] but the references to Bishop Stillington's [7] imprisonment in March, 1478, to the negotiations at Bruges in July, 1478,[8] and to the Scottish expedition in 1482,[9] are perhaps the only political items of importance before the usurpation of Richard III. The two letters which Simon Stallworth wrote to Sir William Stonor from London in June, 1483, are of real value, but they are no longer novel.[10] Francis Lovell's letter of 11th October, 1483,[11] is of interest for Sir William Stonor's political career, but is not otherwise important.

It is thus in the illustration of the public and domestic life of four generations of country gentlemen that the most continuous interest of the Stonor Letters consists. The careful preservation of family papers, not merely the essential Deeds of their property and the useful Accounts

[1] Nos. 70 and 112.   [2] Nos. 152 and 153.   [3] No. 59.   [4] No. 73.
[5] No. 112.   [6] Nos. 113, 170, 172, 220, 239, 287, 288, 313.
[7] No. 204.   [8] No 223.   [9] No 318.
[10] Nos. 331-2; they were printed in *Excerpta Historica*, pp. 16, 17.
[11] No. 333.

of Bailiffs and other Ministers,[1] but also of their private correspondence
and documents of an official kind which came into their hands, was a
characteristic of them all.   To this we owe a series of documents, relating to the office of sheriff, which for their number and variety is probably unique amongst private collections.   For Edmund de Stonor's
shrievalty in 1377-78 we have not only numerous letters, mostly it is
true of a formal character, addressed to him in his official capacity,[2]
but also writs and mandates issued by or to him,[3] a class of documents
which are rare at so early a date.   A Household Account of this year
contains incidentally a record of the expenses of the "jentaculum" or
official entertainment of the justices at Stonor.[4]   For the shrievalties
of the two Thomas Stonors there is only one writ,[5] but on the other
hand we have the detailed Account of the Under Sheriff in 1427,[6] and
the record of the Allowances claimed by the second Thomas in 1466.[7]
Interesting, though less important, is a letter from the Under-Sheriff
to his employer in the latter year.[8]   The work of a Justice of the Peace
did not produce much correspondence, but there are occasional references to legal matters arising out of it.[9]   Even gentlemen of position
added to their income by taking stewardships from the King, monas-
teries and great lords, and Sir William Stonor had many.[10]

Perhaps as a consequence of the diversified character of their property
estate-management figures largely in the correspondence of the Stonors.
A landlord of importance had as his principal servant a Receiver, to
whom the Bailiffs and Stewards of the various properties and manors
were accountable.   John Warfield, Henry Dogett, and Walter Elmes
were successively Receivers for the Stonors.   An Account by Warfield
is printed here,[11] and there is a letter addressed to him by the Bailiff at
Ermington, which is both interesting in itself and of unusually early
date for a private letter in English.[12]   There are a number of letters
from Henry Dogett,[13] though the interest of them is very slight; they
give the impression of a faithful servant, but in other quarters he is
represented as a harsh steward.[14]   The letters from Walter Elmes are

[1] See vol. ii, pp. 177-82.
[2] Nos. 10-12, 14, 16, 17, 22, 23.
[3] Nos. 9, 13, 15, 18, 20, 21.
[4] No. 19.
[5] No. 84.
[6] No. 52.
[7] No. 85, cf. also No. 78, and *Ch. Misc.*, v, 21; ix, 12, and *Ancient Deeds*, C.
5650, 1968; see vol. ii, p. 174.
[8] No. 83.
[9] Nos. 94, 200, 220, 243.
[10] Nos. 136, 199, 237, 239, 240, 244, 255.
[11] No. 41.
[12] No. 42.
[13] Nos. 171, 231, 245, 256, 265.
[14] Cf. Nos. 189, 244.

more detailed and interesting.[1] At Ermington there were frequent difficulties, and as a consequence there are many letters from successive bailiffs.[2] Though Thomas Stonor and Sir William Stonor paid visits periodically, the management of so distant an estate was of necessity left much to servants. To the Gloucestershire estates there are only occasional references.[3] Horton was in the possession of Alice Drayton till 1468; in Sir William Stonor's time it was apparently managed by Richard Page. Of Penton Mewsey we learn a little from the quaint letters of John Shynner,[4] and an interesting communication from Sir William Sandes,[5] a neighbouring landowner. The Receiver was a man of some position; Warfield was one of the feoffees of the elder Thomas Stonor, Dogett had apparently a little estate of his own at Pusey, and Walter Elmes was a cousin of Sir William Stonor, who made him one of his executors. The local bailiffs or stewards were generally humbler persons. But Richard Germyn, who was Devonshire agent for Sir William Stonor in 1480, was an Exeter merchant of importance.[6] Page was apparently tenant of the manor-house at Horton, and his relations with Stonor were those of a legal adviser, who incidentally exercised supervision over the farmer.

Naturally a certain amount of legal business arose out of such extensive estates. Thomas Mull in Thomas Stonor's time, and Richard Page, Thomas Moleyns and Hugh Unton[7] under Sir William Stonor, were all London lawyers, and the regularly feed advisers of the Stonors. From one letter, Moleyns would seem to have held a sort of watching brief to look out for any business in the Courts which might affect his master's interests.[8] Litigation is indeed always a prominent feature in the private correspondence of the time, though it might be rash to assume that it had an equal part in everyday life. Thomas Stonor had one great lawsuit with Richard Fortescue, which went on for six years. Probably it was a revival of an earlier quarrel in 1424,[9] but the actual suit was one for trespass and assault on Thomas Stonor and his bailiff, John Frende. The narrative begins with two letters of complaint from Frende to his employer, apparently in 1462,[10] on the 10th of May in which year Fortescue is alleged to have assaulted Stonor at Ermington. In the following year there seems to have been an Arbitration, with an Award which probably satisfied neither party; it was not to Mull's

---

[1] Nos. 263, 282, 287, 288.   [2] Nos. 63, 64, 71, 81, 126, 174, 184, 270.
[3] No. 193.   [4] Nos. 299, 301.   [5] No. 298.
[6] Nos. 208, 272.   [7] No. 313.   [8] Nos. 291, 311.
[9] Nos. 45, 46.   [10] Nos. 63, 64.

liking[1] and Fortescue broke it almost at once.   In October, 1465, Fortescue got a writ against Frende, and on 12th December following his supporters (the whole countryside seems to have become involved) arrested Frende under its authority.   Frende put up a Bill of Complaint for riot in Chancery,[2] and also began proceedings for false imprisonment in the Common Pleas.   In Trinity Term, 1467, the Chancery Record was brought into the King's Bench.   Thence the dispute was referred to the Assizes at Exeter, where the ordinary jury found a verdict against Fortescue.   The verdict was challenged, and a fresh hearing with a jury of twenty-four was ordered in Easter Term, 1468.   Finally in Michaelmas Term of that year the case was settled.   Thomas Stonor wrote in triumph to his wife "mine adversary of Devonshire hath had no worship . . . he is nonsuited in the Court to his great shame"[3]   The whole is an unusually full record of proceedings in the same case, first in Chancery and in the Common Pleas, then at the Assizes and in the King's Bench.   Its interest is enhanced by the accompanying Letters and other subsidiary documents.

Thomas Stonor's papers include five letters relating to another lawsuit, with which he had no direct concern, viz. the claim of one Mistress Swete to be the heir of Sir Walter Romesey.   The letters by themselves are hopelessly obscure, but they have led to the unravelling of a curiously complicated genealogical dispute.[4]

Sir William Stonor also had his share of litigation; we find him involved in disputes with the Prince's Council concerning the property of his brother-in-law John Barantyne (who was a minor),[5] with the Queen,[6] and with his own mother,[7] besides some minor matters.   A more serious suit seems to have been as to the Manor of Wolveston (part of the Winnard inheritance) which continued after the death of Agnes Stonor.[8]

The Stonor Letters naturally teem with references to the social and domestic life of the time.   The valuable Inventories at Horton in 1425,[9] and at Stonor in 1474,[10] the numerous Household Accounts[11] (beginning with one in 1378) and the actual bills of trades people (there is one for cloth in 1380,[12] others of particular interest are a Wax Chandler's bill[13] to Dame Elizabeth Stonor, and shoemakers'[14] and mercers',[15] bills to

---

[1] No. 69, cf. No. 79.   [2] No. 80.   [3] No. 91.
[4] See Appendix to Introduction, pp. xlviii-lvi below.   [5] Nos. 310, 311.
[6] No. 313.   [7] No. 320.   [8] Nos. 266-68, 313.
[9] No. 50.   [10] No. 140.
[11] Nos. 19, 55, 101, 146, 233.   [12] No. 39.   [13] No. 227.
[14] No. 234.   [15] Nos. 235, 317.

her husband), illustrate the furnishing of the manor-house, where it
" snewed of meat and drink " and there was an abundance of cheer and
company, and gentlemen and ladies ruffled it in fine attire. Sir William
Stonor had a demi-gown of black puke lined with green velvet,[1] and
Dame Elizabeth bought 38 yards of green sarsenet at five shillings a
yard, which she was assured would last her own life and her child's
after her.[2] Food was provided chiefly from the estate, or neighbour-
hood,[3] and the coarser materials for dress were woven from home-
grown wool by a weaver at Watlington.[4] But costlier goods and
delicacies, in particular fish and wine, were brought without difficulty
from London by the bargemen who plied regularly on the river to
Henley.[5] Mistress Jane had no liking for sojournants,[6] but Dame
Elizabeth with her meyny of boys no doubt kept a merry household,
even if it lacked sad wise rule. The fifteenth century country-gentle-
man had plenty of company; at Stonor, besides Dame Elizabeth's
children and the young Fenns, there were a number of wards of Sir
William's.[7] There is not, however, much reference to the children.
Parental rule at the time was generally strict, but the Stonor Letters
give us on the whole a uniform impression of family affection. This is
the more remarkable since matrimony was very much a matter of
business. All three of William Stonor's marriages had been made for
money or position, only from Agnes Wydeslade do we get something
like a love-letter before marriage.[8] Matches were arranged on a commercial footing. Thomas Betson, it is true, seems to have married his
child-wife for love, but we find Dame Elizabeth bargaining for a husband
for another daughter,[9] and her brother John Croke was beholden to
William Stonor for helping him to an advantageous match.[10] Similarly
when Edmund Stonor consults his brother about a possible wife, it is
the suitability of the settlements with which he is concerned.[11] It was
the possibility of securing a good husband (commercially) that made the
father of daughters glad to undertake wardships, as Thomas Stonor did
that of John Cottesmore whom he matched with his eldest daughter.[12]
One might have expected to find some record of wedding festivities,
but the greatest feast in the Stonor Papers is that of the lavish entertainment of worshipful men, priests, and poor people at the funeral of
Thomas Stonor.[13]

[1] No. 222. [2] No. 252. [3] See Nos. 146 and 233.
[4] No. 95. [5] Nos. 164, 209, 210, 225, 313. [6] No. 106.
[7] No. 234. [8] No. 262. [9] No. 176.
[10] No. 183. [11] No. 155. [12] No. 110. [13] No. 138.

There are a good number of letters from neighbouring squires, usually cousins more or less remote, which give a few hints on their mutual relations. Most commonly they touch on business, petty disputes of their own or greivances of tenants.[1] But instances are not wanting of mutual helpfulness. Most of the letters are autograph and inability to write is rare. Thomas Gate, in a letter where he claims that it is reasonable for a gentleman to know his pedigree and his possibility, quotes St. Paul in evidence.[2] There are a few references to sport; Thomas Stonor and his son kept hawks,[3] and they had abundance of game in their park whence they sent presents of venison to friends in London.[4]

Elizabeth Stonor introduces us to another side of life amongst her citizen relatives, and in Thomas Betson we get a pleasing picture of the best type of London merchant. The story of his illness is a strange mixture of affectionate anxiety and sordid concern about money. The friendship of the Duchess of Suffolk enabled Elizabeth Stonor to go to court: "I waited upon her to my lady, the King's mother and hers, by her commandment. And also upon Saturday last I waited upon her thither again, and from thence she waited upon my lady her mother, and brought her to Greenwich to the King's good grace and the Queen's. And there I saw the meeting between the King and my lady his mother. Truly me thought it was a very good sight."[5] It is a pity that Elizabeth was not moved more often to describe what she saw.

However, we have to thank Elizabeth Stonor for the introduction of her husband to the wool trade, which has given the Stonor Letters an interest for commercial as well as social history. Neither Elizabeth Stonor nor Betson are concerned solely with the business, but it is always cropping up in their letters and incidentally Betson has a good deal to tell of his work, of profitable transactions in England and Calais and of his visits to the Mart at Bruges. On more purely commercial matters we learn something from Betson's assistants, Thomas Henham, Thomas Howlake, and Goddard Oxbridge.[6] Thomas Howlake's report on the sales of wool in July, 1478, contains material of particular value.[7] Sir William Stonor had of course a personal interest in the wool-trade as a great sheep grazier on the Chilterns and Cotswolds. Both in his own and in his father's time we get documents relating to the

---

[1] See Nos. 75, 76, 87, 110, 119, 236, 242.
[3] Nos. 86 and 198.   [4] Nos. 269, 274.
[6] Nos. 163, 164, 222, 223.

[2] No. 130.
[5] No. 172.
[7] No. 223, compare No. 159.

hire and purchase of sheep.[1] The information in these Letters is less purely commercial than that in the *Cely Papers*, for we have not for the most part the actual business documents, but the material will be found valuable for purposes of comparison and illustration.

There are some few individual letters to which special attention must be directed. The nearness of Stonor to Oxford brings us fairly frequent references to the University. In Edmund de Stonor's time there is an Indenture of the delivery to Queen's College of the college seal, plate, books, and other articles which had been improperly taken away.[2] About the same date we get an interesting letter from a needy scholar asking for assistance.[3] A writ in 1466 has to do with payments due from the Chancellor of the University, and from All Souls and Exeter Colleges.[4] The sheriff's petition for Allowances in the same year includes a number of payments due from various Colleges.[5] The Petition of the parishioners of Didcot may be included amongst University documents, since the parson was absent at the schools, and the Rector, Roger Bulkeley, was a sometime Commissary of the University.[6] A letter from Sir Richard Graystoke has apparently to do with the exhibition of a poor scholar.[7] In 1480 William Sutton, then Commissary, writes to Sir William Stonor at the request of the Chancellor on behalf of a poor gentlewoman.[8] Stonor had an honourable reputation for his readiness to help needy scholars; from one of these, Master Edmund, we have a letter to his patron, though it has no direct reference to University history.[9] But the most valuable document is the extremely interesting letter from Thomas Banke, which gives us incidentally particulars of Stonor's benefactions, and describes the action taken in the University to settle a complaint which Stonor had made about the treatment of his servants by some of the scholars; it is characteristic of the time to note the deference which was paid to Edward de la Pole and James Stanley.[10]

A document which is probably unique is the letter[11] in which William Goldwyn, a London physician, sends four prescriptions to be made up by the Bucklersbury apothecary. It is noteworthy as giving actual prescriptions for a definite patient, and for their intelligent character, the first is clearly a laxative; the use of the abbreviation an[a] (for ἀνά) is remarkable; though Goldwyn was a man of repute, he can hardly have come under the influence of the Renaissance, and it would seem

[1] Nos. 61, 157, and 196.   [2] No. 18.   [3] No. 31.
[4] No. 84.   [5] No. 85.   [6] No. 74.   [7] No. 181.
[8] No. 280.   [9] No. 195.   [10] No. 303.   [11] No. 271.

to be a traditional survival.   The half-scruple is represented by a long
"s" (for "semissem"), of a form similar to that still used in written
prescriptions; it is printed below as "ss" in accordance with modern
practice.   A second letter from Goldwyn mentions that 15*l.* was due to
him,[1] which would be a handsome fee.   There are a few medical
references in some other letters.[2]

The reader of these Letters is sure to be struck by the curiously
modern note in many chance phrases, such as Mistress Jane Stonor's
lament that "servants be not so diligent as they were wont to be";[2] the
household calling to Betson "Come down to dinner!   Come down to
dinner at once!"[3]   Dame Elizabeth's naive surprise that the bargemen
were "loath to take any stuff of ours, for truly to my knowledge I never
had a thing carried by them but that I paid them truly befoie";[4] the
homely advice of William Harleston to his nephew;[5] or Sir William
Sandes walking in the woods for his recreation.[6]   It is indeed a great
part of the value of such documents for history that they bring home to
the reader how little men have changed in themselves for all the changes
in their environment.   It is easy also to exaggerate the changes of
environment, business and sport, matchmaking and festivities were
much what they are to-day five centuries ago.   Though William
Harleston found the world never uneasier, the troubles of the time seem
to have disturbed social life in the country very little.   It is remarkable
to note how easy communications were.   The barges plied regularly
from London to Henley in four days.   A messenger covered the distance
in a day's ride, and Dame Elizabeth took the journey as a matter of
course.   Even from Exeter to London there seems to have been a
regular service of carriers, by pack-horse.[7]   Both Thomas Stonor and
his son paid frequent visits to their Devonshire estates, and Richard
Germyn urged Sir William to spend the summer in the West[8] without
a hint that it was anything unusual.

In the Introduction to the *Paston Letters*,[9] Dr. Gairdner remarked
that: "No person of any rank or station in society above mere labour-
ing men seems to have been wholly illiterate.   All could write letters:
most persons could express themselves in writing with ease and fluency."
This judgment is fully confirmed by the Stonor Letters.   Dr. Gairdner
thought that the nobility were generally the worst writers of the day.
There are few letters from nobles in these volumes, and Lord Strange

[1] No. 274.   [2] Nos. 188, 250, 275.   [3] No. 166.
[4] No. 176.   [5] No. 260.   [6] No. 298.
[7] No. 268.   [8] No. 272.   [9] Vol. i, p. 318.

could probably do little more than sign his name.[1] Sir William Stonor, his father, and brothers on the other hand wrote their own letters and spelt passably well. Jane Stonor wrote tolerably but spelt atrociously. Her daughter-in-law Elizabeth generally employed an amanuensis, but could write well enough if she pleased; any difficulty there is in her letters seems to be due to the fact that they were dictated. Generally the country squires of Oxfordshire and their women folk, and the better class merchants of London could write with ease. The worst writers and spellers are inferior clergy like John Shynner and the Abbots of Norton and Nutley,[2] or humble mercantile people like Thomas Henham and Goddard Oxbrige;[3] the last named is easily the worst writer and speller in these Letters, though he was no worse than George and Richard Cely.

In printing the Letters the original spelling has been preserved, though "with" has been printed for "wth," and "yat" for "y^t". The modern practice has, however, been followed in the use of u and v and i and j; but in certain cases a partial exception has been made; some writers, as for instance Sir William Stonor,[4] were in the habit of writing "nov" for "now" and "yov" for "you"; this seemed sufficiently characteristic to be preserved. In signatures also the actual spelling has been retained as "Olyuer Wittonstall" and "Ric. Havrecourt". On the whole it has seemed well to preserve the thorn, "þ" for "th," and the soft guttural "ʒ" for "gh" and "^{y}" in such words as "myʒt" and "ʒove"; the latter at all events in such an instance as "ffeizthefull" (which Betson wrote commonly) would defy transliteration. Any little difficulty which these peculiarities might create will be met sufficiently by the Glossary.

As far as possible the Letters and other Documents are arranged in chronological order. But there are many which can only be dated approximately; in some cases with no more certainty than that they were before 1474 (the date of Thomas Stonor's death) or before 1478 or after 1477 (when William Stonor was knighted). Where letters of uncertain date refer to the same subject it has seemed best to bring them together even though they were written at various times[5]

---

[1] No. 230.   [2] Nos. 199, 299-302.   [3] Nos. 163-5, 167, 222, 251.
[4] Stonor commonly wrote "v" in place of "w"; cf. No. 296.
[5] Cf. Nos. 98 and 99, 103-5, 107-10, and 298-301.

APPENDIX TO INTRODUCTION

THE INHERITANCE OF SIR WALTER DE ROMESEY

The case of Mistress Swete which forms the subject of two letters addressed by Thomas Hampton to Thomas Stonor,[1] is too complicated for treatment in one of the usual Notes prefixed to the Letters. Its history goes back to the time when the Romeseys succeeded the Bissets at Rokebourne and Combe Bisset. On 22nd August, 1334, John Byset was found to have held the manor of Kidderminster, Worcestershire, the manor of Rokebourne with a messuage and forty acres at Stapelham in Hampshire, and the manor of Combe in Wiltshire;[2] his heir was his sister Margaret, "quem Robertus Martyn duxit in uxorem," she was aged thirty and more.[3] Robert Martyn died on 24th April, 1355, when it was found that he held jointly with his wife, Margaret, the manor of Rokebourne with half the manor of Combe Byset for the term of their lives under a fine which secured the remainder to John, "filius ipsius Margarete," and his heirs, and in default to the right heirs of Margaret, who was still alive; Robert Martyn's heir was unknown.[4] The implication is that John was son of Margaret by a former marriage,[5] and this is confirmed from other sources.

On 12th October, 1333, Walter de Romesey had been found to have held Fyrnham (Farnham) in Hampshire, and Wynford, Oclee, and Modford Terry in Somerset; John his son and heir was aged thirty and more.[6] Though it is nowhere definitely stated, John de Romesey must

[1] Nos. 65 and 67 below, see also Nos. 66, 68, and 69.

[2] As also did his father, another John Byset, in 1307, *Cal. Inq.*, iv, 431.

[3] *Cal. Inq.*, vii, 605.

[4] *Chancery Inq. p.m.*, Edw. III, File 130.

[5] They may perhaps be identified with Margeria Romesey, "domicella Isabelle Regine" and John her son, who were buried at Greyfriars, London (*The Greyfriars of London*, p. 78).

[6] *Cal. Inq.*, vii, 514.

have died soon after his father, having married Margaret, sister of John Byset; and his widow must have married Robert Martyn before 22nd August, 1334. By John de Romesey, Margaret had two sons, John and Walter. John, who is mentioned in the Inquisition after the death of Robert Martyn, probably died before 12th March, 1346, when Walter, son of John de Romesey by Margaret his wife, was found to be twenty-one years of age and more, having been born on the Sunday before St. Agatha—5th February—in the ? year of Edward II.[1]

In 1350 Walter de Romesey and Joan (Johne) his wife were parties to a Fine concerning lands in Domerham and Morton, which were then settled on them for their lives with remainders to Thomas "filius ejusdem Johne" for his life, then to the heirs of the body of Walter and Joan, then to the heirs of the body of Thomas, then to Cicely and Maud, sisters of Thomas, and the heirs of their bodies, and finally to the right heirs of Walter.[2] This is the Fine to which reference was made by Thomas Hampton, who believed that the Thomas of the Fine was son of Walter and Joan.[3] The terms of the settlement are peculiar, but indicate that Thomas was son of Joan by a former husband. This is confirmed by a fifteenth century Inquisition, where after recital of the Fine of 1350 it is alleged that Walter and Joan had no heirs of their bodies, that Thomas entered into possession under the Fine and had issue, John Northlode, who succeeded and died without heirs of his body, and that, Cicely and Maud died without issue.[4] During the litigation of 1463-64 it was definitely stated that Joan had been first married to Amaric Northlode, and died without issue by Walter de Romesey.[5] In one place she is called Joan Martyn, which suggests that she may have been a daughter of Robert Martyn by a first wife.[6] Joan de Romesey must have died some years before 1370; possibly before 1355, since Robert Martyn's heir was unknown.

In October, 1373, Margaret de Romesey died, and was found to have been seized in her demesne as of fee of the Manor of Rokebourne, and of a moiety of the Manor of Combe, Wilts; Walter de Romesey, "chivaler," her son and heir was aged thirty and more.[7] In June, 1386, it was found on inquisition that Walter de Romesey might with-

---

[1] *Cal. Inq.*, viii, 673; the year of birth is illegible, it cannot have been later than 1325.

[2] *Feet of Fines*, $\frac{265}{48}$, No. 8.   [3] See No. 67 below.

[4] Inquisition for William Horsy in 1448, *Chancery Inq. p.m.*, Henry VI, File 131.

[5] See No. 67 below.   [6] See p. liii below.

[7] *Chancery Inq. p.m.*, Edw. III, File 234.

out prejudice to the King have licence to transfer a moiety of the Manor of Combe Byset to feoffees with a view to a retransfer to himself and his wife Alice and their heirs male, and in default to the heirs male of Walter, and then to his right heirs.[1] In the Inquisition of 1448, to which reference has already been made, it was alleged that Walter married Alice, daughter of William Filoll, and had issue, Thomas and Mary. Though the Inquisition of 1386 does not mention that Walter and Alice had any children, they had been married for many years, since their son Thomas was married before 1382,[2] and had a son in 1389. In 1394 Walter de Romesey acknowledged that the same relief was due from him for Kidderminster, Rokebourne, and Combe as was paid by his mother Margery, daughter of John Byset.[3] This is con-. clusive for the identification of Walter's mother with the sister of the John Byset who died in 1334. On 16th December, 1400, Thomas Romesey was found to have been seised of lands at "Suth Domerham" held by services unknown of John Lovel, William Peytefyn, and Walter Romesey, "chivaler," and of a messuage and virgate of land at Morton and also of a moiety of the Manor of Farnham, Hampshire; he died on the Monday before the feast of St. James the Apostle—i.e. 19th July, 1400; Thomas his son and heir was aged ten.[4] This Inquisition is the "gentlemanly thing," which Thomas Hampton had found[5] and hoped to use with the Fine of 1350 to establish the claim of Mistress Swete. By a Fine in January, 1402, the family estates were settled on Sir Walter Romesey and Alice his wife with remainders to Thomas, son of Thomas Romesey and others.[6] In December, 1403, Sir Walter Romesey was found to have been seised with Alice his wife for their joint lives of the Manor of Rokebourne with remainders under the Fine of 1402, to Thomas, son of Thomas Romesey, and his heirs male, then to his brother Walter and his heirs male, and then to the right heirs of Margery Byset, mother of Walter Romesey, "chivaler"; Walter and Alice were similarly seised of other lands in Hampshire, Dorset, Wilts, and Somerset. Walter died on 25th November, 1403; his heir was Thomas, son of Thomas Romesey.[7] Alice, " que fuit uxor Walteri de Romesey," died on 13th December, 1404; she was seised of Roke-

---

[1] *Inq. ad quod damnum*, 404 (7).   [2] Hoare, *Wilts.* Cawden, p. 13.
[3] Madox, *Baronia Anglica*, 51, 52 (with an account of the early history of the barony of Byset).
[4] *Chancery Inq. p.m.*, Henry IV, File 21.   [5] See No. 65 below.
[6] Recited in Inquisitions for Sir Walter Romsey, William Horsy, and Thomas Payn.
[7] *Chancery Inq. p.m.*, Henry IV, File 44.

bourne, Modford Terry, and other lands; her heir was Thomas, son of Thomas, son of Alice.[1] In February, 1412, Thomas, son of Thomas Romesey, was found to be of full age on the Feast of SS. Simon and Jude (28th October) last passed, having been born at Lye and baptized at Wimborne Minster on that Feast in 13 Richard II—1389.[2] This is the "Sir Thomas" of Hampton's letters.[3] His father, whom Hampton wrongly supposed to be son of Walter by his first wife, married Eleanor and had issue, two sons, Thomas and Walter.[4] Sir Thomas Romesey died in 1420 and was succeeded by his brother Walter, who died in the autumn of 1428,[5] leaving by his wife, Elizabeth, daughter of Walter Sybbeyn (?),[6] a son Walter, who died on 28th February, 1429, aged two or three years.[7] Elizabeth Romesey married, before 13th July, 1430, as her second husband, Henry Champeneys.[8] The Romesey estates then reverted to Joan, daughter of Sir Thomas Romesey; she married Thomas Payne, who in April, 1434, claimed that his wife was of full age, but it was found that she was only sixteen, having been born at Rokebourne on the Feast of St. Petronilla—31st May—1418.[9] On 31st October, 1440, Thomas Payne and Joan his wife obtained licence to settle Rokebourne, a moiety of Farnham, and a moiety of Combe Byset, with remainders to the heirs of the body of Thomas, and to Joan's right heirs; Henry Champeneys was then a feoffee of Combe.[10] By a Fine in October, 1443, Payne and his wife settled Ocle and other lands on Henry and Elizabeth Champeneys, for their lives, but Joan died seised thereof before 1448.[11] On 31st December, 1447, Thomas Payne died, and it was then found that after the death of the last Walter Romesey the lands went under the Fine of 1402, to Thomas Hunteley, now alive and aged forty, as cousin and next heir, being son of Richard, son of Margaret, daughter of Sir Walter Romesey, and "eidem Thome" (presumably Payne); and that Payne entered (se intrusit) on the manor of Ocle without right or title and died without heirs.[12]

[1] Chancery Inq. p.m., Henry IV, File 49.   Id., File 88.
[3] Nos. 65 and 67.   [4] Inquisition for William Horsy.
[5] Id., Henry VI, File 38, the date of death is given as 3rd September or 1st November, 1428.
[6] Inquisition for William Horsy.
[7] Chancery Inq. p.m., Henry VI, File 44.
[8] Cal. Pat. Rolls, Henry VI, ii, 65.
[9] Chancery Inq. p.m., Henry VI, File 67.
[10] Cal. Pat. Rolls, Henry VI, iii, 473.
[11] Somerset Inquisition for William Horsy
[12] Chancery Inq. p.m., Henry VI, File 131, "manerium &c. remanserunt Thome Hunteley &c. et eidem Thome virtute finis".

By the death of Joan Payne the Romesey estates certainly should have gone to the right heirs of Sir Walter, viz. to the descendants of his daughters. It was over the partition of the estates that the dispute in which Mistress Swete was interested arose. After Payne's death Joan, wife of Roger Wyke, as daughter of Mary daughter of Sir Walter Romesey, and William Horsy as son of Eleanor another daughter of Mary, entered on the Romesey estates. William Horsy, who had married Margaret, daughter of John Glenne, died on 1st April, 1448, leaving as his heir his son Thomas, aged seven. On Horsy's death a special commission *ad melius inquirendum* was issued,[1] and the detailed findings which have been so often cited above were the result. After his father's death, Thomas Horsy was seised of Rokebourne (and presumably the other estates) in coparcenery with Joan Wyke. Roger and Joan Wyke by a Fine made an estate to John Browne, John Wyke of Byndon, and Richard Levermore. Thomas Horsy was seised in his share till Thomas and Joan Swete, and Richard Hatfeld disseised him.

In the course of pleadings in the subsequent suit it was alleged by Roger and John Wyke that on 22nd June, 1461, Thomas Swete " de Bradeford juxta Yevell "—Bradford Abbas—Dorset, "glasyer," Joan his wife, and Richard Hatfeld, later of " Adhere," gentleman, broke their close and houses at Rokebourne and did great damage.[2]

In March, 1462, Richard Hatfeld, gentleman, and Thomas Swete and Jane his wife filed a petition in Chancery that, whereas divers variances and debates were hanging and moved between them and Roger Wyke and Jane his wife, upon the right and title of the manor of Rokebourne and other lands late of Joan wife of Thomas Payne, which variances by agreement of both parties be put in compromise, and whereas Roger and Jane Wyke had entered on the manors and taken all evidences touching the suppliants' title, there might be a commission to summon John Popham, knight, and Henry Champeneys of Frome, gentleman, who have very knowledge of the right and title, and have them sworn. A commission was issued accordingly to Humphrey Stafford of Southwick.[3]

In Easter Term, 1462, Roger and Joan Wyke had commenced pro-

---

[1] *Chancery Inq. p.m.*, Henry VI, File 131. Horsy and the Wykes are alleged to have entered on Joan Payne's death, but Thomas Payne was clearly possessed of Ocle till 31st December, 1447. See also *Cal. Pat. Rolls*, Henry VI, v, 187.

[2] *Coram Rege Roll*, 807, m. 56, Hilary Term, 2 Edward IV. On the dorse of the same membrane Thomas Swete's wife is described as " Johannam, uxorem ejus, nuper de Bradeford, spynster ".

[3] *Early Chancery Proceedings*, 29/31 and 32.

ceedings against Thomas and Joan Swete.   Delays were interposed, the Swetes failing to appear, and the hearing was put off again and again till Easter, 1463.[1]   Meantime in Trinity Term, 1462, the sheriff had been directed to produce Thomas and Joan Swete, William Saunderston of London, mercer, William Ratclyff of London, gentleman, and Richard Hatfeld of London, gentleman, to answer for certain trespass, contempt, and forcible entry for which they were indicted.[2]   The other side had retaliated on 5th October, 1462, when Thomas Lyete, late of Lytes Care, Somerset, Isabella Hunteley of Netherattebeare, widow, and others, broke the close of Thomas Swete and Richard Hatfeld at Netherattebeare, did them grievous hurt and so threatened their tenants that they did not dare to continue, to the great loss of Swete and Hatfeld, who thereupon took proceedings in the King's Bench in Hilary Term, 1463.[3]

When the original suit in which the Wykes were plaintiffs came up in Easter Term, 1463, the defendants, Swete and Hatfeld, set up a pedigree alleging that Sir Walter Romsey married one Joan Martyn after banns at Salisbury, and had issue, Thomas and Margaret.   Thomas, they asserted, was grandfather of Joan Payne, at whose death the manor of Rokebourne went rightly to Joan Swete, as daughter of John, son of Margaret, daughter of Margaret, daughter of Sir Walter Romesey. For Roger and John Wyke it was denied that Walter Romesey and Joan his wife had any such issue, Margaret, as the defendants alleged;[4] further that Joan died at Rokebourne in the lifetime of Walter, who then married Alice, daughter of William Fillol, and had issue, Thomas (supposed by the defendants to be son of Joan) and Mary, who married Thomas Byngham and had issue, Joan, wife of Roger Wyke, and Eleanor, mother of William Horsy.   With a view to the determination of the facts a writ was issued for a jury of twenty-four; whether the writ should be issued to the sheriff of Wiltshire or the sheriff of Hampshire was in question, ultimately it was issued by assent to the sheriff of Wiltshire.[5] At the Assizes held at Salisbury in July, 1463, the defendants failed to appear, and the jury found that Thomas was son of Walter and Alice

---

[1] *Coram Rege Rolls*, 804, m. 19, 805, mm. 19 and 32, 807, m. 56.

[2] *Id.*, 805 ; Rex. m. 22.

[3] *Placita de Bancc*, Roll 807. m. 376 dorso; but this may have been a separate dispute relating to the same lands as were in dispute in 1482, see p. lv below.

[4] This does not preclude the possibility that Margaret was daughter of Walter and Alice de Romesey.

[5] A doubt was expressed by Hampton as to whether the " office " was to be found in Wiltshire or Hampshire, see No. 65.

as alleged by Wyke, and assessed the damages at 200 marks.[1] At the same time at the Assizes held at Winchester, Thomas Horsy recovered seisin of Rokebourne against Thomas and Joan Swete and Richard Hatfeld under an Assize of Novel Disseisin with damages of 420*l.* Swete failed to pay, and Horsy sought a remedy in the King's Bench in Hilary Term, 1464,[2] when the record of the Assize was ordered to be brought up. Similar proceedings were taken at the same time by John Browne, John Wyke of Byndon, and Roger Levermore with similar results, the damages being assessed at 1500 marks. In each case the damages were trebled in accordance with the statute, Swete having been in occupation for three years before the issue of the original writ on 21st May, 1463.[3]

The pleadings in this litigation make it clear that Mistress Swete's claim was based on the belief that Thomas Romesey was son of Sir Walter by his first wife, and that her own descent was from Margaret, an alleged daughter of Sir Walter. Thomas Hampton asserted that Sir Walter had two daughters, Margaret wife of John Hunteley and Isabel, wife of John Popham.[4] At an inquisition on the death of Isabel, wife of Sir John Popham, in 1419, it was found that she had married in the reign of Richard II, Thomas Lye, and was jointly enfeoffed with him in the manor of Stanton Fitzherbert, Wilts, by demise of Thomas Romesey and Oliver Romesey. By Lye she had no issue, and after his death she married Sir John Popham, by whom she had a son Thomas, who was twelve years old when his mother died on the Tuesday before Ascension Day in 1419.[5] The Chancery Petition of 1462 suggests that the second husband was the well-known Sir John Popham, who was speaker-elect of the House of Commons in 1449 and died as a very old man in 1463 or 1464;[6] he, however, left no surviving issue, and his heiresses were the daughters of his cousin, Sir Stephen Popham.[7] According to the Inquisition for Thomas Payne, Margaret Romesey was mother of Richard Hunteley, and grandmother of Thomas Hunteley.[8]

None of the documents with which we have so far had to deal give the full descent of Joan Swete. But in 1482 John Hunteley, son of the before-named Thomas, sued Richard Hatfeld and Christine his

[1] *Coram Rege Roll*, 808, m. 80.   [2] *Placita de Banco*, Roll 811, m. 224.
[3] Roll 811, m. 96.   [4] See No. 65 below.
[5] *Chancery Inq. p.m.*, Henry V, File 38.
[6] *Dict. Nat. Biog.*, xlvi, 147, where the fact that he was ever married is questioned.
[7] See p. 69 below.   [8] See p. li above.

wife, Joan Swete, and Margaret Swete as to lands and tenements in Netherattebere, Overattebere, and Homer, which had been settled by Fine in 4 Edward II on David, son of Thomas Huntelegh, with remainder to his brother Thomas and his heirs.[1] The defendants set up a pedigree alleging Thomas brother of David Huntelegh, to have had two sons, John and Richard.[2] John was father of Margaret, mother of John Shete, whose daughter Joan was mother of Christine Hatfeld Joan Swete and Margaret. Richard Hunteley is given as father of Thomas and grandfather of the plaintiff. John Hunteley replied that Margaret daughter of John Hunteley in the alleged pedigree died without issue, and the jury found in his favour. There was dearly something amiss with the Swete descent, and this last suit explains why the Hunteleys (as will be seen) opposed Joan Swete's claim in 1464. Possibly Thomas Hampton's statement that their opponents would have " to breff Margaret bastard "[3] was well-founded. But it is difficult to suppose that Margaret and Isabel, the alleged daughters of Sir Walter Romesey, were not in some way connected with the Romeseys. Whatever the solution may be Thomas Mull was well justified when he wrote in 1463 that the matter " must have witty guiding."[4]

The litigation of 1462-64 would seem to have been conclusive, but Mistress Swete still believed in her case, and ultimately on 29th September, 1467, Joan, late the wife of Thomas Swete, and others, obtained a grant of the manors of Rokebourne, Hants., Northcourte in Combe Bisset, Wilts., Okeley, Overattebere, Netherattebere and Homer, Somerset, for a term of five years without impeachment of waste or rendering any account, with reversion to the King for the use of Joan and her heirs, on a supplication that she and her husband were seised in their demesne in her right, and had enfeoffed the King of the same to the use of themselves and their heirs, and the King was so seised till Thomas Horsy, John Calewey, and John Wyke entered on Rokebourne and Northcourte, Horsy, Calewey, Wyke, and Thomas Lyte entered on Okeley, and John Hunteley, Isabel, late wife of Thomas Hunteley, John Sydenham, and William Lucock entered on the other Somerset manors.[5] In spite of this grant, Thomas Horsy at his death in 1477

---

[1] Wrottesley, *Pedigrees from the Plea Rolls*, p. 462.

[2] The pedigree seems to be faulty; Richard Hunteley was certainly son of Margaret Romesey, whose husband was John Hunteley. Joan Swete's alleged grandmother Margaret was probably daughter of John and Margaret Hunteley.

[3] See No. 65.   [4] See No. 69.

[5] *Cal. Pat. Rolls*, Edw. IV, ii, 33. The appearance of Calewey is possibly explained by the statement in HUTCHINS, *Dorset*, iv, 370, that Joan, daughter of

held Little Domerham, and East Merton, the manor of Okeley, and other Romesey lands, which had been settled in 1467 on him and his wife, Anne, with remainders to his brother John, and to John Wyke ; his heir was his brother John, then aged thirty and more.[1]   Perhaps the litigation ended in some sort of a partition, though the lands in dispute between John Hunteley and Joan Swete's daughters in 1482 do not seem to have been part of the Romesey inheritance.

The reference to Sir John Beynton in Hampton's letters is in part explained by the Inquisition after his death on 20th June, 1465, when it was found that he held in Combe Bisset and Homyngton a messuage, 3 cottages, 30 acres of land, and 5 acres of meadow of John Horsy as of his manor of Rokebourne.[2]

Maud and Thomas Bingham, married Thomas Kelwaye de Rathborne (? Rokeborne).

[1] *Chancery Inq. p.m.*, Edward IV, File 62.   [2] *Id.*, File 17.

John Byset,
d. 1334.

Thomas Byngham   Cicely.   Maud.

Roger Wyke = Joa   John Northlode,
                             o. s. p.

John Wyke.   Walter Romesey,
                      d. 1429.

Thomas Lye (I) = aret.

Margaret = Shete.

John Shete = Beatrice Tremayn.

wete = Joan.   Christine = Richard Hatfeld,

PEDIGREE OF SIR WALTER DE ROMESEY AND HIS DESCENDANTS.

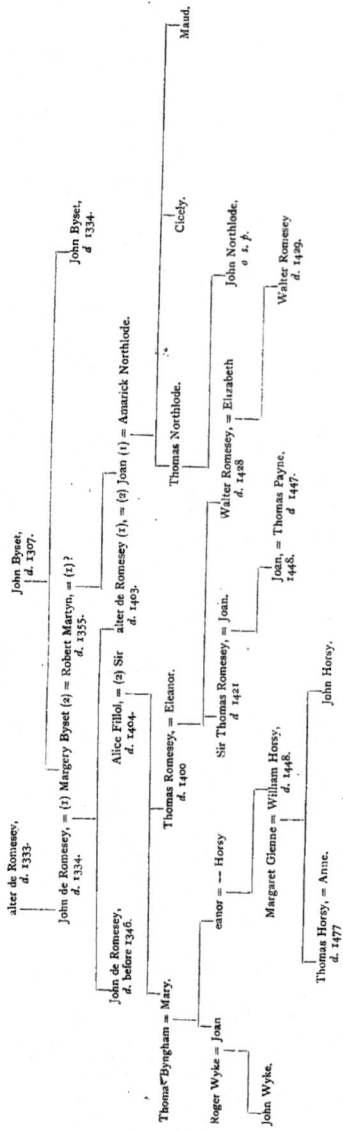
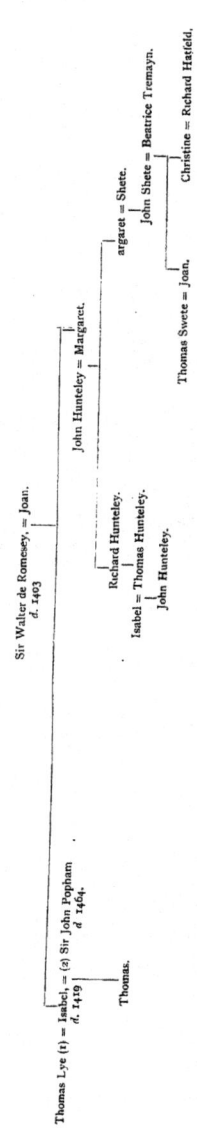

PEDIGREE ALLEGED BY SWETE.

1. CHARTER OF RICHARD I. DE STONOR

[c. 1290]

This is given as the oldest document in the Stonor Papers. It is a grant by Richard de Stonor to his son Richard and the latter's wife Cicely ; Richard and Cicely were the parents of John de Stonor, the judge. From *Ancient Deeds*, C. 221. The seal is lost.

Sciant presentes et futuri quod ego Ricardus de Stonor dedi, concessi, et hac presenti carta mea confirmavi Ricardo, filio meo, et heredi, et Cecilie ejus uxori, dimidiam virgatam terre in Buksebraund,[1] quam quidem terram Gilbertus Herberd et Ricardus Le Has aliquando tenuerunt in eadem villa, cum boscis, pasturis, et aliis ad eandem terram pertinentibus : habendam et tenendam dictam terram cum omnibus qualitercunque ad eandem pertinentibus de me et heredibus meis sibi et heredibus suis de se procreatis libere, quiete, bene et in pace jure hereditario imperpetuum. Ita tamen quod si dicti Ricardus et Cecilia heredes non habeant de corpore suo progenitos, quod post decessum eorum, videlicet Ricardi et Cecilie, ipsa eadem terra ad me sive ad heredes meos legitimos, qui pro tempore fuerint, integre, plene, et sine diminucione redditura. Reddendo inde annuatim mihi et heredibus meis . . . assignatis unam clovam gariofili ad Pascham pro omni servicio, exaccione, et demanda, et faciendo domino feodi servicia debita et consueta : pro hac autem donacione, concessione, et presentis carte mee confirmacione dederunt mihi dicti Ricardus et Cecilia decem libras sterlingorum pre manibus. Et ego Ricardus et heredes mei, ut predictum est, dictam terram dictis Ricardo et Cecilie et eorum heredibus contra omnes contradicentes imperpetuum acquietabimus, warantizabimus, et defendemus, et ut hec mea donacio, concessio, et presentis carte mee confirmacio firma et stabilis imperpetuum permaneat, huic scripto sigillum meum apposui : hiis testibus, Domino Henrico

[1] *I.e.* Bixbrand, one of the manors of Bix in Oxfordshire.

Tyeis, Elya de Wyrefeld, Roberto de Copeford, Willelmo de la Ho, Hugone le Bret, Willelmo de Hattecumbe, Ricardo de Laucnorr, et aliis.

2. JOHN DE STONOR TO [AN OFFICIAL IN ENGLAND]

[11 APRIL, 1325]

On 6 Feb., 1325, Sir John de Stonor, knight, Arnold Gulielmi de Byarn William de Weston, and Peter de Galiciano were appointed proctors to treat for the espousal of Eleanor daughter of Edward II with Alfonso, King of Spain—Castile (*Cal. Pat. Rolls*, Edw. II, v, 103; *Foedera*, iv, 122-6). This letter was no doubt written during the mission, perhaps to Hugh le Despenser. From *A.C.*, xlvi, 1.

PAR MONS. JOHAN DE STONORE

Sire, pleise vostre seignurie qe a la fesaunce de ceste lettre ne avyoms fait nul esploit des busoignes dount vous nous chargastez a faire en Espaigne; qar, sire, le Roy feust greve de maladie a nostre venue, qe nous ne purrioms mie de oyt jours parler ove lui: et auxint, sire, par encheson de la noun venue de les grauntz seignurs de la terre et de ses tutours qe ne furont adonqes venuz, ne de lieur venue, Sire, en certayn ne poioms mie saver. Sire, qaunt le Roy feust allegge de sa maladie et nous venyms devant lui, il se porta sagement et nous fist bien semblant, et a ceo, sire, qe les plus privez qe sont devers le Roy nous disoynt, a lui plust bien nostre venue. Sire, covenable chose y ad il de tutes partez, a ceo qil me semble de ceo qe nous avoms a parler dieu nous doint bon esploit faire. Sire, Dieu vous doint bone vie et longe pur sa mercy. Escrit a Valedolit, le Joedy en la semaigne de Paskes.

No endorsement.

There is a second letter (*A C.*, xlvi, 2) *of the same date in nearly identical terms :—*

Tres cher Sire, vuillez saver qe a la fesaunce de ceste lettre, &c. *but ending*, Sire, de ceo qe novels nous deussont venir des parties, dount vous bien savez, rien ny est venus, de quai, Sire, il nous merveille mout. Sire, Dieu vous doint, &c.

3. ELEANOR LE DESPENSER TO JOHN DE STONOR

[*c.* 1326]

Eleanor, daughter of Gilbert, Earl of Gloucester and wife of Hugh le Despenser the younger. Since she writes from Berkley, the date is probably not later than 1326, for in September of that year the Despensers were compelled to restore the Castle to its rightful owner. From *A.C.*, xlvi, 4.

Ellianor le Despensier a nostre trescher et bien ame monsyr Johan de Stonor, Justice du Banke nostre seignur le Roi, salut et honour. Nous vous prions tant come nous poons qe la requeste que nostre treschere dame la Roine vous fait par ses lettres pour nostre chapelen, nome Johan de Sadyngton, veuillez avoir a cuer e accomplir en si graciouse maniere comme vous savrez et pourrez pour lamour de nous [et] en [tiele] maniere qui sen puisse loer a nous et que nous vous en doiens mercier et tres bon gre savoir. Car par raison ce avoms de mes bien ames a qui il appartient, nous avons ses besoignes mout a cuer. Nostre syr vous garde. Escript a Berklee le vij jour de Fevrier.
No endorsement.

4. EDWARD, PRINCE OF WALES, TO SIR JOHN DE STONOR

[*before* 1351]

ABSTRACT. A fragment of a formal letter addressed to "Johan de Stonor et ses compaignons du Comun Banc" with reference to a suit "parentre le Priour de Merton et les povres tenauntes del auncien demaigne du manoir de Merton," begging them to be "auxi favorables et cedauntes en dit ple come vous purrez par voie de resoun," and not to allow the tenants to be vexed by clerks, serjeants, or other people of the Court. "Don souz nostre prive seal a nostre manoir de Kennyngton le xj jour d'Averil."

Another even more fragmentary letter in the same behalf is from Henry, Earl of Lancaster. Dated "a nostre manoire de Savoye a Londres le ix jour d'Averil, par le Counte de Lancastre". *Addressed:* "A mon chers amys monsyr Jo[han] de Stonore et monsyr Ric. Wyloughby, justices nostre Seignur le Roy en le comun Banc". From *A.C.*, xlvi, 3 and 5.

5. THE MANOR OF BIERTON

[*c.* 1360 ?]

Richard Fitzjohn, who died in 1297, left the manor of Aylesbury and hamlet of Bierton to his wife Emma. His heirs were his four sisters, Maud, wife of William de Beauchamp, Earl of Warwick, Isabel, wife of Robert de Vipont (whose daughters were Isabel, wife of Roger Clifford, and Idonea, wife of Roger Leyburne), Avelina, wife of Walter de Burgh, Earl of Ulster, and Joan, wife of Theobald le Botiller (*d.* 1285), great-grandfather of James le Botiller, 1st Earl of Ormonde (*Calend. Genealogicum*, ii, 540-1, 563; *Cal. Inq.*, iii, p. 283; *Cal. Close Rolls*, Ed. III, ii, 429). The genealogy of the following document is therefore hopelessly wrong. John de Stonor, the chief justice, held Bierton by knight-service of the Earl of Ormonde (*Feudal Aids*). From *A.C.*, xlvi, 6.

Domina Emmota le Mohaute, domina de Beerton, habuit quatuor filias, quarum Dux Lancastrie unam duxit, alteram dominus de March duxit, terciam dominus Warre duxit, quartam Beket, dominus de Ormond, duxit; et s'c quatripartum fuit i'lud dominium de Beerton. Unde dicit dictus Johannes Dalby, senior, quod omnia terra et tenementa que fuere domini Johannis Stonor deveniebant a domino de March pro antecessore dicti domini de Stonor perquisita, et excepta una prepostura jacente inter le Beerton Grene, aliter terre nec prata, neque pasture tenementa de Beket, dominus de Ormond, per redditus et servicia nec racione alicujus tenoris alterius.

6. INDENTURE BETWEEN SIR THOMAS TIREL, STEWARD OF ·ISABEL, COUNTESS OF BEDFORD, AND EDMUND DE STONOR

4 OCTOBER, 1363

From *Ancient Deeds*, C. 2529. The seal is lost.

Hec indentura testatur quod Thomas Tirel, miles, generalis Senescallus domine Isabelle, filie Regis, concessit et dimisit Edmundo de Stonore, nomine dicte domine, maneria de Stonore, Watecombe, Sottewell, Harnhull, Burton et Penyton, existencia in manu dicte domine racione minoris etatis dicti Edmundi ex concessione dicti domini Regis : habenda et tenenda usque ad plenam etatem ejusdem Edmundi : reddendo inde annuatim dicte domine et assignatis suis ad receptam suam London. quadraginta et quinque libras argenti ad festa Nativitatis Domini, Annunciacionis beate Marie, Nativitatis sancti Johannis Baptiste, et sancti Michaelis per equales porciones. Et si contingat quod predictus redditus in parte vel in toto per quindenam post aliquem terminum prenominatum aretro fore, quod tunc bene liceat pre[dicte domine] et assignatis suis in omnibus predictis maneriis ingredere et penes se retinere cum omnibus bonis et catallis . . . eisdem inventis sine contradiccione alicujus. In cujus rei testimonium [huic scripto sigilla] sua alternatim apposuerunt. Data London. quarto die Octobris anno regni Regis Edwardi tercii post conquestum tricesimo septimo.

7. RECEIPT TO EDMUND DE STONOR

5 DECEMBER, 1364

From *Ancient Deeds*, C. 1357. The seal is lost.

Hec indentura testatur quod Willelmus Hulle, generalis receptor domine Isabelle, filie Regis, recepit de Edmundo Stonore, firmario maneriorum de Stonore, Watlynton, Penyton et Harnhull, octo libras bone et legalis monete de festo sancti Michaelis ultimo preterito : de qua quidem summa ipsum acquietat per presentes sigillo [suo] signatas. Data London. v^{to} die Decembris anno regni Regis Edwardi tercii post conquestum tricesimo octavo.

8. NICHOLAS COWLEY TO EDMUND DE STONOR

c. 1365

This may relate to some payment due to Stonor, for the time when he was a ward of the Countess of Bedford : see Nos. 6 and 7 above. From *A.C.*, xlvi, 13.

A mon treshonore et tresreverent syr, je moy recomanke a vous de tout mon cuer, tresentierment endesirant doier bones novelles de vous, come je sui grauntement tenuz. Outre ceo, monsyr, voillez savoier qe vostre argent, qest dues a vous, est cy prest a Dorchestre en la garde del Abbe et serra delivere a les Auditours de ma treshonore dame la Countasse a lour proschein venu a Newenham sur bone acquitaunce. Car je suppose qils serount cy a Newenham cest Symaygne. Et sera dilivere par le mayn dun Johan Warein de Bredicote. Autre chose quant a present, monsyr, ne sai escrire, mais je pri a la Trinite qe vous doigne bone vie et sauntee de corps a long durre. Escript a Dorchestre cest Lundy en graunt hast.

Le Vostre, si vous plest,
Nicholas Couelie.

A mon treshonore et tresreverent Syr, Monsyr Edmond de Stonore.

9. WRIT TO THE BAILIFF ERRANT FOR THE COUNTY OF OXFORD

OCTOBER, 1377

Amongst the *Stonor MSS.* in *Ch. Misc.*, 37, i, there are 21 Writs, Mandates, and Precepts relating to Edmund de Stonor's term of office as sheriff. Many of them are badly damaged, five of the most perfect are printed here (*see* Nos. 13, 15, 20, 21) as examples of an interesting and uncommon class of documents. From *Ch. Misc.*, 37, i, 15.

Edmundus de Stonore, vic. Oxon., dilecto suo Johanni Pentere, ballivo hundredi de Dorchestre, hac vice ballivo itineranti in comitatu predicto, salutem. Ex parte domini Regis tibi mando quod non omittas propter aliquam libertatem in comitâtu predicto, quin capias Johannem Barayte de Bradhinton commorantem apud Brydecote in parochia de Dorchestre, ubicunque inventus fuerit in comitatu predicto, et eum usque Castrum Oxon. duci facias : ita quod habere possim corpus ejus coram Gilberto Wace et sociis suis, justiciariis domini Regis de pace in comitatu predicto, apud Watlyngton die Lune proximo post festum Sancti Luce Evangeliste ad respondendum tam domino Regi quam Willelmo Gryme de Dorchestre de placito transgressionis contra formam statuti.

10. JOHN DE WELTON TO EDMUND DE STONOR

14 November, [1377]

The dates of this and Nos. 11, 12, 14, 16, 17, 22, and 23 can be fixed by the fact that they are addressed to Edmund de Stonor as Sheriff of Oxford and Berks. *A.C.*, xlvi, 19, which is too fragmentary for reproduction, is a letter from the executors of John de Foxle to Edmund de Stonor. From *A.C.*, xlvi, 31.

Trescher Syre, porceque vooz ministres ount pris une destresse de mon meistre, monsyr John de Foxle, pur certeinez summes de deniers chargeez sur lui en lescheqer, vous pri tres cherement depar mon dit meistre et depar moi, come un desconu devers vous vous purra pri er, qil vous plaise comander as ditz vooz ministres de faire deliverance du dite destresse, et plus avant surseere de destresse prendre du dit mon meistre par la cause susdite tanque un resonable jour, quel vous plerra assigner, a quel jour le dit mon meistre ou autres pur luy serront prestez de vous faire covenable surete de vous descharger en lescheqer sur vostre accompt. Trescher syre, ceste requeste vous pleise accomplier a cause du dit mon meistre, qi maintenant est deschayte de grevouse maladie, et par encheson de cestes mes prieres, qi a tout temps serra prest de vous faire plesance a mon poair. Trescher Syre, nostre sۡⁿᵉ SYre dieu vous voille ottrere honurz et bone sancte a treslong durre. Escrit a Merlawe le xiiij^me jour de Novembre.

Vostre Johan de Welton.

A mon reverent homme et sage Esmond de Stonore.

11. JOHN DE BEVERLE TO EDMUND DE STONOR

1 January, [1378]

From *A.C.*, xlvi, 11.

Trescher amy et ffiable compaignon. Pur ce qe je maffie entierment de voz, sieurement espoirant de vostre eide avoir et sage discrescion en

ce qa vous attint dameiste, et bonement faire purrez, a cause de conus-
ance auncien, vous pri affectuousement et de cuer qe vous vieullez a
moi faire certefier des choses a moi tochantz south vostre ordenance,
en voz disposicion et sourveiaunce estoiantz, combien la copie de bref
tochant le manoir de Buckenhull a moi envoier, si ascun y soit, et qanque
a voz y deviendra, ou ascun autre chose le dit manoir au moi tochant,
com suisdit pur lamor de moy.   Outre queux amys ma compaigne
soventz foithz et de cuer vous salue tres volonters faire vorroiantz ce qe
turnereit a voz honur et profit selonc nostre petit poair.   Le senet
espirit vous eiez en sa tressentisme gard.   Escrit a Loundres le primer
jour de Januer.

par Johan de Beverle.

A mon trescher amy et ffiable compaignon, Esmond Stonore, Viscount Doxenfort et Berk.

12. WILLIAM OF WYKEHAM, BISHOP OF WINCHESTER, TO EDMUND DE STONOR

11 JANUARY, [1378]

There are remains of the bishop's seal.   The next letter in the Collection
(*A.C.*, xlvi, 33) is also addressed by Wykeham to " E. Stonor, viscount de
Berkes," but is too fragmentary for reproduction.   From *A.C.*, xlvi, 32.

Trescher et tresffiable amy, Nous vous prions trescherement de coer
qe es busoignes, qe nostre cher amy, Johan Beverleye, ad affaire en voz
parties touchans vostre office en le Counte doxenford, lui veuilletz estre
entier amy eidant et consellant par touz les bones et resonables voies
qe vous purriez.   Issint qe le dit Johan puisse effectuelement sentir qe
ceste ma priere lui purra valoir.   Pur la quelle chose, trescher amy,
nous vous volons tresbon gree savoir et especialement estre tenuz.   Et,
trescher amy, le seint esprit vous veulle tous jours garder.   Escrit a
nostre Manoir de Suthwerk, le xj jour de Januer.

levesque de Wyncestre.

A nostre trescher, et tresffiable amy, Esmond Stonore, Visconte
Doxenfort.

13. PRECEPT TO THE BAILIFF OF CHAD-LINGTON

JANUARY, 1378.

This may have reference to the same matter as the letter from Sir John de Nouwers, No. 12. From *Ch. Misc.*, 37, i, 4, 5.

Edmundus de Stonore, vic. Oxon., ballivo hundredi de Chadlyngton salutem. Summone per bonos summonitores xxiiij [legales] homines de balliva tua de visneto de Keyngham, quod sint coram justiciariis domini Regis ad assisas in comitatu Oxon. [capiendas] assignatis apud Oxon., die Jovis proximo ante festum Convercionis Sancti Pauli, ad re-cognoscendum super sacramentum suum si Willelmus d[e Wynd]esore, chivaler, et Alicia, uxor ejus, Johannes Nouwer, chivaler, Willelmus Hervy, Edmundus Te[ttes worth, Johannes Davy de London, Robertus . . . , Willelmus Hankyn, Johannes Mylyn, et Willelmus Carter de Keyngham, injuste et sine judicio disseisiverunt Johannem atte Halle de Sib . . . de libero tenemento suo in Keyngham post primam, &c. Et interim habeant visum, et nomina juratorum imbreviari facias. Et pone per vadium et salvos plegios predictos Willelmum, Aliciam, Johannem Nowers, Willelmum, Johannem Davy, Robertum, Willelm-um, Johannem Mylyn et Willelmum, vel ballivos suos si ipsi inventi non fuerint, quod tunc sint ibi audituri illam recognicionem. Et habeas ibi summonitores, nomina plegiorum, et hoc preceptum.

Endorsed are the names of the Sureties of John de Nouwers and Hervy, and of Hankyn and Carter. "De omnibus aliis non habeo plegios, quia nil habent in balliva mea."

Attached is a parchment slip headed Hundryde Chadlynton, *with the names of the 24 jurors.*

14. JOHAN DE NOUWERS TO EDMUND DE STONOR

[JANUARY], 1378

Sir John de Nowers of Churchill, Oxfordshire (*Visitations of Oxfordshire*, 114). See the Precept in this matter No. 13. From *A.C.*, xlvi, 24.

Trescher sire et ffyable amy, moi mervoile grauntment de ceo qe vous ne mandez hors nule precept a bayliff pur mon nisi prius : et Sire, vous pry cherement qe vous voilez server le dit nisi prius : et sire, aleyde.de Deux jeo le deserverai enci devers vous qe vous agrerez ceste chose : voilez, Sire, ffeare cum jeo maffy enterement en vous.   La response de cest moy voilez remander par vostre lettre et par le portour de cest.   Trescher sire, deux vous meyntaigne touz jours en joye et sancte.

Johan de Nouwers.

A Esmond de Stonore, Vic. de   Oxinfford.

15. WRIT CONCERNING THE ALIEN PRIORY OF STEVENTON

20 JANUARY, 1378

Steventon Priory was a cell of Bec Abbey.   It was granted by Richard II to Westminster Abbey in 1399 (*Monasticon*, vi, 1044).   From *Ch. Misc.*, 37, i, 6.

Ricardus, dei gratia Rex Anglie et Francie et dominus Hibernie, Vic. Oxon. et Berks. salutem.   Precipimus tibi quod in execucione brevis nostri nuper tibi directi de capiendo sufficientem securitatem pro qua respondere volueris a quolibet Priore, et procuratore possessiones virorum religiosorum alienigenarum extra regnum Anglie commorancium occupante, in balliva tua, quod ipsi nulla bona seu catalla in Prioratibus et possessionibus predictis existencia seu eisdem qualitercunque spectancia aliqualiter elongabunt, set quod ea integraliter conservabunt et custodient absque subtraccione seu diminucione aliquali inde facienda, supersedeas omnino quoad Priorem de Styventon, et districcionem si quam eidem Priori feceris, vel si que bona et catalla ejusdem in manum nostram ceperis occasione predicta, sine dilacione relaxes et restituas eidem, ipsum ea de causa non molestando aliqualiter seu gravando. T. venerabile patre T. Exon. episcopo, Thesaurario nostro, apud Westm. xx° die Januar. anno regni nostri primo, per ipsum Thes.   Hanleye.

16. THOMAS DRU TO EDMUND DE STONOR

11 March, [1378]

Thomas Dru was on the commission of peace for Wiltshire, 1377-81. From *A.C.*, xlvi, 16.

Treshonore Sire, voillets savoir qa nostre Session de la pees tenuz a Malmesbury Willelmus Courden de Tettebury et aultres, qore ount perduz et lez vie liverez a la presone levesque, furount endites en la fourme southescript.   Juratores dicunt quod Willelmus Courden de Tettebury cum aliis, die mercurii in festo sancti Hillarii anno Regis Ricardi post conquestum primo, in Kyngesthernes in parochia de Sherston obviaverunt Johanni Sparghe de Tettebury et Johanni Somerel, famulo suo, et eis insultum fecerunt et ipsos felonice depredaverunt de x. li. auri et argenti ac eciam de tribus equis cum cellis eorum et apparatu precii xl. s., et prefatos Johannem et Johannem ibidem felonice interfecerunt.   Par quei, Sire voillets sauvement garder le dit William tanque vous eyet bref et commaundement de le court de lui mander es Bank le Roy ou altrement devaunt les justices de la deliverauncez el counte de Wilts.   Sire si ren voilletz de moy qe faire puisse ceo serrez prest.   Et sire, le seint esprit vous eit en sa saint garde.   Escript le xj^{me} jour de March.

Le vostre Thomas Dru.

A le Viscounte Doxenfcrt ou son lieu tenaunt.

17. WARYN DEL ISLE TO EDMUND DE STONOR

12 April, [1378]

Waryn del Isle was on the commission of peace for Berkshire in 1377-8 (*Cal. Pat. Rolls*, Richd. II, i. 39, 47, 48, 306).   His sister was married to Edmund de Stonor.   From *A.C.*, xlvi, 23.

Trescher et tresame frere, pur ceo qe William Frensche de Chepinglambourne, qe demouret ovesqes moi en ceste presente viage, le quel

nadguerez fust bailly de Shryvenham, si est alever en son baillie certeyne summe dargent, come apiert par ses estretez, sur quei vous plese
qe vostre baillif arraunt du Counte de Berkes les puisse lever soloin
ceo qe reson soit et purport de sez estretes tanqe verraiez puissent estre
trovez, a fyn qil ne soit pas endamagez en ma service par cele cause, si
verraie soit.   Trescher et tresame frere, vous plese saluer ma tresame
soer, vostre compaigne, et voz enfaunz, qe jeo prie dieu qe vous otroie
bone vie et longe durre.   Escript dedeisoy mon Neif juxte Hamele in
the Rys,[1] le xij jour d'April.

· Waryn del Isle, Seignur Teeys.

A mon trescher ffrere Esmond Stonore, Viscounte Doxenford.

18. INDENTURE OF THE DELIVERY OF VARIOUS ARTICLES AND BOOKS BE-LONGING TO QUEEN'S COLLEGE, OX FORD

13 MAY, 1378

On 6 April, 1378, a commission was issued by letters patent to Sir Thomas
de la Mare, Knight, Edmund de Stonore, and Reynold de Sheffield directing
them to command Richard de Thorpe, clerk, William Frank, and William
Middelworth, clerk, to restore to Master Thomas de Carlol, provost of the
college called Quenehalle, the college seal, writings, muniments, keys, books,
and goods, which they had carried away, and detained, in spite of a mandate
to bring them into Chancery; in default they were to be arrested and brought
before the Council at Westminster (*Cal. Pat. Rolls*, Richd. II, i, 204).
With the possible exception of Queen's College MS. 348 (sec. xii), "Ques-
tiones in librum Genesin auctore Albino," none of the manuscripts are now
at Queen's College.   The "Polucranica Cestrenc." is a copy of the *Poly-
chronicon* of Ranulph Higden.   William Durant was Warden of Merton
College.   From *Ancient Deeds*, C. 1782.

Hec indentura facta apud Oxon. die Jovis proximo ante festum sancti
Dunstani, anno regni Regis Ricardi secundi post conquestum Anglie
primo, in presencia Edmundi de Stonore, vicecomitis Comitatus Oxon.,
inter Magistrum Willelmum Fraunke, capellanum, ex parte una, et

---

[1] Hamelrise or Hamble on Southampton Water.

Magistrum Thomam Carlel ex parte altera, testatur quod prefatus
Magister Thomas recepit in presencia predicti vicecomitis de predicto
Magistro Willelmo per manus Magistri Roberti Hudershale sigillum
commune aule Regine Oxon. sub tribus clavibus, cum septem indenturis de eleccione librorum collegii predicti de anno domini mil-
lesimo CCC^mo lxxij^do.   Item, unam calicem argenti deaurati cum
patena, cum causula pro eadem : unam peciam argenti cum coopertorio
et casula pro eisdem ; unam mazeram cum coopertorio argenti ligato,
cum casula pro eisdem.   Unum librum Catholicum, secundo fo., unde
cela.   Sextum decretall. cum omnibus doctoribus, secundo fo., fervore
caritatis.   Item, unam bibliam, secundo fo., celi Orocheli.   Item,
moralia beati Gregorii super Joob, ij^o fo., quo ordine.   Item, Doctorem subtilem, ij^o fo., Figure.   Item, concordancia, ij^o fo., Abra.
Item Crisostomum super Matheum ij^o fo., . . . spiritus.   Item, Augus-
tinum de civitate dei, ij^o fo., eorum (?).   Item, Doctorem de Lira in parte
super proverbia Salamonis, ij^o fo., in comparacione.   Item, Liram super
salterium, ij^o fo., dominum sedentem.   Item Polucranica Cestrenc'.,
ij^o fo., navigabilis.   Item, Manipulum Florum, ij^o fo., quisque.   Item,
librum super Genesim a diversis tractatoribus, ij^o fo., set bona facere.
Item Originalia Augustini, ij^o fo., ac . . . eleccione predicti Willelmi
Frank.   Item, par decretorum, ij^o fo., aliter agentes.   Item, Thomam
super quartum sentenciarum, ij^o fo., set sol'. effectus.   Item, Adamen-
tem, ij^o fo., fau. . . . Item . . . sentenciarum, ij^o fo., ... Item,
Ricardum de sancto Victore de Trinitate, ij^o fo., aliter.   Item, tabulam
philosophie et theologie, ij^o fo., asina.   Item, Sentencias Augustini
de libro retractation[um], ij^o fo., . . . Item, sanctum Thomam super
primum sentenciarum, ij^o fo., Ipso facto.   Item, repertorium Magistri
Willelmi Durant, ij^o fo., 3. j. iii. 2.   ·Item, parvum librum ru[beum]
  . .[1] proposissiavit [ver]sus Mooat.

19. HOUSEHOLD ACCOUNT OF EDMUND DE STONOR

20 JUNE-29 AUGUST, 1378

On a single skin, *Ch. Misc.*, 37, i, 25—probably part of a larger roll.   The
account relates to the year in which Edmund Stonor was sheriff.   Most of the
entries are formal and uninteresting, e.g.

----

[1] This is quite illegible : probably it should be " ij^o fo ".

"Die Mercurii xxx die Junii in pane, ob., cervis. [de stauro], in carne, iiij d. Die Jovis primo die Julii in pane ob., cervis. de stauro, in carne ij d. Die Veneris xxx die Julii totum de stauro."

The weekly totals are given (1) 5s. 0½d., (2) 2s. 3d., (3) 7s. 3d., (4) 2s. 10½d., (5) 21s. 11d., (6) 10s. 1d., (7) £4 14s. 8½d., (8) 19½d., (9) 4s., (10) 9d.

The entries explain the larger sums for the 5th to the 7th weeks—18 July to 7 August—as visitors and officials were present.

"Die Mercurii xxj die Julii presentibus dominis Roberto Tresilian, Gilberto Sotesbrok, Edmundo Fraunceys et aliis cum familia sua, in pane ix. d., cervisia de stauro, in carne gross. ij. s. vij. d. ob., in ij auc. vj. d., in quinque capon. xx d., in ix pull. xj. d. ob., in quatuor lagenis vini, xl. d., in pane equino empto j. d., in j. lecto conducto pro garcione, j. d., in pipere, croco, et zingibe, v. d." . . . "Die Jovis quinto die Augusti, quo die deliberacio facta fuit coram Roberto Tresilian, Gilberto Wace et Johanne Kentwode justic., panis de stauro, in j quarteria bone cervisie ij. s. in carnibus bovinis mutulinis et porc., v. s. j. d., in viij capon. iiij. s. j. d. ob., in quatuor ancis. xv. d., in iiij porcellis, ij. s. vij. d. Item in j. p.[1] salis iiij. d., in pane equino vj. d. Item in diversis speciebus emptis x. s. vj. d. ob. Item in xxiij lagenis et j quart. de vino empto xv. s. xv. d. ob. Item solutum est pro custagiis Johannis de Kentwode xij. s. vj. d. Item solutum est barbitonsori vj. d. Item solutum est hominibus Prioris Sancte Frideswide et Edmundi Gifford portand. signos v. s. iiij. d. In lacte pro furmente iij. d. In pull. et columbariis emptis, xviij d." . . . "Die Sabbati septimo die Augusti presentibus vicecomite, Adam Hertyngton, Ricardo Filongle et aliis, in pane viij d., in cervisia empta pro dominis v. d. ob., in diversis piscibus emptis pro prandio eorundem xij. s., in j. quart. vineg. et sanap. iij d., in allio et sepibus ij. d., in farina j d., in prebend. equorum domini iij. d. ob., in lectis conductis pro garcionibus, iiij d., in j carcata bosci empta ij. s. j d., in j. quarterio carbonum xiiij. d. Item solutum est Johanni Tutte pro labore ejus xij. d. Item solutum est lotrici pro labore ejus per di. anni ij. s. Item ij li. candel iiij. d. Item in pane equino iij. d. Item solutum est pro j quarto de verceuse ij. d. Item pro ciphis emptis ix d. Item in suis empt. vj. d.

---

[1] Perhaps for "pondere".

20. MANDATE TO THE BAILIFF OF DORCHESTER

JULY, 1378

See No. 9. From *Ch. Misc.*, 37, i, 7.

Edmundus de Stonore, vic. Oxon., ballivo libertatis hundredi de Dorchestre salutem. Mandatum domini Regis in hec verba [recepi · Ricardus], dei gratia Rex Anglie et Francie et dominus Hibernie, vic. Oxon. salutem. Precepimus tibi quod distringas Hugonem Chastillom et Matilldim, uxorem ejus, per omnes terras et tenementa in balliva tua. Et quod de exitibus eorundem nobis respondeas. Et quod habeas corpora eorum coram justiciariis nostris apud Westm. in Octabis sancti Michaelis ad respondendum Thome Camoys et Elizabethe, uxori sue, de placito vasti de tenemento in Cheselhampton cum pertinenciis &c. Et ad audiendum judicium suum de pluribus defaltis. Et habeas ibi hoc breve. T. R. Bealknapp apud Westm. x° die Julii anno regni nostri secundo. Quare tibi mando quod mandatum istud diligenter executaris, et de execucione michi respondeas in Castro Oxon. inde &c [?] cum hoc mandato.

21. WRIT TO THE BAILIFFS OF THE TOWN OF OXFORD

JULY, 1378

From *Ch. Misc.*, 37, i, 8.

Edmundus de Stonore vic. Oxon., ballivis libertatis ville Oxon. salutem. Mandatum domini Regis in hec verba recepi : Ricardus, dei gratia Rex Anglie, et Francie, et dominus Hibernie, Vicecomiti Oxon. salutem. Pone per vadium et salvos plegios Robertum Wattlyngton, carnificem Oxon., quod sit coram Justiciariis apud Westm. in Octabis sancti Michaelis ad respondendum Priori sancte Frideswide Oxon. de placito, quod t[ene]at ei convencionem inter eos factam de toto prato australi ipsius Prioris de Bunseye cum le Hok eidem annexo, eidem Roberto per prefatum Priorem ad terminum annorum dimisso ad eundem terminum tenendo. Et ad ostendendum quare non fuit coram Justiciariis nostris apud Westm. a die sancti Johannis Baptiste in xv dies, sicut summonitus fuit. Et habeas ibi nomina plegiorum, et hoc breve. T. R. Bealknapp apud Westm. xij° die Julii anno regni nostri secundo &c.

Endorsed : Nos Thomas Somerset, et Johannes Shaw, ballivi de la ville Oxon., vobis sic significamus.

Plegii Johannis Watlyngton, carnificis Oxon.: Ricardus Burgh, Johannes le Noble.

22. GILBERT TALBOT TO EDMUND DE STONOR

1 September, [1378]

Gilbert Talbot of Goodrich, third baron Talbot, died in 1387. He was grandfather of John Talbot, Earl of Shrewsbury. From *A.C.*, xlvi, 30.

Trescher et tresame cosyn, molt vous merciouns de ceo qe vous avetz ease noz tenauntz de Aston par cause de nostre preyer, queux furent pris et areynez, pur quele chose molt sumes tenus a vous. Et tresame cosyn, tochant ceux qe ne sunt pas pris, vous priouns cherement qils puissent trover maynprise destre devaunt monsyr Robert Treselyane, Justice, le luyndy proschain apres la seynt Michel, issint qils puissent avoir deliveraunce de les bienz queux Thomas Galyan ad arestuz deins le dit Aston, et cariez hors de lours tenementz demesne. Ceste chose, tresame cosyn, voillet faire a nostre requeste ; et sur ceo envoiouns deverz vous nostre bien ame Thomas atte More pur vous certefier plus a plain, a quil vous plese doner foy et credence de ce qil vous certefiera tochaunt noz dites tenauntes. Et si rien soit devers nous qe feare puissouns fiablement, nous voillet euci certefier et nous le ferrouns de lee coer. Enpriaunt a dieu qe vous ait en sa garde. Escrit a nostre Chastiell de Godrich le primer jour de Sept.

Gilbert Talbot.

A nostre trescher et tresame Cosyn Esmond Stonore, Viscounte Doxenfort.

23. SIR NICHOLAS SARNESFELD TO [EDMUND DE STONOR]

1377-8

Sir Nicholas Sarnesfeld occurs as the King's knight and standard-bearer on 5 March, 1377 (*Cal. Pat. Rolls*, Richd. II, i, 136). From *A.C.*, xlvi, 26.

Trescher syr, Je vous salue enterement, et vous pry cherment qe vous croies le portour de cestes, Esmond Gifford, de la matere tochant une prestre, qe a nom syr William Drayton, qe demert ou mon trescher frere, mon syr Richard Alberbury, et ou ma dame sa femme, qe fausement est emprisone : et vous pry cherment qe vous ly fases le ben qe vous poes pur lamour de moy et de mon syr Richard. Le sente espirte (*sic*) vous encrese en honours.

De par mon syr Nicol Sarnesfeld, chevaler.

A le vicomte d'Oxenford.

24. THE ABBOT OF ABINGDON TO EDMUND DE STONOR

15 June [? 1379]

This may possibly relate to the Poll-tax of 1379. From *A.C.*, xlvi, 9.

Trescher amy voilletz saver que nostre seignur le Roi nous ad maunde certeyns commissions a vous et autres directes pur taxer et assesser totes maneres de gentz en le counte d'Oxenfort, ovesque un brief de prendre le serment de vous et vos compaignons ove tote le haste que purra estre fait. Pur quei nous prions et chargeons de par mon seignur le Roi que vous soietz a nous a Abyndon sur ceste dymaynge proscheyn avenir apres la date de cestes a prendre vostre serment et vostres commissions saunz ascunes delay ou excusacion : issi quee nostre defaute notre syre le Roi ne soit disseu tarye ne ni delaye de ceo qest a vous graunte. Trescher amy la seint esprit vous eit en sa garde.

Escrit a Abyndon le xvme jour de Juyn.

l'abbe d'Abyndon.

A notre trescher amy Esmond de Stonor.

C

25. PHELIPPOT BOOT AND WALTER ESTHAM TO EDMUND DE STONOR

[*c.* 1380]

It is impossible to fix the date of this and the thirteen following letters ; they are therefore placed in the order in which they appear in the *Ancient Correspondence.* The dates probably range from 1370 to 1382. From *A.C.,* xlvi, 10.

Treshonore et tres ffiable amy, voyles savoir qe Sir Aloen, vostre chapeleyn, veint a Phelippot Boot ycee samedi et a moy a Dorcestre ove vostre lettre de credence, et nous ayt dit qe vous ne purres performeir le jour qe vous aveies assingne ycee lunde par diversces ocupacion qe vous avoystes de deverces boyseyunes a feare : pourquoy Monsyr mat grauntement blame et auxi Phelippot avant nome; pour quoi fiablement vous pry, si vous y voyles feare et performir, qe vous maundes par vostre lettre jour et lu de performir totes nostres parlauxace : car monsyr par cause de performeir est venu a Bamton ove tote maner evidence tochauxs la dite matir, et nous ayt graunt blame de coostes, car en certayn il purra meylour bargain feare si nous navor un Secrete cum nous avouns. A dieux, treshonore sire, qe vous doingne ben encres. Escript a Bamton le jour de seint Agnes.
Par de vostres
Phelippot Boot et Water Estham.

A mon treshonore Esmond Stonor.

26. GREGORY, PARSON OF BOURTON TO EDMUND DE STONOR

c. 1380

Stonor had estates at Condicote and Bourton on the Water, in Gloucestershire ; see vol. ii, pp. 180-2 below. Gregory, rector of Bourton, was one of Edmund de Stonor's feoffees for Harnhull and Condicote, and for Penyton Meysy (*Ch. Inq. p.m.,* Richard II, File 21). From *A.C.,* xlvi, 12.

Trescher et treshonore seignour, vous plese a savoir de la covenante qe John Condicote fait a Dodecote de vers vous de venier a Stonore

oveske Richard Galewayn a vostre rezvenowe de Hantechyre null per-
formeit ne fuit par eng fait tanke a ore.   Et pur ceo, treshonore
seignour, jeo fai a Condicote le jour de Synt Andrew lapostel de en-
parleer de le dit covenaunt, et dunke ils moi promys certeyment [de]
estre a vous a Stonore en le jour de C[once]pcione nostre Dame pour
pleynment acorder oveske vous ; mes apres en le veyle de syn Nicholas
vent John Cundicote a Cundicote et dit au dit Richard, qe il ne puet
aver license de soun seygnour labbe de Haye au dit temps vener ; par
quey, treshonore seignour, le dit Richard et Marjorye sa femme vous
prie enterement, si il soit a vostre voluntee qe le jour puet estre pro-
longe tanke a le Chandelure, pur cause qe il ne at mye seme tot soun
semaile de furment, et auxi pur ceste temps est pluviouse et bret jours.
A deu, Trescher et Treshonore seignour, le seynt esprit soit garde de
vous.

le vostre Chapelayn Gregori, parsone de Bourton.

A mon treshonore seignour Esmond de Stonor.

27. [TO EDMUND DE STONOR ?]

[c. 1380]

From A.C., xlvi, 14.

Trescher Sire, si vos plese a savoir qe jeo serra a Measton le Marsdy
proschein devaunt le feste de Seint Luce ; pourquoi, si vos plese, voilez
mander a le baillif illeqes de sumoner le Court de Merston a Puttenham
encountre le mesme jour.

28. HENRY DOUNHAM TO EDMUND DE STONOR

c. 1380

Henry Dounham occurs as yeoman of the wardrobe to Ingelram de Coucy,
Earl of Bedford, in 1378, and as a squire of the Countess Isabella in 1381
(*Cal. Pat. Rolls*, Richd II, i, 184, 601).   He was one of Edmund de Stonor's
feoffees for Harnhull and Condicote, and for Penyton Meysy (*Ch. Inq. p.m.*,
Richard II, File 21).   From *A.C.*, xlvi, 15.

Treshonore Sire et Meistre, jeo me recomanke a vous si avaunt come soit ou plus puisse : vous enmerciant ovesqe tres tout mon coer dez grauntes bien faitz et naturesses quex vous mauez endurrez devaunt ces hures, dount voz treschers merciez, desirant tout dys affectuelment bones novelles de vous oier et de vostre estate et de ma treshonore amie vostre compaigne et dez toutes vostres enfantz, le quele jeo pri le dieu tout puissaunt qil voille maintenir en croissaunce et multepliaunce dez toutes honurs.   Et si de mon estat vous plese assavoir, al departier du cestes jestoie en sancte du corps, le mercie dieu, tout appareillez ovesqe tout mon corps et biens de feire ceo qe vous plesest a voz comandementz.   Treshonore Sire et Mestre, le filz nostre Seignur Jhesu Crist vous eit tout dys en sa gard.   Escript a Brustwyk en Holdernesse le xxj jour davarell.

Trestout de vostre Henry Dounham.

Et vous pri, treshonore Sire. qe vous plese envoier novelles devers moi du celle chose qe nous parlames a nostre darreyn entreparlaunce.

A mon treshonore maistre Esmond Stonhore.

29. BROTHER EDMUND TO EDMUND DE STONOR

c. 1380

From *A.C.*, xlvi, 17.

In Christo domino salutem et sanitatem sempiternam.   Domine reverende, gratias, si placet, quod toto tempore nundinarum Oxonie non inveni vel percepi aliquem interveniente Bokyngham et Oxon. ; postea ivi Bokyngham et vidi pannos vestros inde dimissos satis salvos et servatos, quos vobis duxi detulisse Oxon. si pot[uissem] ; et consideravi quod erant.ibi plures pannos quam credidi, et multe particule de diversis generibus dijudicavi ; consultum est mihi, quod non assumerem tantum pretium ad curam meam et tot diversa ante mihi ignota, nisi vos [mihi] mandaretis expressius quam fecistis.   Si quidem aliquis eorum, qui pannos detulerunt illuc, veniret ad veraciter recipiendum eorum numeros et videret valorem, ne forte aliquis et aliquis posset mihi impingere et taliter imponere . . .; cui nescirem respondere sicud custodes pannorum. Tum pro rogatu domine Margerie mecum . . . portavi, et modo igitur

misi clamidem, camisiam, et caligas. Item inquisivi de numeris sacer-
dotum et de facto et modo eorum ; et sic feci illis singillatim et ordinate,
quod sunt omnes bene contenti, et, ut dicunt, vobis obligati ; et credo
quod vobis placebit quod feci, cum venero et computem vobis predicta.
Isti sunt parati : eligatis vos de judicio vestro an malletis [un]um de
vestris mittere, vel quod ego in nomine vestro faciam pannos deferri
Oxon. et sic ad vos dem[itte]re. Infra natalem domini intendo per vos
venire et perficere facienda. Valeat vestra caritas in domino, et anime
prosperitas in deo salutar. nostro. Amen. Per vestrum fratrem
Edmundum.
Venerabili viro Edmundo de Stonor.

30. BROTHER EDMUND TO EDMUND DE STONOR

c. 1380

From *A.C.*, xlvi, 18.

Domine et deo devote, noveritis, si placet, me vidisse filium vestrum
Edmundum, et statum suum per duas noctes et diem considerasse :
cujus infirmitas decrescit de die in diem, nec jacet in lecto ; set, cum
calor accesserit, quiescit modicum distemperatus non per duas horas,
post quas surgit, et, sicud exigit tempus, intrat scolas, et comedit et
spaciatur sanus et jocundus, ita quod nullum periculum in eo videtur.
Et ipse motu proprio seipsum vobis recomendavit, et domine sue ; et.
alios aliasque salutavit. Et incipit Donatum adiscere lente et modeste,
sicud adhuc oportet. Et habet illum Donatum, quem timui fuisse per-
ditum. Et vero nunquam vidi puerum talem custodiam habere, sicud
ipse infirmitate durante. Magister et ejus uxor vellent aliquos de
pannis suis esse domi, quia nimis multi sunt et pauciores sufficiunt, et
leviter possunt, illis invitis, demoliri et deturpari. Item vobis transmitto
nomina et modos librorum in uno volumine contentorum, quem librum
non vult pro minori vendere possessor quam pro xij. solidis, sicud et
valet judicio meo et aliorum ; et si vendat, habere solucionem cito re-
quirit. Et ideo faciatis, si placet, mihi responsum per puerum istum de
voluntate vestra circa predicta. Valete in Christi virtute et meritis
virginis et matricis Marie, per vestrum ad votum Fratrem Edmundum.
Venerabili viro Edmundo de Stonore.

31. JOHN HALONTON TO EDMUND DE STONOR

c. 1380

From *A.C.,* xlvi, 20.

Reverencias cumulatas et honores, graciarumque laudabilium repetitas acciones cum mei interioris hominis affectu animose fulminatas. Cum humane nature racio interius dinoscatur exigere angustatum quemlibet suis amicis secularibus, a quibus sui tedii vel gravaminis medela queat fiducialiter impertiri, querimoniam debere sue angustie intimare: hinc est quod, in vestra dominacioni honorabili specialem et precipuam pre ceteris hujus patrie hominibus habentes confidenciam, vestre benignitati confidendo, mei instantis gravaminis querelam, de ejus minime diffidendo relevamine, duximus liquilenter declarandam. Vestra igitur benivolencia scire minime dedignetur, quod in villa Oxonie magna debiti mole existo presencialiter pregravatus ; eo quod a Johanne Baret de mei prioris disposicione x. libras pro mea in universitate Oxonie exhibicione pre-teritis temporibus infallibiliter recepissem, de quibus quidem x. libris, **xx.** solidis duntaxat exceptis, a prefato Johanne nunquam mihi extiterat denarius numeratus : igitur vestram dominacionem deprecor et exoro, in qua fiduciam immensam omnibus aliis pretermissis habeo, quatinus meam necessitatem pio animo considerantes x. marcas cum dimidia, in quibus predicto Johanni Baret in festo Invencionis sancte Crucis proximo solvendis existis per indenturas obligatus, per latorem presenciarum mihi mittere dignaremini, quia si predictam summam vero sive incommode ad presens nullatenus solvere valeatis, saltim centum solidos de pecunia predicta vestram benignitatem mihi exorarem destinare ; omnemque securitatem, quam pro mutua predicta discrecio desideraverit postulare, tempore per vos quocunque limitato ad domum vestram, si vestre dominacioni placuerit, accedendo fiducialiter faciam et exponam : si vero x. marcas cum dimidia prelibatas in presenti solvere vestre placeret benivolencie, predictas indenturas obligatorias vobis per latorem pre-senciarum transmittavi arbitrio vestro disponendas. De beneficiis vero ecclesie de Perton necnon v[ic]ario ejusdem et persone me multipliciter ex parte vestra impensis regratiare vestre dominacioni non sufficio, set Deum, ut vestram benignitatem [perf]iciat, ut vester devotus orator cotidie deprecor et exoro.

Per vestrum Capellanum Johannem
Halonton, Canonicum de Norton.

Reverendo magistro suo Edmundo de Stonore domino.

32. EDMUND DE LA POLE TO EDMUND DE STONOR

[*c.* 1380]

Edmund de la Pole (1337-1419) was son of Sir William de la Pole, and brother of the first Earl of Suffolk. He owned the manor of Borstall, Bucks, in right of his first wife, Elizabeth, daughter of Richard de Handlo (Napier, *Swyncombe and Ewelme*, pp. 291-2). From *A.C.*, xlvi, 21.

Trescher sire et amy, endroit de ce qe mavez envoie qe vous vodroiez savoir jour et lieu a ou nous puissoms estre ensemble pur faire fyn de le Manoir de Pottenham des diverses choses entre nous parlez touchant le dit Manoir, dounte vous plaise savoir qe si vous plaise estre a Borstall ice mescredy prochein avenir, je froy John Bracy et le persone de Pottenham vous encountrer illoqes. Et en cas qe vous ne plaise illoqes venir, veuillez menvoier ou qe vous veuillez qe je vienge a vous, et a qil jour et lieu : issint qil soit devaunt le xvij° jour de ceste presente mois de Marche : et je serroi prest de venir en ayse de vous. Et trescher sire, de cestes vous plaise menvoier respounce par le portour de cestes. Qe nostre seignur tres puissaunt vous encresse en honur a treslong durre. Escrites de ma maneys mayne a Borstall le ixme jour de Marche.

Vostre Esmon de la Pole.

A mon trescher et tres   Monsyr Esmond de Stonor.

33. RICHARD LE SCROPE TO EDMUND DE STONOR

c. 1380

The writer is presumably Richard, first lord Scrope of Bolton (*d.* 1403) ; his cousin Henry will then be Henry, first lord Scrope of Masham (*d.* 1391). In that case the hostel which Henry had purchased may be Scropes Inn in Thames Street, which belonged to Stephen, second lord Scrope of Masham, in 1406 (*C il. Inq. p.m.*, iii, 307 : Stow, *Survey*, ii, 13, 359). On 11 March, 1395, a writ for livery of dower to Joan, widow of Sir Ralph de Stonor, was issued to the Mayor and escheator of London in respect of a messuage in the City valued at 100*s.* (*Chanc. Misc.*, 37, i, 31). This latter is no doubt the tenement in St. Peter by Paul's Wharf, which Sir John de Stonor held in 1354, and is probably the one which Scrope wished to hire.   From *A.C.*, xlvi, 22.

Trescher et tresames, voillez savoir que mon tres honore cousyn, Monsyr Henri Lescrop, ad purchace une hostell a Londres, pur sa demeure illoeqes, mais il ne poet avoir le dit hostell a luy delivere a son ease tancqes une certeyne temps : et pur ceo vous prie cherement qe vous voillez lesser a mon dit tres honore Cousyn vostre hostell a Londres, en quele Syr William Mulso nadgairs feust demeurant, tantqes il poet avoir son propre hostell a luy delivere : entendant certeynement, Sire, qil vous ferra pur vostre dit hostell pur mesme le temps ceo qe reson demande, et qe vous vous tendrez bien content.   Et trescher Sire, cestes choses voillez faire par cause de ceste ma request, et charger un de voz proch. entervenant de luy deliverer vostre dit hostell.   Et luy toutpuissant vous eit touz jours en sa garde.   Escrit a Londres le xiiij jour de Januer.

Richard Lescrop.

A trescher et tresames Esmond de Stonore.

34. WALTER ROUS TO EDMUND DE STONOR

c. 1380

From *A.C.*, xlvi, 25.

Honoures et totes maneres de reverence. Trescher sire, vous pleise entendre qe Ricard Hoghes de Dudecote ad fait fyn pur xl. s. pur ses tenementz illoesqes, et qe vous averez la vache de beriet Johan son piere : et Cristine Beiteres, vostre neife, femme Johan Toughe, chapelayn, si ad graunte de fyn pur ses terres et tenementz reaver xl. s., et pur ij acres de furment iij acres dorge et ij acres de puls vij marcs dargent : et Rauf Kyng, le graunt seignur, si ad graunte vij marcs pur le detenue de Michel, vostre bercher, pur deux jours ; dount nous sumez acordez, si vous le volez assentir par bones [p]legges a moi troves ; mes ils demaundent longe jour de paiement, de quele chose nous ne sumez acorde saunz vostre assignement.   Et Henr. Pighurde, vostre provost, et moi ne poomps acorder par nule voie de sa fyn unqore, et je luy ai graunte

destre descharge de son office par treys ans proscheyn avenir pur xl. s.,
au quele demande il ne voet assentir : pur quei, trescher Sire, vous
plese envoier par vostres lettres a moi par le porteur de cestes tote vostre
volonte des choses avauntdites, auxi bien des jours de paiement des
fyns, com del fyn vostre provost illoesque, sil serra ataunt ou nennye
cest assavoir xl. s.   Trescher sire, luy trespuissaunt vous encresse en
honours et bountees, et vous doigne bone vie et longe a tous jours.   Et
graunt a la meme del garsoun voillez entendre qe son piere luy de
            et encountre resoun, et dist qils sount . . . : de . . ., mes mest
dist de verite qils serrount troves vos . . . vostre Wauter Rous.

A mon treshonore Sire et Maistre Esmond Stonor.

35. MICHAEL SKYLLYNG TO EDMUND DE STONOR

c. 1380

Michael de Skyllyng was appointed King's Attorney in the Common Bench
on 20 November, 1377, and was on the commission of peace for Wilts. and
Hants. (*Cal. Pat. Rolls*, Richd. II, i, 47, 50, 72).   From *A.C.*, xlvi, 27.

Trescher sire, jeo vous requeor si tendrement de coer come jeo puyse,
qil vous pleise remembryer coment jeo parlay a vous dun Nich. Pallyng,
qest neyf a mon treshonore seignur, monsyr Mich. de la Pole, come de
son Manoire de Ramerygge, vostre veisyn en Suthampton, qest demeurant deyns vostre seignurie de Stonor ou pres a ycele : et purceo,
trescher sire, qe le dit Nich. adz este futyf et absent hors de son nye :
sure qel jay charge les tenauntz mon dit seignur affaire venir le dit
Nich. en la seignurie mon dit seignur oue ses biens meobles et nyent
meobles et sequeles.   Mes, treshonore seignur, purceoqe les ditz
tenauntz sont symples et de petit pouerwe affaire ceo qe atyent par la
loy, si vous pry entierement de coer sur la graunde affiance qe jay en
vous et en vostre bone seignurie, qe les ditz tenauntz mon dit seignur
portures de cestes puyssent estre en vostre protexcion et defens affaire
execucion de ceste ma lettre en salvacon de droit mon dit seignur, et
qe les ditz tenauntz mon dit seignur ne soient grevees par la cause del
execuscion susdite, mes par vostre bone mediacion soient de peril et de
damage en touz poyntz gardees par reson de vostre bone seignurie.   Et

si rienz soit, sire, qe faire puysse je vous purra plesure ou vailer en sem-
blahle cas ou en aultre, fiablement le fray solonc mon powere.   A dieux,
treshonore sire, soietz, qe vous deynge grace de bienz faire

le vostre Mich. Skyllyng.

A mon trescher Sire Esmond Stonor.

36 JOHN STOKE TO EDMUND DE STONOR

c. 1380

The following letter in the Collection (*A.C.*, xlvi, 29) is also addressed by
John Stoke to Edmund Stonor, but is too mutilated for transcription.   From
A.C., xlvi, 28.

Treshonoree sire, et trescher cosyn, moult vous merci de touz voz
grauntez bountez et naturesses, queux de jour en aultre mauez fait
saunz nulle desert.   Entendaunt, treshonoree sire, qe jai receu voz
lettres a moi directez, merci, touchant la bargayn des terres et tenementiz
de Johan Babby en Clayore, les queux lettres jai pleinement entenduz.
Pur quei, treshonoree, vous requeor, si pleiser vous soit, si vous semble
qe la bargaigne serroit pur nostre proffit, qe faire voillez la dite bargaigne,
et jeo vous envoiera xx. li. deinz la feste de seint Hiller prochein avenir.
Et les aultres xx. li. serront paiez a quell heoure qe nous sumus sure
dez ditiz terrez.   Endroit, sire, del lautre bargaigne, de quelle nous
entreparlamus a nostre derrein entreparler, vous requer qe vous moi
plese certifier vostre voluntee en escript a pluis toust qe vous bonement
purre.   Et si rienz voillez devers moi, tout temps prest moi trouverez
comme le vostre.   Lui seint esprit vous eit en sa gard, et voz honurs
encresce en bon sauntee et long dure.   Escript a Bristuyt le xv jour de
Decembre.

Vostre Johan Stoke de Bristuyt.

A son treshonore syr et cosyn Esmond Stonore.

37. [EDMUND DE STONOR TO ?]

c. 1380

The absence of any signature, and the corrections and alterations indicate that this is only a draft of a letter. From *A.C.*, xlvi, 35.

Trescher et ffiable amy, jay bien entendu vostre lettre de ceo qe vous moy avez envoye de [aver]¹ mettre ultre le jour, le quele fust mys entre vous et moy de estre a Stonor en la comte de Oxon ² en la veye de seynt Mathieu procheyn avener, a perfourmer les covenauntes [des]¹ queux vous et moy ffuroms entrefiez a Merston en la countee de Hertford, tanque a le Dismeigne procheyn apres la feste de seynt Michel adenqe procheyn ensuiaunt. [Pur quoi]¹ voilletz saver qe jeo su prest de performer iceo jour de seynt Mathieu tous les covenauntes qe furount acorde entre vous et moy a Merston, et ultre jeo a vostre requeste voil attendre tanque a la dit Dismeigne appres le feste de seynt Michel, esteaunt come ils furount faites a Merston. Issynt qe totes les covenauntes entre vous et moy soient pleynement accomples a iceo dis-meigne, come [acorde fust parentre vous et moy]¹ ils dussount aver este a le dit fest de seynt Mathieu a devaunt.

A Stonore [en] le dit Conte de Oxon.

38. MARGARET, COUNTESS OF DEVON TO EDMUND DE STONOR

[*c.* 1380]

The Countess must be Margaret, widow of Hugh Courtney, second Earl of Devon, who died in 1377. She survived till 1391. Ermyngton was held of the Earl of Devon as of the Castle of Plympton. From *A.C.*, li, 57.

Salut et bon amour. Voillez savoir qe come nous avions entenduz yl ya une brief le Roi purchassez devers vous touchant le Manoir de Ermyngton : mes nous ne savions pur qi ne a quel noun : pur qei soiez vous bien avisez et garniz, et nous tenetz pur excusez de nostre

¹[ ] *these words have been struck through.*
² en . . . Oxon, interlineated.

promesse du temps passez touchant ceo qe nous vous promettames de vous garnir en cas qe nous purroioms oier dascun tielle briefe.   A dieu, qe vous garde.   Escript a Exmere le xiij jour de Januere.

La Contesse ⎱
de Devans ⎰ la Mere.

A nostre Cher et bien ame Esmond Sto[nor].

39. BILL FOR CLOTH SUPPLIED TO EDMUND DE STONOR

[*c.* 1380]

From *Ch. Misc.*, 37, i, 26.   Somewhat damaged.

Parcell en[tre] Edmund de Stonore et Raulyn de Swanton   le xiiij [jour de] Novembre dilevere a Tomes son valet.

Primis. pur [ij anes] et j quart. de Sanguyn m . . ., pris lane iiij. s. viij. d, x. s. vj. d.   It., pur ij anes et di. de . . . bruskynmell, pris lane iiij. s. viij. d. [xj. s. vj. d.].   It., pur iij anes et di. de Ray bron chaump, pris lane, ij. s. vj. d., summa, viij. s. ix. d.   It., pur iij anes de tane aparter o le Ray, pris lane iij. s. iiij. d., summa x. s.   It., pur j. ane et di. de Ray, pur j. Garson, pris lane xxij. d. [summa ij. s. ix. d.] It., pur j. ane de tane aparter o le Ray. ij. s ij. d.   Summa, xlv. s. viij. d.

It., pur j peire chans de Skarlet a countre Nowel, pris [vj ?] s. viij. d.

40. WRIT TO THE SHERIFF OF BUCKS ON BEHALF OF EDMUND DE STONOR

25 MARCH, 1381

From *Ch. Misc.*, 37, i, 27.

Ricardus, dei gratia Rex Anglie et Francie, et dominus Hibernie, vicecomiti Buks. Salutem.   Questus est nobis Edmundus de Stonore quod Simon Gardener, Ricardus Sadelere, Johannes Clyfton, brasiere, injuste et sine judicio disseisiverunt eum de libero tenemento suo in

Aylesbury post primam transfretacionem H. Regis, filii Regis Johannis, in Vascon. Et ideo tibi precipimus quod si predictus Edmundus fecerit te securum de clameo suo predicto, tunc facias tenementum illud reseisiri de catallis que in ipso capta fuerunt, et ipsum [*sic*] tenementum cum catallis esse in pace usque ad certum diem quem dilecti et fideles nostri Johannes de Cavyndissh et Johannes de Holte tibi scire faciant: et interim facias xij liberos et legales homines de visneto illo videre tenementum illud, et nomina eorum imbreviari: et summoneas eos per bonos summonitores quod tunc sint coram prefatis Johanne et Johanne, et hiis quos sibi associaburt, ad certum locum quem iidem Johannes et Johannes tibi scire faciant, parati inde facere recognitionem. Et pone per vadium et salvos plegios predictos Simonem, Ricardum et Johannem, vel ballivos suos si ipsi non inventi fuerint, quod tunc sint ibi audituri illam recognitionem. Et habeas ibi summonitores, nomina plegiorum, et hoc breve. T. me ipso apud Westm. xxvº die Marcii anno regni nostri quarto.

41. ACCOUNT OF JOHN WAREFELD, RECEIVER FOR THOMAS STONOR

1416-17

This account is of sufficient interest to justify a fairly full summary. It is for the year from Michaelmas, 1416, to Michaelmas, 1417, and is written on five skins of parchment. Attached is a small supplementary account of payments, and a well-preserved wooden tally from the bailiff of Wattecombe. The document is now in *Ministers Accounts*, 1120/15; but, as the office stamp "Chancery" shows, originally formed part of the Stonor Papers.

· Compotus Johannis Warefeld, Receptoris Thome de Stonore a festo sancti Michaelis &c.

Stonor. Arrears of Dodecote, £20. 2. 2. Bailiff of Dodecote, £25. 2. 2. Bailiff of Sottewell, £10. Farmer of Bensheves, £12. Farmer of Penyton, £12. Bailiff of Aillesbury, £5. Farmer of Condycote, £3. 6. 8. Bailiff of Bourton, £1. 6. 8. Bailiff of Harnhull, 6s. 8d. Farmer of Hembury, £13. Bailiff of Watlyngton, £12. 6. 9. Robert Charyngworth, farmer of Westminster, 6s. 8d. From the collector of the fifteenth " pro denariis per dominum Regi prestitis," £12. 6. 8. " Rec. de domino pro Willelmo Lyncoln," 13s. 4d. " De

domino ad solvendum lez Flemynges pro opere de Stonore,"
£13. 13. 4. Total receipts, £141. 11. 1.

Allowances: to Michael Warwick in full payment for making
200,000 " de Brykes," £40; "ac pro operacione ejusdem materii"
£5. 3. 4; for carriage of the "brikes" from Crokkernende to Stonore,
£15; to Thomas Tiler "pro antiqua barg. sua," £1. 3. 4; to Thomas
Carpenter "pro factura columbarii " 6s. 8d.; to John Penne "pro iiij
serris manual. et pro j carect. pro lez Flemyngges 10s.; to Roger
Ormesley "pro stipendio suo primi termini," 6s. 8d.; to Drue Wiker
for reaping, £1; to Thomas Plomer of Oxford, "pro bargennia facta
arte sua super turrim, in parte solucionis xj marc," £4. 13. 4. Total
of Allowances, £77. 12. 4½.

Emptiones:—"pro una tabula cum uno pari trestell, pro domino,
London," 4s. 6d.; "pro equo griseo domini," £3; "pro ij ciphis
argenteis pro domino," £2. 11. 8—total, £10. 13. 2.

Expenses of Receiver:—holding Courts &c, £3. 10. 0; fine for
reversion of manor of Borewescote, 12s.; expenses of lord and lady in,
London, 14s. 9d.; paid to the lord there, 20d.;—total, £5. 19. 5.

Fees, £6. 19. 0.

Other payments: part of debt to Richard Wyot, £40; debt to
Edmund Hampden, £20—total, £72. 6. 8.

Livery money to the lord—at London on 8th Oct., £8—total,
£58. 8. 4.

Total of allowances, expenses, and liveries, £233. 18. 11½.

A supplementary account shewed: £11 received and outgoings
£10. 13. 4.—"pro cariagio domini a Henle usque London " 6s. 8d.—
Clear excess £92 1. 2½.

The other four skins are: (2) Reeves accounts: for Cundycote (John
Cook), Bourton (Richard Henry), Harnhull (John Ryver), and Hembury
(Thomas Saundres). (3) Account of John Kent, collector of rents at
Wattecombe, Hoo, Thame and Standelve. (4) Reeves accounts: for
Dodecote (Richard Howes), Sottewell (Thomas West), Bensheffes,
(Reginald Sheffeld) and Penyton Meysy (John Paty). (5) Account
of John Kent, collector of rents at Stonore.

42. JOHN DYMMOK TO [?]

This letter, which is much injured, and very difficult to decipher, is written by a bailiff at Ermington, and is apparently addressed to an officer (probably John Warefeld) of Thomas Stonor in London ; Stonor himself was perhaps absent in France. Accompanying it is the " bille of expenses and alowans " ; the latter is too much injured to reproduce in full, but it is not as a whole of great interest, though important as supplying Dymmok's name, and the date ; it is headed :—

Ermyngton

Expense et allocaciones Johannis Dymmok, a⁰ Regis Henrici quinti viij⁰.

In primis pet*it* all*ocacionem* de xlv. s. pro operibus liberorum [tenen-cium]. It., pet. all. de xxviij. s. j. d. pro piscaria voc. Madyngstad.

Other items are :—

iiij. d. pro j twest pro hostio panterie ; viij. s. iiij. d. pro v. mill. lapid. tegul. ; vj. s. viij. d. de expensis Willi. Mayne eundo et redeundo versus London. ; iij. li. quos Willelmus Mayne solvit domino apud Stonor.

There are also legal expenses incurred by William Penbrygge, with his expenses on going to London ; and expenses for John Hals in London. The total of receipts with expenses and allowances was £41 18s. 3d. ; and Dymmok had apparently £21 8s. 0d. in hand.

The Account is probably for the year ended at Michaelmas, 1420 (8 Henry V) ; so this letter was presumably written late in 1420. In an Account rendered by John Warefeld, Stonor's receiver, for that year appears the receipt of £15 from John Dymmok, farmer of Ermyngton, and the payments include :—

expense facte London. in Curia Admirallis pro wrecco maris apud Erm. in mari provecto, viz. primo die Augusti xxvij. s., et in aliis custubus in eadem Curia mense Novembr., ut pro fine xx. s., et senescallo Curie vj. s. viij. d., et pro feodis Clerici Curie pro ij procurationibus vij. s. iiij. d., et in feodis budell dicte curie iiij. d. (*Ministers Accounts*, 750/17).

An Account by John Dymmok for 1419-21 mentions William Mayne and John Hals (*id.*, 822/35, see vol. ii, p. 179 below). Dymmok appears on a commission in Devonshire in Feb. 1419 (*Cal. Pat. Rolls*, Henry V, ii, 274). John Fortescue was father of Richard Fortescue of Ermington (see No. 45) ; he was a justice of the peace for Devon from 1418 to 1422. John Hals, who was on the commission of peace for Devonshire from 1420 to 1431, was a lawyer of some prominence. The paper on which the letter is written is so mutilated at the foot that it is impossible to obtain anything of its meaning ; a continuation on the other side is equally hopeless (*Ch. Misc.*, 37, i, 32, 33).

Ermyngton.

Syr, as touchant þe ffynes þat ʒe sende to me, syr (?), I knowe ham noʒht what þay be, what is I-payd ne what is to payng, but I have aspyd among ham yn presence of Thomas, your messynger, [who] can enfourme you : and þay wil noʒtt paye . . . with oute hure dedis enselyd and . frynd is . . . and his wif hath ʒulde up hure e . . . d. Symon Lode doþ no fors f[or he] is febel and yold, Paulisfot, Ray, John at Wille, this persons[1] use makyth ham fulfulle alle [þis]. John Hals welle haþ enformyd me of ham, and therfore Thomas can enfourme [you] of all hit : but ʒut I shal enquere among ham better, yf y may eny þyng gete yn hast : and þerfor sendith [unto me a] bille of hur namys and what is to pay and touchant R. H[a]lle &c. Thomas can enfourme you by mouthe fully of J. Fortescu, Raff Hatt and Woder, god frendis, of the whiche spareth noʒtt to speke boþ for youre worchip and profet : and touchant my payment I sende by Thomas, your ʒeman, to my maister and Cosyn Hals a letter and a bond to delyvere you, excepte divers expenses and alowans, of þe whiche I send to you a bille. And as touchant myn endentur, reson wolde that þay were had aredy, for drede of changyng of þe world þat is bretell, as sone as hy[t] myth be mad and enselyd effectually, savant my maysteris profit and worchip : for truly ʒe knowe wel, and knowe also þat I am a profitabel Reve for hym and have a gret charge and labor. Saunz rien apprendre. For why comyth, so moche as the clothyng þat was spoke (?) þer of is by hynde, but ʒut I chalynge hit noʒth but after [my] maysteris oune governanse at þis tyme : for me þynkyth h[it] bote a febel reward, for wel I wot he haþ no servant [yn] Engelond þat servyth hym yn suche a labor and travayl [as] I do, payng more to hym þanne þe value ʒerly amontath, takyng ryth noʒth for my travayl, þe which as ʒut I faith wel safe yn hope of amendement aftir his discrecion and . . . . And touchant my maysteris beyng at London, and . . . ns . . . at mois michel ;[2] I wot wel ʒe most nedes be þer, [for] ʒe shalle save my maysteris enheritance, his profit and his worship, for to answer to þe false sugestion þat is mad [yn] þe admyral is Court : for every man here know[eth] wel þat þe wreke is

---

[1] The reading is doubtful.
[2] Or perhaps "mes Michel," for Michaelmas.

parcel of þe enheritance of Ermyngton and is fre   amend, noþer
pledeþ to a Countre is payment for me . . . my Styward and yours;
and þer for John Fortescu is worth and tenementes (?)   and
leeches yn þis be . . . .   never yn my lyf, for. . . . .

43. LEASE OF THE MANOR OF PENYTON MEYSY

1ST MAY, 1423

From *Ancient Deeds*, C. 3536. A small octagonal seal, ½ inch across,
with a device, is attached ; it is presumably that of William Whythygge.

Hec indentura facta inter Thomam de Stonore, armigerum, et
Thomam Chaucere et alios cum eodem Thoma Chaucere per predictum Thomam de Stonore feoffatos in et de manerio de Penyton
Meysy ex parte una, et Willelmum Whythygge de Enam ex parte altera,
testatur quod predicti Thomas de Stonore et feoffati sui predicti tradiderunt, concessere, et ad firmam dimiserunt predicto Willelmo
manerium suum de Penyton Meysy cum omnibus terris, redditibus, et
serviciis, pratis, pascuis et pasturis cum suis pertinenciis, boscis ibidem
et advocatione ecclesie ejusdem ville omnino exceptis et prèdictis
Thome de Stonore et feoffatis suis semper reservatis. Habenda et
tenenda omnia predicta Manerium, terras, redditus, servicia, prata,
pascua et pasturas, cum suis pertinenciis, exceptis preexceptis, predicto
Willelmo a die sancti Michaelis Archangeli proxime futuro usque ad
terminum septem annorum proxime sequentium et plenarie completorum.
Reddendo inde annuatim predictis Thome et feoffatis suis predictis,
heredibus et assignatis eorum, durante termino predicto, viginti duas
libras bone et legalis monete ad festa Annunciacionis beate Marie
virginis et Sancti Michaelis Archangeli per equales porciones. Et si
contingat predictus redditus viginti et duarum librarum in parte vel in
toto aretro fore non solutis post aliquod festum festorum predictorum
per duodecim septimanas, quod tunc bene licebit predictis Thome de
Stonore et feoffatis predictis in omnia predicta manerium, cum terris, redditibus, serviciis, pratis, pascuis et pasturis cum suis pertinenciis reintrare,
et ea in suo pristino statu habere hiis indenturis non obstantibus. Et
predictus Willelmus omnes domos manerii predicti durante termino

predicto manutenebit, reparabit et sustentabit quociens et quando necesse fuerit; aula cum cameris suis dicte aule annexis, coquina, et pistrina, et alia domu vocata le Knyghtchambre, jam ruinosis, exceptis: quas predicti Thomas et feoffati sui predicti reparari facient infra primum annum. Et predicti Thomas et feoffati sui predicti dictum Willelmum durante termino predicto exonerabunt de omnibus redditibus et serviciis forinsecis ultra viginti et duas libras predictas. Et predictus Willelmus Senescallum et Receptorem predictorum Thome et feoffatorum suorum ibidem bis per annum recipiet et eos honeste inveniet in omnibus expensis suis pro Curia et recepta ibidem faciente durante termino supradicto. Et predictus Willelmus in predicto manerio, domibus, gardinis, boscis et gravis ejusdem manerii non vastum nec dampnum faciet durante termino predicto, nisi habendo rationabiliter lignum focalem et meremium pro housbote et housbondria sua sustentanda, et hoc per deliberacionem et assignacionem Senescalli vel Receptoris dicti Thome et feoffatorum suorum predictorum. Et dictus Willelmus predictum Thomam et feoffatos suos predictos et heredes et assignatos eorum erga dominum Regem de quintadecima concessa vel concedenda durante termino predicto exonerabit et acquietabit. Et predictus Willelmus in firma predicta in propria persona sua, si vixerit, cum familia sua inhabitabit, et statum suum non dimittet sine assensu et voluntate predicti Thome et feoffatorum suorum predictorum. In cujus rei testimonium partes predicte sigilla sua alternatim apposuere, hiis testibus Thoma Sakevyle, milite, Willelmo Doyly, Petro Feteplace, Willelmo Wyot, Johanne Warefeld, et aliis. Datum apud Stonore primo die Maii anno regni Regis Henrici sexti post conquestum primo.

44. J. HURLEGH TO THOMAS STONOR

28 SEPTEMBER [1424 or earlier]

The writer, who was clearly connected with Salisbury, is probably the John Hurlegh, who was prebendary of Ramsbury in 1414, Warden of the Hospital of St. Nicholas, Salisbury, from 1418-20, and rector of Kingston Deverell; he died in 1425 (Wordsworth, *Cartulary of St. Nicholas Hospital*, p. 211 ; for another reference to him see *Cal. Pat. Rolls*, Henry VI, i, 234). Golafre, Warfield and Hurlegh were three of Stonor's feoffees of Ermington (see p. 36 below). Warfield was also Stonor's receiver (see No. 41). A Nicholas Cassy of Gloucester occurs in 1427-29, and a John Cassy of Gloucester in 1434 (*Cal. Pat. Rolls*, Henry VI, i, 376, 515 ; ii, 372). William Alisaundre of

Wilts. occurs in 1423-34 (*ibid.*, i, 571 ; ii, 219, 343). This letter may possibly have some connexion with the presentation of one John Hurle to Bourton in Hemmersh, diocese of Worcester, in 1421 (*ibid.*, Henry V, ii, 399). From *A.C.*, xlvi, 44.

Wurshipfull Sire and maistre, I recommande me to ʒow ; and do ʒow to wite þat I am enfourmed þat Osebarn and Cassy have pursued a new writ of *quare impedit* aʒeyns ɪ. Golafre, ɪ. Warfeld, and þe incumbent, and þoghten, as I suppose, to have hade a pryve recovere : for as Gyles, our attorne of þe chapitre, told me, þat þe processe is at distresse now retournable at þe oeptes or þe quinzisme, I [? know]not qwether. I seend syr John to Gloucestre to þe under-shirreve to have hade a copie : and he said to hym, " kame none write " : and so and I suppose þe retourne be pryvele made at London : here is koynt craft. William Alisandre semes most bost and wurship, for all syde þat þai be onward at þis terme. And if I may ride for þe crikke, I shall kome to ʒow, praing with all myn hert þat ʒe wold be þer &c. Also I send ʒow a copie of þe letters of Institucion and Induccion at þe kynges presentacion &c., praing hertely þat ʒe will vouchesave to konnen with ʒore counseill : for I suppose þai be now at more laiser þen at London &c. Also, Wurschipfull Syr, Cassy hase disabeied þe Juggement of Wilcotes : I send ʒow a copie þerof, and of þe endenture made, þe obligacions be in mennes bondes þ [1] dar not delyver ham for hym : I seend ʒow a copie of ham. And truly I wold full fayn þat he were chawfed. Man of lawe say here þat þe parson, my cosyn, and ʒore bedeman, has his accion as for his reparacons, and þe payne of þe obligacion shuld I have : for truly þat was þe entent, þat if my cosyn hat disabeied þe juggement I had forfaited myn obligacion. And me semes þat he shuld be in þe same caas to me. He settes noʒght be noman. And þerfore truly, syr, I wold the poure parson hade resonable reparacion after þe juggement, and þe avantage of þe obligacion stonde in governance of ʒow and ʒore frendes &c. I pray ʒow lette all be seen with gode avys, as my holly trust is in ʒow. Also, syr, I send John to Mr. Gilbert for þe sale of þe land, and he sais Lang, the corser, has been with hym, and if hit shuld be soold be parcelles he wold undertake of vj C. markes and moore &c. And he sais my lord of Duresme has write to hym for a cosyn of his, Mr. ɪ. Fytan. And I shall be at London now at þis terme for finale sale þerof, I suppose. And Mr. G. says, if he may for his foote, he will also. And see ʒe what is best

---

[1] There is a hole in the MS.

for зore entent, and I shall help faithfully as mycull as in me is.   And I beseche зow seend me som wurd be þe brynger of зore will and avys. Also I have be sore diseised in my bakke, and elles I shuld have spoke with зow er þis: for certeyn þer was never matier þat I þoght so mycull apon &c.   T. Halling told me he wold speke with зow.   And I pray Gode kepe зowe in hele of body and sowle with encresce of wur-ship.   Writen at Sarum apon þe seynt Michell even,

зore prest, J. Hurlegh.

Venerabili viro Thome Stonore, armigero, domino suo speciali.

45. THE INDENTURE FOR RICHARD AND AGNES FORTESCU

29 SEPTEMBER, 1424

This is a draft, on paper, of the deed which Thomas Stonor enclosed in the following letter.   The original (*Ancient Deeds*, C. 3015) has some altera-tions which it was not worth showing.   The last three l nes are added in another hand.   The deed has a certain interest as having been drafted by the famous Sir John Fortescue, then quite a young lawyer : it is perhaps too much to assume that any part of the draft is in his handwriting.   Ri· hard Fortescue was the third son of Sir John Fortescue, the father of the Chief Justice ; he was killed at St. Albans in 1455 (Stow, *Annales*, p. 399) ; the deed shows that it was he who married Agnes, daughter of Richard Holcombe, and not his son as commonly stated (*Works of Sir J. Fortescue*, ii, 151-2, ed. Lord Clermont).

This Indenture was possibly the sequel of an earlier dispute, as to which there was a Petition in Chancery by Thomas Chaucer, John Golafre, John Hurlegh, " chapeleyn," John Warefe.d, and Thomas Berdelegh, showing that they were seised of the manor and hundred of Ermington, ti l one Richard Fortescu of great malice and forethought made a forcible entry and broke down hedges and ditches.   The Petition mentions " John Fortescu, pier a dit Richard, et 'John Bosan, son frier en ley" (*Early Chancery Proceedings*, 69/24 P.R.O.).

Hec Indentura facta apud Ermyngton in Comitatu Devon. in festo sancti Michaelis Archangeli, anno regni Henrici sexti post conquestum Anglie tercio, inter Thomam Chaucer, Johannem Golafre, Hamonem Belknap, dominos Manerii de Ermyngton predicto, ex parte una, et

Ricardum Fortescu et Agnetem uxorem ejus ex parte altera : testatur quod cum iidem Ricardus et Agnes, ut in jure ipsius Agnetis, clamaverunt communam pasturam in grosso ad omnia animalia sua temporibus apertis depascenda per tctum dominium Manerii predicti in parte occidentali cujusdam fossati, quod vocatur la Yalthadych, quod vero fossatum jacet per divisa de aqua de Ermyn versus terram de Prutaston inter dominium de Ermyngton et sanctuarium ejusdem luci,[1] et ultra linaliter a capite ejusdém fossati versus ad terram de Prutaston, ex concessione cujusdam Johannis Peverell, nuper domini Manerii predicti, facta cuidam Ricardo de Holecombe antecessori predicte Agnetis, cujus heres ipsa est, prout in eodem scripto inde confecto plenius continetur, ubi predictus Ricardus de Holecombe nec aliquis heredum vel assignatorum suorum unquam aliquam communam pasturam in Manerio predicto habuerunt seu de jure habere debuerunt, prout ex parte predictorum Thome Chaucer, Johannis Golafre, et Hamonis Belknap asseritur. Et pro eo quod iidem Ricardus Fortescu et Agnes renunciaverunt omne id quod eis pertinet seu quov smodo pertinere poterit in futurum in predicta communa pastura virtute concessionis perdicte, et eciam remiserunt et relaxaverunt pro se et heredibus suis per presentes predictis Thome Chaucer, Johanni Golafre et Hamoni Belknap totum jus suum et clameum quod habent seu quovismodo in futurum habere poterint in Manerio predicto : ita quod nec predicti Ricardus Fortescu et Agnes, nec eorum heredes aut assignati aliquam communam pasturam in Manerio predicto aut in aliqua parcella inde de cetero habere vel clamare poterint, set inde per presentes in perpetuum sint exclusi : iidem Thomas Chaucer, Johannes Golafre; et Hamo Belknap tradiderunt et concesserunt et hac presente carta indentata confirmaverunt predictis Ricardo et Agneti duodecim acras et unam rod terre arabilis per perticam mensuratas, qualibet pertica continens sexdecim pedes et dimidiam, simul jacentes in longitudine inter viam legalem que ducit in Ermyn in parte boriali et abbuttant in longitudine in terram predicti Ricardi et Agnetis ex parte australi, et jacentes in latitudine inter Holecombeslad ex parte occidentali et viam regiam que ducit a Saneford usque Prutastoneslond ex parte orientali : habendas et tenendas predictas duodecim acras et rodam terre cum pertinenciis predictis Ricardo et Agneti et heredibus de corporibus eorum procreatis sub forma, condicionibus, et declaracione subsequentibus : reddendo inde annuatim predictis Thome Chaucer, Johanni, et Hamoni, heredibus et assignatis suis sex denarios ad festa sancti Thome Apostoli, annunciacionis beate Marie Virginis, nativitatis sancti

---

[1] Probably an error for " loci ".

Johannis Baptiste, et sancti Michaelis Archangeli, equis porcionibus. Et si predicti Ricardus et Agnes, aut heredes sui predicti, aut eorum aliquis in aliqua Curia domini Regis, heredum aut successorum suorum, de recordo in futuro clamaverint aliquam communam pasturam in Manerio predicto vel in aliqua parcella inde vel aliqua pastura ibidem usi fuerint, vel predictas duodecim acras et rodam terre vel aliquam parcellam inde per judicium Curie Regis perdiderint, aut alicui alien- averint: quod tunc bene licebit predictis Thome Chaucer, Johanni Golafre, et Hamoni Belknap, heredibus et assignatis suis in predictas duo- decim acras et rodam terre cum pertinenciis reintrare et in pristino statu suo retinere, presentibus indenturis et sesina inde habita non obstantibus. In cujus rei testimonium uni parti hujus scripti indentati penes predictis Thoma Chaucer, Johanne et Hamone remanenti predicti Ricardus et Agnes sigilla sua apposuerunt: alteri vero parti hujus scripti indentati penes predictis Ricardo et Agnete remanenti predicti Thomas Chaucer, Johannes, et Hamo sigilla sua apposuerunt.   Data loco et festo et anno supradictis.

Noverint &c nos Johannes Speke de Bramford in Com. Devon., Henricus Fortescu de Wodelegh in eodem Com., et Johannes Fortescu de Helewille in eodem Com. gentilmen.

46. THOMAS STONOR TO [SIR JOHN FORTESCUE]

[30 OCTOBER, 1424]

The reference to "my uncle Belknap" shows that the writer of this letter was Thomas Stonor (d. 1431), whose mother was a daughter of Sir Robert Belknap. The previous document (which is clearly "your son Richard's" in- denture) gives the date 1424, and shows that the letter was addressed to Sir John Fortescue, the father of the Chief Justice : the Chief Justice first appears as "gubernator" at Lincoln's Inn in 1425, so that this letter is perhaps the earliest extant reference to him in his legal career. Richard Fortescue, the judge's younger brother, is noticed on p. 36 above. Wytbury is probably the John Wydbury of Cornwall, who occurs in conjunction with John Crokker of Lyneham, near Ermington, in February, 1422 (Cal. Pat. Rolls, Henry V, ii, 423); he may be the same as the John Wydbury of Southampton, squire, who died before February, 1423 (ibid., Henry VI, i, 48). The letter like the foregoing deed seems to be a draft kept by Stonor for reference ; this explains the absence of any endorsement. From A.C., xlvi, 37.

Ryth welle belovyd syr, I grete yow well, doyng yow to undurstonde þath yowre son Jon and I beth fully acorded as towchyng to the ferme of the Maner off Ermyngton, as hys endenturys þerof beth enseylyd. And ye shall have þe lawe Court of Mychellmasse last passed.   Furþurmore I send yow be the berer of þys letter endenturys betwene yowre sone Rychard and my feffeys, þe wyche ben made be avyse and asent of yowre son Jon : prayinge yow that ye delyver nat the party of þe same endenturys enselyd be my feffeys into the tyme that yowre sone Rychard have enselyd hys party of the same endenturys : and thanne hys party soo enselyd that ye delyver sesyng unto the same Rychard and hys wyff aftyr the fourme cf the endenturys : to wyche endenturys lakketh þe selyng of my uncle Belknap, wyche shall ensele þem whanne he com fro beyonde see.   And seeth that yowre forseyde son Rychard duly ensele þe same endenture, for yowre son Jonys honestie hanketh theron. And as towchyng the warce of Wytburyes heyr, and of þe londys, the wyche longen to me, I pray yow that ye soo see þerto that my ryth be saved, that I and my frendus schull have yow thonke therfore.   And yf ye see that hyt may lawfully be sesyd þath ye sesed [hyt][1] as my trust ys in yow.   Nomore y wryte unto yow at thys tyme, but the holy gost have yow in hys kepyng.   I-wrytte at London the Monday nexte before alle-halwenday.

By Thomas Stonore.

No endorsement.

47. EXPENSES OF A FUNERAL

[*before* 1425]

Since this funeral clearly took place at Rippinghale in Lincolnshire, the date must be earlier than 1425, in which year Thomas Stonor sold all his estates in that county (*Ancient Deeds*, C. 1223).   It may therefore be safely assumed to refer to Thomas Stonor's own mother, Joan daughter of Sir Robert Bealknap.   As to the possible earlier date of her death see p. xix above.   Presumably Rippinghale formed part of her dower.   The original is on a sheet of paper folded lengthwise to make four pages.   It is printed here in full, except for the omission of " Itm." before the various particulars. From *Ch. Misc.*, 37, i, 35.

---

[1] " hyt " afterwards erased.

Payd to the smythe of Rypyngall. Item primis: for ij fyches, —.
Payd the smythe of Ripynghall for deverce thynges, xj. d.   Payd to
Rad. Foole, ij. d.   Payd for halfe a beeffe, v. s. iiij. d.   Payd for
breede, viij. s.   Payd for waxe, after vij. d. þe li., x. li. v. s. x. d.;
and the resedue of the waxe here anone.   Payd for iij torches, viij. s.
For fysche at Burie, xiij. d.   For fysche at Stamforde, —.   For wyne,
xxij. d.   For clarett wyne, ij gallantes, xvj. d.   For a vele, iij. s. iiij. d.
For a brawne, iij. s. iiij. d.   For ij geece, x. d.   For iij pygges,
xij. d. ob.   For plovers, vij. d.   For blake couton for the herse clothe,
vij yardes, ij. s. xj. d.   For an elne of lynen clothe, v. d.

The vijth day.

Md. delyvered to Wyllm. Wayrd to be dalt in almes for my moders
soule.   First to the towne of Morton, iiij. s.   To Hacomby, ij. s.
viij. d.   To Douysby, delyvered to Thomas Barwyke of Rypyngall this
some, ij. s.   Delyvered Tourner for Aslaby, ij. s.   Delyvered to Moris
for þe towne of Sempryngham and Poynton, ij. s. viij. d.; to Kyrby,
xviij. d.; Douysby, ij. s.; to the towne of Loughton, xx d.; to Greyby,
viij d.; to Myllinethorpp, vij d.   Delyvered to the preestes of the vijth
day, vj. s. viij. d.   To clarkes and chylldren and pore peple the same
day, x. s.   For ix dozen of breede the berying day, ix. s.   For a vele
the vijth day, ij. s. viij. d.   For ij swannes, iij geece, iij capones, iij
pygges, halffe a hox & vj cople of cones —.

The xxxth day dalte in Almes.

Delyvered to William Warde for Mourton, this some, iiij. s; for
Hacomby, ij. s. viij. d.; Douysby, ij. s.   Delyvered to John Torner:
for Aslaby, ij. s; Kyrbye, xviij. d.; Loughton and Loughton, xij d.;
for [Gr]ayby, viij d.   Delivered to Thomas Barwyke for Ryppyngall,
ij. s.; for Sempryngham, ij. s. viij. d.; Douysby, ij. s.

Vetalls þe same day.

Halfe a oxe, iiij. s.   Halfe a porke, xij. d.   Also croppe of beeffe
and the surloyne, x d.   A swane, iiij geese, ij pygges, iij capons, v
cople of cones, xvj plovers, a moton (*no prices*).

The berying day.

Receavyd of my mothers mony in golde and sylver thys som ffoloyng.
In Kyng Hary pence this som xxx. s. xij. d.   In golde v. li.   In
grotes and pence ij^{te}, xiij. s. iiij. d.   Summa totalis vij. li. iiij. s. iiij. d.

Payd to the sheryff servand for sheryff tenthe, ij. s. vj. d.   Payd for ij boxes of conserves, tryacle, and souger candy, x. d.

Delyvered for wages to the herdsmen and other.

To the nettherde for his quarter wage, xx. d.   To Rich. Clay vij. d. Payd to John Hosbourne for a quarter wages.   Payd for coloryng of xxij^{ti} yardes of clothe, v. s. x. d.   Payd to the ffuller for fferyng of the same stuffe, —.

Endorsed on p. 4.   In grotes, xv. s.   In pence and pence of ij, iiij. li. vij. s. vj. d.   Payd of my mony this some folowyng the berying day and þe vij^{th} day; Summa iij. li. xiiij. s. vj. d.

48. TO THOMAS STONOR

[*c.* 1425]

This is a fragment of a letter, which from the mention of "master Chaucer" (Thomas Chaucer, who died in 1434) must have been addressed to the first Thomas Stonor. The reference to "Dymmok" indicates that the letter had to do with Ermington. "Wonard" may possibly be William Wynnard, grandfather of Agnes Stonor (see No. 261). John Cottesmore, who was afterwards (1429-1439) a judge of the Common Pleas and chief justice in 1439, was on the commission of peace for Devonshire from 1424 to 1427; he had lands in Berks and Oxfordshire, and his grandson married a grand-daughter of Thomas Stonor (see No. 107).   From *A.C.*, xlvi, 87.

so Wonard sende me yn a letter that he koude not speke wyth Dymmok att noe leyser sethen my last beyng at home; boot att the assisis, yf he koude entrete hym to an ende resonable, he and I wuld make an ende alle so wel after oure day as afore: which assis begynnyth a goode while after the decollacion above said: boot I may not be there: wherefore my conceile ys fully that ye yn alle hast doe sende thether letters, or froe my maister Chauceire, or froe my lord of Wyn-chester, or rather than to faile froe your selve, by good avice concevid, and that my maister Cotysmore, that is there justeice &c., may do your erant by mouthe unto Wonard, and so I wote. . . .

A mon treshonore et tres reverent Sire et Maister Thomas Stonor.

49. JOHN HAMME TO [THOMAS STONOR]

[*c.* 1425]

There is no indication of date in this letter, nor is the name of the person to whom it was written given.   But the writer is probably the John Hampne who was bailiff at Horton in 1419-20 (*Ministers Accounts*, 1250/2, see vol. ii, p. 179).   It must therefore have been addressed to the first Thomas Stonor. With this the reference to John Martyn agrees, for there was a John Martyn on the commission of peace for Kent from 1413-36.   In any case it would have been difficult to assign the letter to the time of the second Thomas Stonor ; for Alice Drayton owned Horton till her death in October, 1468, and John Forth was bailiff in October, 1469 (see No. 101).   The letter is now separated from the Stonor papers, to which it no doubt belongs, and is in *A.C.*, li, 63.

To my Worshipful lord.   I recomaunde me to ȝow with alle my herte.   I beseche ȝow þat ȝe wille þenke on my lord of Caunterbery, for me feryþ sore of hym.   Als I beseche ȝow, ȝif ȝe mow naȝt tary, þat ȝe wolde speke with John Martyn þat he myȝt be mene betwene my lord of Caunterbery and ȝow þat it myȝt be concevyd forþ in þe best maner for ȝour profyt and worshyp.   Also I beseche ȝow þat ȝe willyn speke to John Martyn as towchyng þe mater of Chertone þat he wolde take non distresse, and þat it myth be conceyved in leyser unto þe tyme þat ȝe and John Martyn mowe speke to-kedyr ate ȝour bothe esement. Also I wold fayn wete what ȝe wyllyn do with Mannemede, for it must be ordeynyd for for ȝour owne profyt.   Also I beseche ȝow with alle my herte þat ȝe willen leve word atte ȝour ynne of alle þese materys I wrete in a scrowe : and I sshal sende þedir a Saterday next comyng.   I beseche ȝow þat ȝe wil tary þe lenger for þese maters aforeseyd, and I sshal helpe to bere sum of þe costes.   Almythy God have ȝow ever in his kepyng body and soule.

Be Johr Hamme
ȝoure pouer servaunt.

No endorsement.

50. INVENTORY OF FURNITURE, ETC., AT HORTON

[*c.* 1425]

John Hamme was farmer at Horton in 1419-20 ; see last letter. From *Ch. Misc.*, 37, i, 34.

Memorandum quod ista billa indentata facit mensionem de certis parcellis subscriptis post egressum Johannis Hamme, nuper firmarii de Hortone, remanentibus Thome Stonore, Armigero, ac domino ibidem.

In primis in le Parlour j longa tabula cum j pari trestell. It., alia parva tabula cum j pari de trestell. It., ij formill. It., j plate de ferro pro candel. It., j dosere cum j banker, semble de colore rubeo et nigro. It., in pantria j giste pertinens pro cervisia. It., j hangyngbord. It., ij alii bordis. It., j pype kokyr pro panetria. It., in boteria j gyste pertinens pro cervisia. Itm., in principali Camera j lectum de colore albo et nigro cum j seler, j coverlyt, iiij curtynys, j canevas, j materas, ij blankettes, j pare linthiam., j linthiam. pro capite. Itm., j longa tabula cum j pare de trestell, iiij plate de ferro. It., j scala in camera predicta. It., j plate de ferro in alia camera. It., j candelebrum de ferro. It., vij lecti i-bordyd in diversis cameris. It., j scala pro pullayle. It., j longa tabula de beche, cum j long formill in le tresauns juxta coquinam. It., j longa tabula cum j pare trestell in le chesehous. It., in le Bakhous j buntyntunne, ij knedyng trowes, j muldyngbord cum covertore ad idem, j plumbum, j cacabus in le wallys. It., ij zeeltonnys, ij mashfattes, iij kemelyns, ij tubbys, v barell pro cervisia, j heryngbarel, ij verjuis barell. Itm., j tonne pro dreye malt. Itm., in le larderhous, j saltyngtrowe, j magna cista pro carne. It., alie ij magne ciste. Itm., in coquina ij dressyngbord, j gret morter cum j pestel. It., j magna olla de eneo continens viij lagenas. It., alia olla continens ij lagenas et di. It., alia olla enea continens ij lagenas. It., ij pannys de eneo feble. It., j broad basyn. It., in le chesehous, j plumbum in le wallys, ij stoppys platys. It., ij plates de plumbo. It., in diversis stabulis v mangeris cum iiij rackys. It., iij rynggebordes pro le Molle Whel. It., vij bordys de Elme in le Schepens.

51. EXPENSES AT HORTON

1425-6

These accounts are contained on three slips of paper.   The first and third are given in full.   From *Ch. Misc.*, 37, i, 36-8.

(*a*) Horton.. Expense forinsece.   In primis lib. Willelmo Olyver equitando ad Stonore ad certificandum dominum de meremio molendini cariato ad Horton, xvj. d.   It., ın domibus nuper, Galfridi Kyrkeby tectandis, vj. s.   It., in expensis domini existentis apud Horton ad xv^m Pasche A° iiij^to regis Henrici vj^ti, iiij. s. ij. d.   It., in expensis ejusdem ibidem, xx. d.   It., in falcacione ix acrarum prati ad usum domini, vj. s., pro acra viij. d.

(*b*) Horton.   Expenses of building the Mill between Michaelmas, 1425 and Michaelmas, 1426.   To R. Palmere carpenter, for repair "per convencionem in gross," £4. 13. 4.   Carriage of timber from Hadloo, 16s.   For 150 large nails, 4s. 6d.   For 150 nails, 6d.   For 100 "leadnaill" 3d.   For 100 nails 3d.   "In ij Curtenis ad cariandum ffimum et compestum per duos dies ad obstupandum stagnum Molendini ad retornendum cursum aque per aliam viam ad dictum opus proficiendum, iiij. s., qualis capiens per diem cum custagiis, xij d."   Two men hired to fill the carts, 16d.   "In fodicione luti ad idem opus, xij d. In iij carectis ad cariandum dictum lutum ad dictum opus per j diem, iiij s.´   In calce fodiendo, iiij d."   Carriage, 2d.   Nicholas Walshmom, for labour, 17 days, 8s. 6d.   Stephen Attewelle, 8 days, 3s. 4d.   Two labourers, 4 days, 1s. 8d.   Three men, 4 days, 4s.   Three men, 1 day, 1s.   Summa, vij li. vij s.

(*c*) Horton.   Custus tegulacionis domus de la Seyer.   In primis in M'M' de latt. quercinis emptis ad idem, xj. s. iiij. d.   Item in cariagio eorundem de Fyelston, xij d.   Item in x^m de prigis emptis ad idem, x. s.   Item in iiij quarteriis calcis adhust. emptis ad idem, v. s. iiij. d., per quarterium, xvj. d.   Item, in cariagio ejusdem calcis, viij. d.   Item in sabulo fodiendo et cariagio ejusdem, viij. d.   Item, in xiiij^m' de tegulis emptis ad idem xlvj. s. viij. d.   Item, in cariagio earundem ix. s. iiij d., per M'. viij. d.   Item, in tegulatori et servienti suo conductis per j diem ad emendendos alios defectus super tectum ejusdem domus x. d.   Summa, iiij. li. xix. s. x. d.

Md. quod in festo purificacionis beate Marie Virginis anni infrascripti Andreas Howe liberavit domino de Horton pro Maneriis suis ibidem de termino Nativitatis domini, aᵒ regis Henrici sexti apud London in ffriday strete apud signum Ursi viij. li. vj. s. viij . d. Item, lib. Willelmo Olyver servienti suo, xvj. d. Item. lib. domino ad signum Ursi predicti in xvᵃ Pasch. tunc prox. seq. Cvj. s. vilj. d. de termino Pasch. tunc preced. pro firma Manerii predicti. Item., lib. eidem per manus Thome Beardeslee ad festum Sancte Margarete pro firma predicta lxvj. s. viij. d. Item, cie Lune prox. post festum omnium Sanctorum tunc prox. seq. lib. eidem per manus ejusdem Thome lxvj. s. viij. d. Summa, xx. li. viij. s.

52. ACCOUNT OF JOHN COVENTRE, UNDER-SHERIFF FOR OXFORD AND BERKS

1427-8

Thomas Stonor was sheriff in 1423-4 and 1427-8. He and Thomas Chaucer sat for the county of Oxford in the Parliament of Sept. 1427. Consequently this account must belong to his second term of office as sheriff. The original is on a single sheet of paper. From *Ch. Misc.*, 37, i, 39.

Inter Thomam Stonore, Vicecomitem, et Johannem Coventre.

Idem Johannes *recepit* de firma hundr. Belle Crucis et Kentebery, vij. li. vj. s. viij. d.

Et de firma hundr. de Okke cum amerciamentis com. Berks. ac amerciamentis turni vic. ibidem ix. li. vj. s. viij. d.

Et de firma hundr. de Mortan cum blad. et turno Vic. ibidem vj. li. xiij. s. iiij. d.

Et de firma hundred. de Pough cum finibus et amerciamentis com. Oxon. xij. li.

Summa xxxv. li. vj. s. viij. d.

Item r. de xxxiiij s. de hid*agio* liber*tatis* de Redyng: Et de xlix. s. de hid. hundr. de Compton: Et de C. s. de hid. hundr. de Wantyng: Et de lxiiij. s. de hid. hundr. de Shrivenham: Et de vj. li. de hid. hundr. Belle Crucis: Et de lxxv. s. x. d. de cremento ibidem: Et de xl. s. de hid. hundr. de Kentebery: Et de xxiij. s. viij. d. de cremento ibidem: Et de ij. s. de visu de Shefford: Et de xij. d. de cremento de Baletston: Et de iiij. s. ij. d. de hid. hundr. de Lambourne: Et de xix. s. de hid. honoris Leic. in Fifhide et Kyngeston: Et de xx. s.

de Vic. de Stevynton : Et de lxxvij. s. de hid. hundr. de Wotton : Et de Cx. s. ij. d. ob. de hid. hundr. de Chad. : Et de iiij. li. iiij. s. iiij. d. de cremento hid. et palfr. in hundr. de Bloxham : Et de xxx. s. de hid. honoris sancti Walven in hundr. de Bolynden &c. : Et de C. s. de hid. hundr. de Okke : Et de lvj. s. vij. d. ob. de cremento ibidem.

Summa ——[1].

Et de turno Vic. hundr. de Pough nihil hoc anno quia ballivi habent in firma sua. Et de turno Vic. hundr. de Bloxham cum vic. de Bereford ij. s. ij d. Et de turno vic. hundr. de Chadlyngton nihil hoc anno quia nulla amerciamenta fiebant. Et de turno vic. hundr. de Want. et Shryvenham xvj. s. viij. d. Et sic vend. Rogero Merlawe et Johanni Coursey. Et de turno vic. hundr. de Okke nihil hoc anno quia ballivus habet in firma sua. Et de turno vic. hundr. de Morton nihil hoc anno quia ballivus habet in firma sua. Et de turno hundr. Belle Crucis ——.

Et de turno vic. hundr. de Kentebery, xiij. s. iiij d. Et sic. vend. Johanni Goolde. Summa ——

Et de blad. Vic. videlicet xix quarteriis frumenti in hundr. de Okke prec. b$_{\text{3}}$. viij. d.—Cj. s. iiij d. Et de x. quarteriis siliginis prec. b$_{\text{3}}$. v. d. —xxxiij. s. iiij. d. Et de gall. vend. hoc anno, xx. s. Summa ——.

Et de xlvij. li. xij s. de expensis Militum Com. Oxon. pro Thoma Chaucer et Thoma Stonore. Summa xlvij. li. xij. s.

Et de denariis manucaptionibus diversorum hominum prout patet per unam cedulam. xvj. li. xiiij. s. vj. d. Summa ——.

Summa totalis clix. li. x. s. x. d.

[*In dorso.*] E quibus sol. in Scaccario domini Regis, iiij^{xx} iiij. li. xvj. s. x. d. Et Priori Sancte Frideswide Oxon. vj. li. xiij. s. iiij. d.

Item in feodis et donis in Scaccario cum jantaculo Vic. ut patet per cedulam, xij. li. ij. s. ij. d. Et in feodis comp. ex convencione facta, vj. li. xij. s. iiij. d.

Et de denariis solutis Ricardo Calday ut de expensis Militis per preceptum Magistri, xiij. li. vj. s. viij. d. Et de ballivo honoris Walyngford iiij^{or} hundr. et di. viz. W. Borde, xj. li. xviij. s. Et de Johanne Jaket, ballivo hundr. de Thame ut de expensis Militis, lxxvj. s. viij. d. Et de ballivo hundr. de Dorchestr. de expensis predictis, lx. s.

Et in perdicione assartorum in foresta de Wyndesore, iiij. li. xvij. s. Et de munit. firmis que requir. super Vic. in Berkes. v. s. Et in perdicione redditus in Clyware, v. s. iiij. d. Et in perdicione redditus super terris nuper Henrici Deye, xx. d. Et in perdicione firme vij hundr. liij. s. iiij. d. Et in perdicione redditus in Hanney, xv. s.

---

[1] Blank in original.

Summa omnium solucionum et expensarum cli. li. iiij. s. v. d.   Et sic debet viij. li. xvj. s. iiij. d.

53. ALYS, LADY SUDELEY TO THOMAS STONOR

before 1431

The writer is Alys, daughter of Sir John Beauchamp of Powyk, who married (1) Thomas Boteler of Sudeley (*d.* 1398) and (2) Sir John Dalyngrygge of Bodiham, Sussex; she held Sudeley in dower, and died in 1442-3. The letter must therefore have been addressed to the first Thomas Stonor and be earlier in date than 1431. From *A.C.*, xlvi, 39.

Right trusty and entierly welbeloved frend y commaund me unto you: and, where as y of singler trust in you have before this enfeffed you with other in my Maners, londes and tenements withyn dyvers shires, wole and hertely prey you, for gret consideracions and causes touching my worship and gret profyt, that ye seale the deedes, made yn youre name and other, of the seid Maners to suche persons as be named in the same, wheche seid deedes the berer of this shall shewe unto you, as my full trust ys and bathe be unto you, like as the berer hereof shall enfourme you: to whom y prey you geve credence.   And, sir, yf ther be anything that y may do for you in any mater in tyme comyng, y wole do yt with all myn hert, and that knoweth God, who have you in his blessed kepyng.   Wreten at Sudely the iiij day of Avrell.

Alys, lady Sudeley.

To the worshipfull and my trusty frend Thomas Stoner.

54. THE WILL OF THOMAS STONOR

1431

Ch. Misc., 37, ix, 8-9, contains an abstract — in Latin — of Thomas Stonor's will, with a valuation, on four pages, the last being blank. Though reproducing no doubt the whole substance and often the exact words it does not appear to be a complete copy. It will be sufficient to give its purport.

" Voluntas T. de S. scilicet quod "—Alice his wife to have in dower the Manor of Ermington, the Manor of Harnhull with the advowson, the Manor of Beerton juxta Ailesbury, and the Manor of la Mote in Westminster, their value being £402. 13. 4.   His wife is to have for life all lands and tenements acquired in Clyve, Westbere, Chestelet, Hopelond, Stureye, and Horton in Kent, and the Manor of Penyton Meysy with the advowson, for the sustinence and finding in food, clothes and education (*in victu, vestitu et doctrina*) of his daughters. Thomas Chaucer, whilst alive, is to have the governance and supervision of his son and heir Thomas, with the issues and profits of the Manor of Hembury for his sustinence till the age of twenty-one.   The marriage of his said son is to be sold by Chaucer, his wife Alice, his brother John Hampden, and John Warfeld.   The proceeds are to be applied for the marriages of his daughters, Elizabeth, Maud, Philippa, Joan, and Anne, together with the issues and profits of the Manors of Dodecote, Sottewell, and Bensheves, Berks, and Stonor, Watlyngton and Cleyore in Oxfordshire.   His daughters are during their minority to be in the governance of his widow, Chaucer, Hampden and Warfeld. Each daughter is to have 200 marks at least for her marriage.   They are to be married in order of age.   If one or more should die unmarried (*quod absit*), her portion is to be divided equally amongst the survivors. If through the death of his said sons[1] under age without legitimate issue, his daughters inherit his lands, the payments of the said 200 marks are to lapse.   His wife, Chaucer, Hampden and Warfeld are then to dispose of the profits of the marriages of his male heirs and of the said Manors during the minority of his heirs in discharge of his conscience, according to the will and ordinance of his parents and ancestors as in their last wills more fully appears.   In the event of his wife's death his son John is to have the reversion of the Manor of Burewardescote on condition that he release to his brother Thomas his right in gavelkind to all lands in Kent, as well those which Thomas Stonor held in right of his wife as those newly acquired.

On the second page is a valuation :—

Debita qúe debentur Thome de Stonore per estimacionem Johannis Warfeld.

De finibus de Hembury, xxx. li.   De reddit. de Hembury, xxx. s. ultra terminum.   De reddit. de Harnhull, x. li.   De reddit. de Bourton, x. marc.   De reddit. de Condycote, v. marc.   De finibus ibidem xl. s.

---

[1] " Predicti filii mei ; " but only Thomas has so far been named.

De finibus de Dodecote, xvj. li. De reddit. ibidem, xxj. li. De reddit. de Sottewell, ix. s. De finibus ibidem, xxx. s. De Watlyngton cum finibus, viij. li. De finibus de Thame, xx. marc. De finibus de Stonore, x. marc. De redd. de Stonore, C. s. De Rypyngale, iiij. li. De Ermyngton, xx. marc. De Aillesbury cum Stoke, C. s. De Penyton, C. s. De Horton, xij. marc. De Will. Clyfforde, xxxv. marc. Summa ———.

Further particulars of the estate are given on the third page :—

Glouc. : Harnhull cum Doughton, Hembury in Saltmarsshe, xxix. li. Berks. : Dodecote, Sottewelle, Bensheves cum membris, C. marc. Nove perquisite : reversio manerii de Burewardescote in com. Berks. Suth : Penyton Meysy, Shipton, xxij. li. Devon : Ermyngton cum membris, iiij^{xx} marc. Oxon. : Stonore cum membris, Watlyngton cum membris, Cleyore ; nove perquisite, Harlyngrugge, Adameslond, lvj. marc. Bucks : Beerton, Ailesbury, Walton, Stoke, xx. li.[1] Lincoln : Rypyngale cum membris, xiij. li.[2] Midd : La Moot in Westm. x. marc. London : hospicium in Peter Lane, viij. marc.[2] Nove perquisite :[3] Clyve, Molendinum de Darentt, nove perquisite in Horton voc. Kyrkebyesplace, Westbere, Chestelet, Sturye, et Hopelond, xxvij. marc. Summa CC. xlij. li. xiij. s. iiij. d.

55. ACCOUNT BOOK OF ALICE STONOR

1432-3

A paper book of 29 leaves, *Ch. Misc.*, 37, ii. The earlier leaves are much damaged. Thirteen leaves only are written on and most are filled with ordinary household accounts of Alice Stonor. The last entry is :—

Die jovis proximo post festum sancti David in vij wytynges frescese, ix. d. Itm., in iij rogettes and in j gournarde, xviij. d. Itm., die cene domini in xij podryd wytyng viij d. Itm., in vj makrel recent. viij d. Itm., in vj rogettes recent., xiiij. d. Itm., in iij botell of wynyger, xv. d. Itm., in vj. bz : avenarum ij. s. Itm., soope iiij. d.

Summà totalis—xix. s. j. d. facta apud Stonor die lune proximo ante festum Sancti Alphegi et soluta eodem die.

On two other leaves there are accounts for corn and brewing.

---

[1] The last three have been struck out and viij. li. xiij. s. iiij. d. substituted.
[2] These have been struck out. [3] I.e. in Kent.

56. AGREEMENT FOR THE MAINTENANCE AND EDUCATION OF ISABEL, DAUGHTER OF THOMAS STONOR

1ST DEC., 1432

This deed is in pursuance of Thomas Stonor's Will—see No. 54. The original is *Ancient Deeds*, C. 1229. Only the tags for two seals remain.

Omnibus Christi fidelibus ad quos presens scriptum indentatum pervenerit, Ricardus Drayton, armiger, et Alicia uxor ejus, que fuit uxor Thome Stonore, nuper de Comitatu Oxon. armigeri, salutem in domino. Sciatis nos prefatos Ricardum et Aliciam concessisse Johanni Hampden de Hampden, Edmundo Hampden, Ricardo Restwold, Petro Feteplace, et Thome Ramsey quendam annuum redditum octo marcarum percipiendum et levandum de et in Maneriis nostris de Penyton Meysy in Comitatu Suth., Beerton juxta Aillesbury in comitatu Buk., ac in omnibus terris et tenementis que habemus in villa Westm., et alibi ubicunque in Comitatu Midd. Habendum prefatis Johanni, Edmundo, Ricardo Restwold, Petro, et Thome, et assignatis suis a festo sancti Gregorii pape proxime futuro usque finem trium decem annorum ex tunc proxime sequentium, ad festa Pasche, Nativitatis sancti Johannis Baptiste, sancti Michaelis archangeli, et Nativitatis Domini equis porcionibus annuatim. Et si contingat predictus redditus ad aliquod festorum predictorum in parte vel in toto aretro fore in futuro durante termino supradicto, extunc bene licebit prefatis Johanni, Edmundo, Ricardo Restwolde, Petro, et Thome, et assignatis suis in omnibus predictis Maneriis, terris, et tenementis per omnia bona et catalla in eisdem maneriis distringere, et districciones sic captas asportare, abducere, et effugare, ac penes se retinere, quousque eis de omnibus arreragiis predicti redditus plenarie fuerit satisfactum. Proviso semper quod quamdiu durante termino predicto nos prefati Ricardus Drayton, et Alicia sufficienter-et honeste invenerimus et sustentaverimus Isabellam Stonore, filiam predicti Thome Stonore et Alicie in victu et vestitu ac doctrina etati et gradui suis convenientibus eidem Isabelle sufficienter administrari fecerimus, tamdiu nos prefati Ricardus et Alicia et assignati nostri de predicto annuo redditu ac solucione simus, et dicte Maneria, terre, et tenementa sint, exonerati et quieti. Proviso eciam quod si predicta Isabella infra terminum predictum maritata fuerit vel obierit, aut Thomas Stonore et Johannes Stonore, fratres predicte Isabelle, infra terminum

predictum obierint, quod tunc presens scriptum pro nullo habeatur.
Proviso eciam quod si prefata Alicia obierit vivente me prefato Ricardo
Drayton, quod extunc presens indentura omni suo careat robore et
vigore et pro nullo habeatur.   In cujus rei testimonium hiis scriptis in-
dentatis partes predicte alternatim sigilla sua apposuerunt.   Datum
apud Stonore in Comitatu Oxon. primo die Decembris anno regni Regis
Henrici Sexti post conquestum undecimo.

57. THOMAS PORCHET TO THOMAS (?) STONOR

[*before* 1450 ?]

To judge from the writing this letter is probably not later than 1450.   The
Latin superscription rather favours an early date.   From *A.C.*, xlvi, 248.

Ryght worschypfull Mayster y recommaunde me evermore hertely
unto your Maysterschyp : doyng you to understande þat y have done þe
message þat ye sent to me for : that ys to sey y have bowght for you
xx^{ti} hogges, and the pris of ix^e ys xvj. d. a pease, and the pris iij hogges
xiiij. d. a pease, and the pris of vij xij. d. a pease, and j Borepegge pris
viij. d.   No more to you, but Jhesu have you in his kepynge, Amen.
Wretyn atte Wodefforde, the Thors daye next after Seynt Luke daye
                    Be your syr[vant] Thomas Porchet.
All so, Mayster, y certefye you for very trowght þat þe xx^{ti} of hogges
are worsse now than they were whanne y bowght hem be ııj. s. ıııj. d.

Tradatur ista litera magistro Stoner.

58. THOMAS WHITBORNE TO THOMAS STONOR

c. 1450

There is no positive evidence for the date, other than that it cannot be later
than 1473.   But the Latin superscription suggests an early date, and the
character of the writing is consistent therewith.   Cuxham is close to Watlington.   From *A.C.*, xlvi, 220.

Rygth reverent and wurschypfull Mayster, I recommende me unto ȝow : besekyng ȝow to have worde whan I schall enter into ȝour myll at Cuxham : for my syster wyll nat lete me to goo to halfe parte of ȝoure myll at Watlyngton no lengger : wherefore y pray ȝow to have worde, and that I myȝth enter at Cristemasse nexte comyng : and ell I wyll provyde me for a noder, and that were me loyth, and yt plesyd ȝoure good maysterschyppe &c.   Also ȝyffe sche wyll nat ocupy ȝour myll at Watlyngton, y wyll provyde for ȝow a good tenaunt, to more ȝour profyyt and avayll for ever. · Sennys I was with ȝow I have be ryȝth seke, bote nowe, blessyd be God, off amendment.   No more at thys tyme, bote all myȝththy God have ȝow in hys kepyng.

By youre Servaunt Thomas Whitborne.

Venerabili et magne discrecionis viro, magistro Thome Stonore, militi, magistro suo speciali tradatur hec littera.

59. THE BATTLE OF ST. ALBANS

21-22 MAY, 1455

Amongst the *Ch. Misc.*, 37, iii, 4-11, there is an English narrative of the Battle of St. Albans, which seems to have been written and circulated in the interest of the Yorkist party.   It was communicated to *Archæologia* (vol. xx, pp. 519-22) in 1822 by John Bayley, keeper of the Records in the Tower, who attributed it to Sir William Stonor, misled as it would seem by the fact that Sir William Stonor was 24 years afterwards steward of St. Albans Abbey at Wallingford (see No. 244).   The presence of the document amongst the Stonor MSS. seems to be accidental.   Dr. Gairdner reprinted the text from *Archæologia* in the *Paston Letters*, No. 283.   There is thus no need to reprint it here, though it seems right to record the source whence it was derived. Apart from some slight variations in spelling the printed text is accurate, except at two points.   The name of the place in St. Peter's Street, where the King's banner was pitched, should be " Goslawe " not " Boslawe ".   In the list of Lords who were hurt there should be inserted between Buckingham and Stafford : " the lord of Dudle with an arowe in the vysage ".   The original is on a large sheet of paper folded to make 16 pages ; the narrative is written on the first 6½ pages.

60. JOHN ELMES TO THOMAS STONOR

6TH FEB. [? 1457]

The 6th of February fell on a Sunday in 1452, 1457, 1463, and 1474. If the writer may be identified with John Elmys, the merchant of Henley, who occurs in 1443 (*Cal. Pat. Rolls*, Henry VI, iv, 169), the most likely date is 1457. "My lady your sister" is clearly Isabel, wife of Thomas Sackville of Falley or Fawley, which is halfway between Stonor and Henley. Thomas Sackville died in 1466, and if this letter is read as implying that Isabel Sackville was a widow, the date must be 1474. From *A.C.*, xlvi, 43.

Right wurshipfull syr, and my good Maister, y Recommaunde me to yow : and please hyt your Maistershyppe to wete that the Sonday next after my departynge fro yow I come to Hendeley at vij of the clocke in the mornynge, and whan I had herde masse John Mathew come to me fro my lady youre syster, and told me that there had be certain persones at my place at Falley and have take a distresse thre horses of my tenauntes, whiles that he was at the Chyrche at matyns and have caried hem away : and they have seled up the halle dore with a wrytynge ther apon, what the wrytynge is I wot not as yet : and thys was don wythoute any knowliche or wetynge of my lady, or of any oficer of bereys : wherefore my lady, your syster, wuld that I shuld wryte to yow of this mater, for she feryth that here fraunchese shuld be hurt or broken, becawse of this doyng &c.   And syr, I beseke yow to be my goode Maister : for be my trouth I nevir dede any thynge in the mater syne I was with Maister Fowler, and suche promys as I have made on to yow and to Maister Fowler y shall trewly kepe hyt.   Also syr, my tennant, Robert Cockes, is a hevy man becawse his hors be take away.   I can nor wyll not gefe hym no comfort, onto that I have wurd fro yowr Maistership, that wote Almyght Jhesu, who have yow, Right worshipfull syr, evyr in his blessed kepyng, Amen.   Writen at Hendeley in hast the same Sonday that the dede was don, the vj day of Feverer.

By your servaunt John Elmes.

To Right worshipfull syr, and my goode Maister Thomas Stonar, this be delivered.

61. AN AGREEMENT FOR HIRE OF SHEEP

27 DEC., 1460

From *Ancient Deeds*, C. 8834.

Thys yndentur made at Stonore the xxvijth day of December the ere of Kyng Herre the Sexte xxxixth : wytnysseth þat Thomas Stonore, Esquier, hath delyveryd to Symon Cooke yn the pariche of Newnam yn Counte of Oxford iiij^{xx} Ewe Schepe, price the polle xij. d., for the terme of iiij ere next folowyng, peyyng erly to the sayde Thomas Stonore, esquier, at the translacyon of Synt Thomas the martyr yn Julii next folowyng after the date of thys present wrytyng xiij. s. iiij. d. st., at fest of Sent Mychell next folowyng xiij. s. iiij. d. ; and after the terme of iiij ere the sayde Thomas Stonore, Esquyer, to chese whether he wol have for the sayde schepe ende of the terme the pris above rehersyd for the poll or the scheppe.

62. JOHN GOODMAN TO [THOMAS] STONOR

[? before 1461]

The reference to the Duke of York makes it likely that the date is not later than 1460. It is possible, however, that the letter may have reference to the intended sale of Bierton to Sir Ralph Verney which took place in 1469. From *A.C.*, xlvi, 245.

Ryʒth worchypfull maystyr, y hertyly recomaund me unto youre maistyrchyp, desyryng to here of your wele fare and prosperite, the wych God encrese. The ca[use of] my wrytyng unto your maystyrchyp at thys tyme ys thys : I have enqueryd of certen men yn Beerton and Aylesbury of all the poyntes that ʒe toke unto me on by . . . of, and of old Balky of Aylesbury y have enqueryd : and he seyth that xx yere hys fadyr held yt, os ʒe wot what y mene : and he then aftyr held xxx yere and more and never was callyd upon nodyr for sewte ne servyse, nodyr hys lord at that tyme beyng, nodyr amercyd but only in the Duke of York court, and so seyth payd never rent for the same to hym (that ʒe know of) savyng xviij. d. for an preposture, lyyng in the Grene of the seyd towne that ʒe know of ayens youre close. And yn rental yn Gooldes tyme, and before yn Abraham tyme, and yn Balky tyme the yongge, beynge Bayllys of Aylesbury, there was none payd savyng the seyd xviij. d., nodyr yet savyng the clayme that ʒe know of. Moreover, I have be at Bysschopyston with Wyllyam Gourney and he seyth that ʒe have yn Bysschopyston the iij part of a close callyd Bondmannys Wyke, and yn on othere callyd Hanketes Wyke, and yn on othere callyd the Merch Close, and in vj score acre of lond and mede : and the mede ys yn all ix acre savynge on yerd. And yf ʒe wole wyte yt, yn case yt schuld be departyd, how many acre the closys conteyn, y schall yn wrytyng send unto Yngram, and he schall convey yt unto you. Moreover Ingram hath a rentalle of me, that was made yn Abraham tyme. And yf ʒe kowde have yt of hym, ʒe schuld know all : ffor yn hys fadyr tyme, that ʒe know of, the seyd Abraham was Bayly and yn the yong dayys of the seyd man that ʒe know of. And y schall enquere more there of. No more unto youre maystyrchyp at thys tyme, but Jhesu kepe you, be your man and servaunt,

John Goodman.

To maystir Stonor be thys byll dylyveryd.

63. JOHN FRENDE TO THOMAS STONOR

[? APRIL, 1462]

This seems to be the earliest letter relating to the dispute between Thomas Stonor and Richard Fortescue. We know that Stonor was at Ermington on 10 May, 1462. In this letter Frende seems to desire his master's presence, and it is possible that the date was soon after Easter (18 April) in that year. It seems to be earlier than Nos. 64 and 71. The Richard Fortescue of this letter was the eldest son of the Richard Fortescue of No. 45, and was therefore a nephew of the Chief-Justice. Stonor's mother, who was married to Richard Drayton, had rights of dower at Ermington—see p. 48 above. For the further history of the dispute see Nos. 64, 71, 72, 79-82 and 91. From *A.C.*, xlvi, 49.

Right worshipfull maister, I comaunde me unto yov : praying yov to sende me word by your letter where ye wil come in to Devenshire to abide other no &c : and what I shall do with the corne, syder, and wyne : yf ye come nought, hit were best, me semeth, that hit were sold betyme &c. Also tenentes of Modbury, that is to sey John Torryng

and other, have made an ende with Ric. Fortescu in your defaute, understondyng to them that ye wold have come, and kepe not your promise
at no tyme &c. Item, waen Ric. Fortescu was there in lente nov last
past he sende to Modbury by John Saunder seyng, that he badde re-
coveryd of Thomas Stonore a C. li: and wel a wist they schuld be cast
in suche daunger as they schuld never abere: and for fere of suche
langage the seid Torryng and other have made there ende under this
condicion, what they schall paie, though &c hit passe ayenst them.
Item, the mede I kepe in your honde unto tyme ye sende me word
what I schall do. Item, I do yov to wete that my maister Drayton
hath sende me word that I schulde fylle a grete parte of the Southwode:
I pray yov sende me word where hit be your will or noo.

By John Frende of Ermyngton, Boucher.

To my worshipful maister Tho. Stonor in hast.

Endorsed is a list:

Inter Stonor et Fortescu.

Will. Courtenay.   Johannes Courtenay.   Willelmus Halewell.   Henr.
Pomeray.   Walterus Reynell.   Ote Gylberd.   Johannes Gybbes.
Gilbertus Yarde.   Nicholaus Kyrkeham.   Reginaldus Werthe.   Johannes
Hache.   Oliverus Hache.   Thomas Gylle, jun.   Willelmus Corun.
Robertus Roklegh.   Robertus Pyperell.   Johannes Halewell.   Hugo
Champernoun.   Willelmus Wollecomb.   Willelmus Mileton.   Johannes
Bolte.   Johannes Hinychurche.   Hugo Forde.   Johannes Smale.
Johannes Holdeche. · Willelmus Fountayn.   Thomas Prendyrgyst.
Willelmus Calman.   Robertus Shyner.   Johannes Brusshford.

64. JOHN FRENDE TO THOMAS STONOR

[*c.* 1462]

This seems to be later than the previous letter, and probably earlier than
No. 71. From *A.C.*, xlvi, 50.

Right worshipfull maister, I recomaunde me unto yov: letyng yov
wete that Thomas Baron, John Peperell, the son of Robert Peperell,
mauneseth me dayly, and put me in suche fere of my lyffe, that with
other the servauntes of Ric. Fortescu, that I dere not go to cherche ne

to chepyng. Also now late the seid Baron and Peperell have sklaunder me that I schuld sende divers men to the bous of the seid Thomas; and ther and at that tyme the seid persons, that is to wete John Gune, John Cleveff and other, schuld take theefly xxvj. s. viij. d. of the godis of the seid John Peperell, vj spones of silver of the godis of Thomas Barons, and a girdell with silver harnes of his susters, and divers polen, and brynge althis to the hous of John Frende of Ermyngton : and there and at that tyme then schuld recette : uppon the whiche sklaunder and untrue noyse the seid John Frende hath made his purge with meny worshippfull gentilmen and gode yoman. Wherefore I pray yov that ye see a meane that I may be in ese : for hit is worse than ever hit was : for ye have seid many tymes that ye wold come thether, and dwelle ther : and that thay putteth in uterance daily that we schalbe undowe, for ye nel never come to helpe us. Also I pray yov that my maister Drayton may se this letter, and be enformyd thereof. And also I pray yov to take hede above, and make gode wacche for Thomas Baron. And Thomas Horne bethe come uppe to London a fote, for make labour ayenst me. Also but ye come and defende me, I wille do the service no lengher, for I may not ne dernot. And for the sege for my maisteres is made after your device.

By your servaunt John Frende of Ermyngton.

To Thomas Stonor, squyer, in hast.

65. THOMAS HAMPTON TO THOMAS STONOR

[1462]

The history of Mistress Swete's case is too complicated for treatment here and has therefore been given at length in an Appendix to the Introduction— see pp. xlviii-lvi above. This and No. 67 were clearly written whilst the litigation was pending, and since No. 67 is dated 31st August both letters must be ascribed to 1462 ; after July, 1463, Mistress Swete's friends could no longer have believed that Thomas Romesey was son of Sir Walter and his first wife Joan. The writer was Hampton of Kimble—see Nos. 68 and 76. It is difficult to tell why he calls Mistress Swete his sister, unless Hampton's wife was a sister of Thomas Swete. Stapulham (now Staplefarm) was a vill or tithing in the Hundred of South Damerham, Wilts. I have not discovered what place is meant by Sylverton. From A.C., xlvi, 54.

Rytht wurschypfull and my tender welbelovyd Cosyn, I recommaunde me to yow : letyng yow wyte þat my Suster Swete recommaundyth her to yow, and hertyly thankyth yow for her chylderyn, and so do I as well for owr venyson.   Syr, sche prayth yow specyally to make your effectuell labor un[to] the parson of Sylverton þat he wull in weye of Crystes charyte loke up all suche evydens as in eny wyse may make eny proffe Thomas to be þe son of Syr Water and Jahne his ffurst wyff.   Of Margete and Isabell : Margete was weddyd un[to] John Hunteley : Isabell was weddyd unto John Popham.   That þese persons, all or some of þeyse wer þe chyldryn of þe seyde syr Water and Jahne : lete hym schewe hit in the wey of good and of concyens.   Þe parson, þe Kynges Chapeleyn, when he was with hym sye a full fayre Dede and Sealle of Armys : and when þe parson of Sylverton sende his ffolke to London, þey wulde in nowyse schew þat dede.   And þyff my Suster Swete mochte hafe had mony at here wyll, the parson schulde haf com over to yow ; hit wulde nat be.   Moreover, syr, we haf a ffyn reryd unto Syr Water and Jahne terme of þer lyvys, þe rem. þerof unto Thomas, þe son of Jahne, and thit [sic] he was þe son of þem boþe, of Domerz and Morton : [1] but Wykes wuld haf þe ffyn servyd in Stapulham, because hit ys in þe same parische, surmyttyng þat Jahne schulde furst hafe ben weddyd unto Amaryke Northlode, and he to be ffader to þe sayde Thomas. And for certeyne Stapulham came nevyr by þe ffyn, þe wyche was reryd A° xxiiij Regis E. iij : but by a latter tytull.   Lete hym geder all þe dedys of Stapulham to geder, þat hit may be provyd þat hit ys no parcell of þe ffyn : and lete þem be schewyd, and by here trouth to haf all þe dedes þat consernyth here enherytaunse þat he hath in his kepyng : sche wull þat he haf Stapulham as sure &c., as we all can make it.

Moreover, Syr, I wryte aparte þat hit may be kette away, þyff ye lust to schew þis above unto þe parson of Sylverton.   The case was soo when my Suster Swete man schulde go sche kowth haf no money as for þe ffyndyng of þe Offyces, unneth to make hym bryng yow þis my sympyl byll.   Nevyrthelese here we praye yow that ye make some redy apoyntement with the Eschetor, þat he wull not fayle yow, but be redy at suche tyme as ye and we schall sende unto hym both to haf hit fond ýn þe Com. of Suth. as well as in Wylschere : and what he wull haf to ffynde hit in on, and what in the toþer Schyre : for per case þe on schall suffyse.   Anoþer poynte, þat ys we kepte not sende þe Dede aboute

[1] I.e. Domerham and Merton, now Damerham and Marten.

into þe tyme hit were enrowlyd, for drede of losyng &c., Syr, we haf ffonde a gentylmanly thynge, a copy of þe Kynges Recordes þat Thomas, ffader to Syr Th., was seysyd and dyde seasyd Aº regis H. iiijᵗⁱ ijº, the wyche schall make owr ffyn gode.   And so thys fondyn, he most breff Margete, Suster to Th., bastard, wych was ffader to Syr Th.   Nomore to yow at þis tyme : but almythty Godd haf yow in kepyng.   Amen.

By your owne Thomas Hampton.

To my ryght wurschypfull Thomas Stonor, be þis delyvered.

66. H——— TO [THOMAS] STONOR

22 July [? 1462]

Since this relates to Attebare it probably has reference to the affairs of Mistress Swete—see Note on No. 65, and p. liii above.   The date is therefore probably 22 July, 1462.   The writer can hardly be Hampton, for the writing differs from that of Nos. 65 and 67 ; nor is Hampton likely to have addressed Stonor as " syr ".   The right side of the letter has been torn away. From *A.C.*, xlvi, 250.

Riht worshepful. Syr, after all du recommendacion had unto you and to my mastres your [wife, letyng you wete] that as for Attebare, I am in pocescion þerin wiche takyn pesybely, as   . more playnly can enfourme you, to whom that yt wooll please you to g[ive credens in what] he woll schowe unto you for þe exspedicion and wele of þis matyer. A[lmyghty Jhesu] ever preserve you.   Wryt at Attebare uppon Mary Mawdelyne Day.

H.

To Mayster Stonor be þis delylyvered.

67. THOMAS HAMPTON TO THOMAS STONOR

31 Aug. [1462]

This seems to be later in date than No. 65.   For the reasons stated in the Note on that letter the year must have been 1462.   As to Sir John Beynton, see p. lvi above.   From *A.C.*, xlvi, 56.

Rythe wurschypf[ull Co]syn, I recommaunde me to yow, letyng yow understande þat my Suster Swete ffulherteyly dayly praying Godd for yourre gode. S[yr, sche recomaunds] her to yow, s[pec]yally prayng yow to do your tender dyligens as unto the parson of Sylverton for þe hafyng of p[rofe . . .]. Syr, ye were no rather gon fro my house but þe parsons man came unto us and lete my Suster understande þat his mayster had ff[ound] fayre evydens under seale to profe Thomas to be sone of syr Water Romsey and Jahne, his ffurst wyff, and with þat sche wuld ordeyne a suffycyaunte persone to be bounde with here in maner and forme, as we ben boundyn and as ye must nedys see : ffor þe sayde Obligacion moste nedys be delyveryd by your hands or by þe hand of Phylyp Pymme acordyng to an endenture made betwene þe parson man and [. . . Mo]reover, Syr, in eny wyse þat we may haf notyse of þe parson what maner tytull Wykes made ffor Stapulham ayenst hym and ayenste Syr J. Beynton, Knyth, and thyf hit were by d[er]ayng,[1] þat in eny wyse þat we may haf a copye of hit; and thyf hit be by wey of ple, þat we may haf þe Record and wͭ at yere hit was, and what terme : and þat þe parson wull stere theym þat were of Beyntons Counsell and his to be of owr Counsell for owr mony. And also, Syr, I lete yow wyte þer schall no more be don to þe offyse ffyndyng in no wyse. Hyth wat ye may þat ye were wyth uns, ye schall understande a beter meane &c. on. Remembre . . . my lord of Suthfolke wull be in the mater and he be made on of þe ffeffes, as ye wull desyr hym ye or naye, or m . . . ch on as ye dar truste : the mater ys beter þen we understode, a grete dell, þankyd be Godd. No more to yow at þis tyme, but he þat made both yow and me preserve us in perpetuyte, Amen.

Wrytyn at London in Our Palys of the Flete, þe laste daye of August.
                              By your owneThomas Hampton.

Gode syr, I pray yow remembre Mowne in your comyng homward þat he woll be my gode Cosyn, þer ys non oþer mene, but þe. Kyng wull haf mony me semyth by Fowler.   •

Unto my ryght Wurshypfull Cosyn, Thomas Stonor, be thys de-lyveryd in hast.   •

[1] Hampton wrote "dayng " with an otiose abbreviation mark at the end (as also appears in " ffyndyng " and " Kyng " lower down) ; he probably meant " derayne "

68. H. UNTON TO THOMAS STONOR

[? 1462]

The mention of Wykes and Hampton or Hampden of Kimble suggests that this letter may have to do with Mistress Swete's affairs—see Note on No. 65. If so it may be assigned to 1462 or 1463. Unton was a lawyer, see No. 313. "Maister Mylle" is presumably Stonor's brother-in-law Thomas Mull—see No. 69—who was also a lawyer. "Maister Fouler" is perhaps Richard Fowler—see No. 150. From *A.C.*, xlvi, 81.

Right worshipfull Maister, I recommaunde me unto you &c. And thanket be God that my Maistres is amendet. Letyng you wete, Syr, that Maister Mylle and I have ben dayly with Maister Fouler and Maister Danvers, and as yet Nassh is not comyn. And syr, as for Wykes, he is not here, nor on Kene nayther. And so Hampden of Kymbell movet us that ye shuld have had all Wykes landez in your hand, and have assignet old Wykes a certeynte to lyf apon ; but I sup-poset ye wold not so, and I durst take opon to chaunge your opynyon. Mayster Mylle wold ye shuld have take an annuite of xl. s. yerly of old Wykes and his wif, and yong Wykes and his wyf, and of all the feffez : bot I supposet ye wold not so, for by cause of the penalte of the pay-ment of the xl. s. yerly. And I told Hampden, withoute we dro to an end that ye wold execute your exigent ayeynest yong Wykes : and so I trowe we shall draw to an end. And all myghty God have you in kepyng.

Your owne servaunt H. Unton.

To my right worshipfull Maister, Thomas Stonore.

69. THOMAS MULL TO THOMAS STONOR

[MAY, 1463]

The date is fixed by the reference to the "Award of Devonshir," which from No. 72 seems to have been made on or soon after 12th May, 1463 ; see also No. 79. The Swete lawsuit, in which Thomas Hampden or Hampton of Kimble was interested, was at this time in a critical position—see p. liii above. Unlike most of Mull's letters it is not autograph ; this circumstance, combined with the rather formal tone of the letter, suggests that relations were somewhat strained. From *A.C.*, xlvi, 61.

Ryght worshipfull Brother, I comaund me unto you. And thogh it so be that, as me thynkyth, ye do not remembre me in suche. thynges as is me dewe, my sylver not payd me as yet of oold, a new payment nowe ron bothe : to long burthyn makyth wery bonys &c : Yet to remembre you of thynges which shold concerne you, I wold not that ye, nor noon of your welwyllers, took non thynges but such as myght be to your worship &c. Sir, I avise you that in al hast possible ye dispose you to London, bryngyng with you Thomas Hampdene, your Cosyn, as ye woll his welfar and moo &c. Sir, I knowe him not, and thogh I did, yet it must have wytty gydyng, which in no wyse I woll medyll of withoute it be so that ye or sum other sadd man mo then he be heer : the mater requyreth haste, for such that ye woll not ymagen, and thynges that I woll to no man utter but to you or such as I knowe &c. Sapienti pauca. As for your owne maters, when ye cume ye shal understond al as requyryth : it hath noon hast, but when ye woll, com yourself : the Award of Devonshir is not such as I wold it wer. God preserve you &c. Ye know your seson, kepe it and ye woll &c.

T. M^{ll}.

To my worshipfull Brother, Thomas Stonor.

70. JANE STONOR TO THOMAS STONOR

[2ND AUGUST, 1463]

The endorsement is illegible, but the letter was clearly written by Jane Stonor to her husband. The most probable date is 1463, when the Scots had recovered Alnwick and Edward IV went north to Northampton, where he remained till 28 July, which was the Thursday after Langforth came to Stonor. Langforth was probably the son of Edward Langford, the writer of No. 119. From *A.C.*, xlvi, 73.

Syr, I recommende me to ʒow. Plesyth ʒow to wete þat upon Wednes-day last passyd my cousin Langforth ys sone browthe ʒow a privy sele, and to all þe jentylmen off þe schyre. So I resseyved sore akenyn my wyll. Y þesyryd of hym to have kept ytt stylle, for ʒe were not at home : butt he wold nott so doo, but counsellyd me to sendyd ʒow in all hast. And he promysys me þat he wold informe þe kyng þat·ʒe were not at home, and he told me þat upon þe Thursday folwyng þe kyng remevyth northward, and purposyth into Schottland, ef þen he com akeyn. For þat oþer party hathe bysechyd þe castell þat was late rescuyd, and þer ys of þam moo þen V. m., as þe Kynge hath word. Other tydynges y can none send : but y beseke þe holy gost be ʒour gyde. I-wrytyn at Stonor þe Tuesday after seint Annis day.

Yowr owyn J. S.

71. JOHN FRENDE TO THOMAS STONOR

[? 1463]

This would seem to be later than Nos. 63 and 64, and probably of nearly the same date as No. 72. Ugborough is 3 miles N.E. of Ermington, Modbury 2 miles S.E. Aveton Giffard and Churchstow are between Modbury and Kingsbridge. Dodbroke is close to Kingsbridge. Holbeton is about 2 miles S.W. of Ermington. The names are written in three columns ; the top of the paper above the third column has been cut away, but there is nothing to indicate that any names are missing. From *A.C.*, xlvi, 51.

Willelmus Champernound de Modbury, armiger. Willelmus June, armiger. Johannes Shynner, nuper de Modbury, clerk. Willelmus Franke de Modbury, yoman. Willelmus Wyllyng de Ugburgh, yoman. Willelmus Luysh de Ugburgh, yoman. Thomas Robyn, nuper de Dodbroke, yoman. Rogerus Wyot, nuper de Dodbroke, yoman. Walterus Mathue de Kyngysbrygge, yoman. Johannes Torrynge de Modbury, marchant. Radulphus Gybbe de Modbury, yoman. Robertus Shynner de Modbury, marchant. Henricus Hyne de Modbury, carpenter. Edwardus Pound de Modbury, mercer. Thomas Stenlake de Modbury, yoman. Henricus Lyveger de Modbury, draper. Petrus Carsewyll de Modbury, mercer. Willelmus Kevelyn de Modbury, weever. Henricus Pyers de Modbury, mason. Willelmus Lyveger de Modbury, shyrman. Ricardus Croppyng de Modbury, weever. Ricardus Sperte de Modbury, cordeweener. Adam Lovetorre de Modbury, marchaunt. Johannes Lede de Modbury, marchaunt. Johannes Bastard de Modbury, baker. Johannes Crewbere de Modbury, marchaunt. Thomas Hervy de Modbury, tayllour. Johannes Cryspyn de Modbury, fysher. Walterus Lovecrofte de Modbury, weever. Johannes Rouwell de Modbury, cordewayner. Johannes Apeldorn de Modbury, bocher. Johannes Dyver de Modbury, cordewayner. Johannes Rugge de Modbury, wever. Henricus Ryche de Modbury, glover. Thomas Ryche de Modbury, glover. Willelmus Cokke de Modbury, cordewayner. Johannes Rouss de Modbury, ffrankelyn. Matillda Legh de Modbury, vidua. Willelmus Adam de Modbury, yoman. Ricardus Leghe de Leghe, bocher. Thomas Veyse de Leghe, bocher. Willelmus Spycer de Aveton Gyffard, yoman. Ricardus Frende, senior, de Ermyngton, drover. Johannes Frende de Erm., bocher. Robertus Frende de Erm., toker. Willelmus Forde, senior, de Holbeton, husbondman. Willelmus Forde, junior, de Holbeton, laborer. Henricus Denyell de Aveton Gyffard, taillour. Johannes Corset de Kyngsbrygge, cordewaner. Willelmus Mowne de Modbury, wever. Walterus Frende de Ermyngton, bocher. Willelmus Betyn, nuper de Sadlyngton, yoman. Johannes Rogger de Holbeton, milward. Johannes Huchyn de Erm., toker.[1] Johannes Sturne de Modbury, yoman. Johannes Coyte de Modbury, laborer. Johannes Sayer de Modbury, carpenter. Willelmus Rowe de Modbury, grome. Ricardus Marshall de Modbury, yoman. Willelmus Skowte de Modbury, laborer. Johannes Tybbe de Modbury, husbondman. Johannes Wyse de Modbury, taillour. Willelmus Vygge de Modbury, laborer. Thomas Gow de Modbury, laborer. Henricus Skryche de Modbury, smythe. Johannes Hayman de Modbury, carpenter. Willelmus Maddok de Modbury, corveser. Johannes Hyrward de Modbury, corveser. Ricardus Cokke de Modbury, tanner. Michael Fawke de Modbury, carpenter. Johannes Cook de M.,[2] steynour. Willelmus Manevon de M., mason. Rogerus Hayman de M., corveser. Johannes Frode de M., corveser. Johannes Argent de M., wever. Johannes Ryse de M., tanner. Johannes Terry de M., bocher. Willelmus Hempston de M., taillour. Hugo Ryse de M., laborer. Ricardus Rede de M., laborer. Ricardus Mewy de M., taillour. Johannes Smale de M., laborer. Johannes Whyte de M., jowter. Willelmus Cook de M., kerver. Ricardus Hylle de M., corveser. Johannes Roche de M., tayllour. Willelmus Coyte de M., corveser. Johannes Lovecrofte de M., clerke. Ricardus Iwayn de M., laborer. Johannes Skowte de M., corveser. Nicholaus Jay de M., tayllour. Thomas Broun de M., laborer. Willelmus Crokker de M., yoman. Johannes Credon de M., toker. Robertus Covyn de M., laborer. Thomas Hylle de M., bocher. Willelmus Hylle de M., wever. Henricus Bray de M., smythe. Ricardus Bease de M., smythe. Johannes Mewy de M., tayllour. Thomas Leveger de M., yoman. Johannes Whyte de M., corveser. Johannes Pyers de M., corveser. Johannes Kevelyn de M., corveser. Willelmus Clerke de M., laborer. Robertus Kelowe de M., glover. Johannes Kelowe de M.,

---

[1] The first column ends here.
[2] From this point the original has only " M.," no doubt for Modbury.

glover. Johannes Berse, nuper de Plymstoke, yoman. Willelmus Ryder de Leghe, yoman. Henricus Peche de Aveton Gyffard, yoman. Walterus Wakeham de Aveton Gyffard, yoman. Johannes Redhode de Aveton Gyffard, laborer. Thomas Emery de Aveton Gyffard, laborer.[1] Stephanus ffelipp de Aveton Gyffard, bocher. David Tope de Aveton Gyffard, husbondman. Willelmus Sheccote, nuper de Ugburgh, yoman. Johannes Richard de Dodbroke, yoman. Jacobus Langmede de Dodbroke, husbondman. Johannes Kydeway de Dodbroke, laborer. Robertus Kente de Dodbroke, miller. Johannes Carsewill de Dodbroke, mercer. Johannes Strawe de Dodbroke, cordewaner. Johannes Wynsore de Dodbroke, wever. Ricardus Wynsore de Dodbroke, taillour. Thomas Parker de Dodbroke, crokker. Walterus Wynsore de Dodbroke, wever. Ricardus Tynner de Dodbroke, dyer. Willelmus Webber de Dodbroke, fisher. Ricardus Coshe de Dodbroke, mason. Willelmus Campe de Dodbroke, brewer. Robertus Broke de Southpole, carpenter. Johannes Tayllour de Dodbroke, seman. Willelmus Herward de Dodbroke, tayllour. Johannes Olyver de Dodbroke, laborer. Johannes Groby de Dodbroke, cordwayner. Willelmus Wynde de Staverton, yoman. Ricardus Wakeham de Kyngysbrygge, yoman. Andreas Costard de Kyngysbrygge, yoman. Johannes Corset, junior, de Kyngysbrygge, cordewayner. Johannes Lange, junior, de Kings., tayllour. Henricus Ayshlegh de Dodbroke, mercer. Robertus Dyer de Kyngysbrygge, corveser. Johannes Dever de Kyngysbr., bocher. Johannes Pralle de Kyngysbr., bocher. Johannes Mey de Kyngysbr., brewer. Ricardus Bakkelegh de Kyngysbr., smythe. Willelmus Yoman de Kyngysbr., smythe. Thomas Jowde (?) de Aveton Gyffard, seman. Henry Vygge de Aveton Gyffard, seman. Petrus He . . . e de Churstowe, husbondman. Johannes She . . . e de Churstowe, yoman. Willelmus Davels de Churstowe, bocher. Johannes Milward de Ermyngton, carpenter. Thomas Chapelman de Erm., carpenter. Johannes Davy de M., wever. Johannes Thryste de Modbury, laborer.

Right worshipfull and reverent syre, y recommaund me unto you, praying you hertely that ye will fochesafe to holde me escusyd of that y p[ro]mittyd you atte Ermyngton to be with you atte London thys terme: for y am seke, and ly style yn my bede; where y shall leve or day y wete noght, but y sende you yn thys paper the names of all ham that ·wyll desyre to have a quytans of Richard Fortescu for your mater.   No

---

[1] The second column ends here.

more to you atte thys tyme, but the holy Trinite have you yn hys kepynge.

Your servant Jon Frende.

Tradatur Thome Stonor ad signum vocatum Wolsak in Flete strete.

72. STONOR v. FORTESCUE: BILL OF NAMES

28TH AUGUST, 1463

This is the Bill of Names referred to in No. 79. It was consequent on the award to which reference is made in Nos. 61 and 79. From *Ch. Misc.*, 37, ix, 11.

This bille endentyd witnesseth that Thomas Stonore, Esquier, bathe deliveryd to Richard Fortescu of Holecumbe, Squier, the Sunday afore the decollacion of Seynt John the Babtyst these names here undyrwrytyn in the thryd yere of Kyng Edward the iiij^{th}, the wych the forseyde Richard shall reles unto all accions of trespas done by fore the xij^{the} day of Maye last past: William Champernone of Modbury, Squier, William June of the same, Squier, John Shynnor, late of [Mod]bury, clerk, John Frank of Modbury, yeman, &c. (*The rest of the names are the same as in* No. 71 *down to* Richard Frende, *who is described as* of the pariche of Ermyngton, drover, *with the substitution of* Petyr Coleswell of Modbury, mercer, *for* Petrus Carsewyll, *and the insertions of* Petyr Caswell of Modbury, mercer (*after* Henry Pyers *or* Pers) *and of* Richard Frende, of the same pariche, the younger (*added after the elder* Richard Frende). *There are a few varieties in the spelling of names:* "Uxeborough" *for* "Ugburgh," "Veysy" *for* "Veyse," "Lussh" *for* "Luysh".)

73. PROCLAMATION OF A TRUCE BY SEA

24 APRIL, 1464

This Proclamation is given in a writ, dated at Westminster, 24th April, 1464, and addressed to the Sheriff of Oxon. and Berks., requiring him to publish it. The negotiations to which the Proclamation refers are given in *Foedera*, xi, 520-2. The original has endorsed on it a receipt by William

Bekyngham, collector of the tenth, for a payment from the vill of Stanlake, dated 10 October, 1464.   From *Ch. Misc.*, 37, iii, 16.

" Forasmuch as betweixt the right trusty and right welbelovyd Cosyn to our soverayn lord the kyng, Richard, Erle of Warrewik and Sar., grete chamberleyn of England, and the right trusty and welbelovyd knyght, John Wenlok, Lord Wenlok, oure seid sovereyn lordez deputeez and commissarez on that oon partie, and the noble and worthy lord, the lord Lannoy, ambassiatour and Comyssarye of the excelent and myghty prynce Lowes of Fraunce cosyn and adversarye to our seid soverayn lord, on that other partie, certeyn abstinence of Werre by the see, stremez and fresshwaters, for the partie and in the name of oure said soverayn lord and the partie and in the name of his seid cosyn of Fraunce, be appoynted, taken and concluded under certeyn maner and forme, as other trewes by land late were accepted, accorded, and concluded by the ambassiatours and Commissariez of bothe parties in the Toun of Hedyn : the seid trewes be see, stremez and fresshwaters to begynne the xx day of Maii next comming, and to endure to the sonne goyng down of the first day of Octobre than next suyng : the kyng oure seid soverayn lord strectly chargeth and commaundeth all his liegemen and subgectes and everye of theym wele and duely to observe and kepe the same abstinencez of Werre by see, stremez and ffresshwaters duryng the tyme abovesaid, accordyng to theffect, tenure, and contenue of the seid appoyntement, nothyng doyng or attemptyng to the contrarie therof, as they woll aunswere at theyr parell and eschewe to be punysshed as brekers of the seid abstinences accordyng to the lawes of oure seid soverayn lord and statutes ordeyned and made in that behalve."

74. A PETITION OF THE PARISHIONERS OF DIDCOT TO THOMAS STONOR

[*c.* 1465]

The only clue to the date is the reference to Dr. Bulkeley, i.e. Roger Bulkeley, D.D. of Oxford, who was Proctor in 1433, Principal of Hare Hall in 1450, and Commissary of the University in 1450, 1461, and 1464.   He was Rector of Didcot in 1465-67 (*Ministers Accounts*, 1240/10, 11 ; see Vol. ii, p. 182) ; he may have held the rectory for some time previously.   The original is badly damaged in the lower left-hand corner.   From *A.C.*, xlvi, 41.

Unto oure worshipfull and reverent Maister, Thomas Stonor, esquier, or to such as it plesith him in tbis behalf to assigne.

Besechethe lowly and mekely unto youre gracious Maistership youre pore bedemen and tenauntes off youre lordeship off Dudcote, wich beth gretly wronged and ungodely entreted by the parson off Dudcote foresaid: wich parson desired off the Township foresaid, that is to say off Thomas Frocwell, Richard Colleman, Williham Harries, and off other mo, to go to scole to Oxonford, and the said parson to fynde his depute and his attorney for alle sacramentes and necessaries in his absence there treuly to be observed and kept. Herapon this was graunted to the said parson, and then the parson yeed to Oxford, and the dyvyne service and other sacramentes wer not kept as thei aght to be, to gret unese to the parish. Ferthermore the chirchemen of Dudcote wer in bargenyng off a ryke off weete for the welfare and help off the chirch: the seid parson undirstode this, and unkyndly labored to Doctor Bulkley, that was awner off the reke, and prively bargened with and put the chirchemen aparte. And when the parson com home he declared in the polepitt openly, that it was the Doctor wille the parissh shuld by the straw off the reke, because thei had but litell stuff among hem this yere: God knoweth full evell penyworthes thei had and sharp. And but because off him the parish wer like to have more favor off the straw, the said parson toke to him Richard Colleman and Williham Harries to be parcenars with him after the price he bought itt, and fully agreed: and the next day after the parson denyed it, and wrongly to put hem from the bargeyne. Also the said parson yeed to Oxonford, and graunted to Williham Harries a dayes thress off straw off the same for ix. d. And he remembred him, and wold not let him have it after under xvj. d. a daies thress, and ever sold so and derrer: he myght have do better, for the straw was not his, and it was the Doctoures will that the parish shuld have penyworthes better then he shewid: ffor this unkyndnes the parish wer displesid, and thought greet unkyndness; for what that ever he wer to by straw, he must pay in honde or fynde surete as it wer a straunge man. And mo this langage and contenciones is betwix the said parson and his parishioners, with other maters moo, to greet heveness off the parish the parson to be so unkynde. Item, Robert Dobson, the parson's man, repreved and ungodely in the moost unhonest wise called diverse men knaves and harlettes and charles, and said thei wer so everychon. And the said parson mayntened him therin. Thei wer so bold that tweyne off the parson's men lay awayte apon John Pepwite in Bagley; and ther thei bete him, and, except pepull of Abendon, likly to have kylled [him] : this man rekevered and come home. And apon a Sonday after evensong the moder of [this] same man, Bett, and the man also, made an oute cry apon the parson amonge all the parisshe . . . whiche were bevy to here off, iff it shuld be written. Item, Richard Browne com, and openly [declare]d afore the parson and the parisshe that Richard Colleman shuld have be beet, iff he had come . . . . . . wey : the parson said he wold put on aventure the valure off his parsonage, but at the last . . . . . . vjs. viijd., that Browne wold nat awow this : and Browne at all tymes will · . . . [awo]w itt, and testifie it at alle tymes. The parisshones, for goode tranquillite, reest, and . . . [fe]ryng the greet hurt off the chirch ale at that tyme, beside alle other offences . . . . and his preest to go in to the parsonage to kepe peas, and the parson redde a greet . . . bully, and called Maister Stonors men, and said stonde, wich we, Williham . . . . and off this, and come to Dudcote and made peas unto the tyme Maister . . . . . . at. Wherfor we wyll beseche youre maysterschip to have knowleche how and . . . . en yet to make a new dyvvysion ayen. Ther was a mason wroght on the . . . the parson wold have sett his horse on the chirchyerd in the night tyme, and it in his horse, and desiryd him to put hym noon there by cause off the off the scafoldys that were aboute hytt.

No endorsement.

75. THOMAS AND MARGERY HAMPDEN TO THOMAS STONOR

[c. 1465]

Since Thomas Stonor, the elder, had not been dead (as it would seem) forty years, this letter cannot be later than 1470, whilst the reference to " your sons " makes it unlikely that it was earlier than 1465. Thomas Hampden's father, John Hampden, was half-brother of the first Thomas Stonor. The writer of the postscript is clearly his wife Margery, daughter of Sir Stephen Popham ; when appointing her to be an executor of his will (*P.C.C.*, 27 Logge), Hampden described her as " my wife whom of youth I have know wele conscienshid, and to me a trew and lovyng wife ". From *A.C.*, xlvi, 53.

Ryght worchepefull cossyn, y recommand me unto yow : and y pray yow, asse y may do any theyng to yowr plessur, that 3e wolle grant me

the nexte avoydanys that ffallethe yow of any benyffys off yowrys that ys
off valew off xx. li., or ӡeffe hyt be better then xx. markes; and y werr be
hold unto yow, ӡeffe hyt lyke yow to do sso moche ffor me, and allso ӡe
hynde me to do ffor yow yn that that yn me ys : y wysse, Cossyn, y have
a beneffysse that ther bathe benne prest ther yn at my unkyll your faderys
dessyr and yowrys alle moste theys xl. wynter, and onne I putte yn at
yowr dessir my selffe.   Y wryte unto yow for a jantylmane, that I darr
promysse yow schall do yow tru servysse and plesurr, and he ys a wor-
chepeffull man and a well rulede, prayng yow to sende me a answerr by
wrytyng.   And allmyty God have yow yn ys kepyng, and all yowrys.   Y
beseche yow thys sympyll byll may recommand me unto my cossyn your
wyffe.   Y-wrytyn at Hampden onne Newyerys day.

Your cossyn T. Hampden off Hampden.

(Postscript in another hand).

Cossyne, I recomaund me untoo yow, and I beche yow of yowre gode
cossyne hode yn þe performyng off my husbondes dessyr &c.   Cossyne,
and ӡe had desyred me or myne soo ofte as I have desyred yow and my
cossyns, yowr sones, I wold have sene yow offtener.   I wesse, cossyne,
het greveth me &c.   Ther may no man hold þat woll awaye : and ther
for I moste take het as weele as I can, and thenketh thes delyng under
wissedome ne kyndnes all thyngys consederbred to be soo strange &c.

To my right worchepefull cossyn, T. Stonore.

76. THOMAS HAMPTON TO THOMAS STONOR

[c. 1465]   •

The writer is Hampton of Kimble : see No. 65.   The date is certainly later
than 1460, but perhaps only a few years.   John Hampton of Staffordshire
occurs as a squire for the body from 1437 to 1459 (*C.P.R*, Henry VI, iii, 45,
vi, 532) ; in the last year he was rewarded for his long service to Henry V and
Henry VI. From *A.C.*, xlvi, 55.

After almaner of due recommendaciouns, in my most tender wyse I
recommaunde me to yow.   S[yr . . . .] haf knowlyche whether
þe sute be takyn ayenst Will. Tystede ye or nay, and W . . . for as hit
was law, tolde me he scholde sey he sette not þer by : What hit menyth

I can not sey. My moder, my wyf, and all my douchters, your pore kynnyswymmen, tenderly recommaundyn þem to yow, of whos prefer-ment I pray yow to haf rememberaunce, þyf eny fortune may grow in eny plase. Syr, I haf late been in the Counte of Stafford with my Cosyn John Hampton, sometyme Squier for þe body with Kynge H., and in my þer beyrg he hath made estate of xl. markes of his lond, and takyn estate of me ayen ther of his lyff and of his wyffes, þe remaynder to me and to myn heyres, with all þe evydens acordyng, where of I haf the more parte at home, wyche þey schall enyoye with al oþer of my londes. Syr, when and what tyme we schall see yow and my cosyn W., I pray yow sende me worde. Syr, þat tyme I haf worde by my Cosyn Waller, brynger of þis my sympull byll, Gode Syr, whether Palmer be delynge ge . . . ye, and how my Suster Swete doth. No more at þis tyme, but almythty godde have yn hys kepyng, Amen.

By your owne T. Hampton.

To my Rythe Wurshypfull Cosyn, T. Stonor, be Wylyam be þis delyveryd.

77. WARRANT FOR COLLECTION OF KING'S SILVER

[c. 1465]

Thomas Stonor purchased Rotherfield Peppard from his step-father Richard Drayton in 1465, but agreed to reconvey it to Drayton and his wife for the term of their lives (*Ancient Deeds*, C. 6944, see Vol. ii, p. 174). The reconveyance was possibly effected by a fine, in which case this warrant may have reference thereto. The original is in *Ch. Misc.*, 37, iii, 20.

Stephanus Coksettur, Thomas Stokfeld, et Robertus Mercer, collectors of the Kyngges sylver chosin in þe hundird of Benfeld &c. To John Wylkys, Constabull off Ritherfeld Pippard. In þe kyngges name We commaunde yow to levey of the persones underwrityn the summes uppon them sett in all the hast possibill.

Rotherfeld Pippard. De Thoma Stonor pro decima parte terrarum et tenementorum suorum ibidem, xxxviij. s. xj. d. De Willelmo Freme, j. d. De Alicia Rolf, x. d. ob. De herede Willelmi Bryne, vij. d. De Johanne Mathew, viij. d. De Roberto Clerk, j. d. De Willelmo

Lawrence, j. d.   De predicto Th. Stonor pro manerio de Blountes, xiiij. s. x. d.   De domino principe pro quieto redditu exeunte de Blountes, j. d. ob.   Summa, lvj. s. iij. d.

78. PÉTITION BY THOMAS STONOR TO EDWARD IV

1465

The date of this is clearly just before Thomas Stonor was sheriff for the second time in 1465-66. Stonor obtained a grant of 100 marks from the issues of Oxon. and Berks. by Letters Patent on 20th Nov., 1465 (*C.P.R.*, Edw. IV, i, 479; see also p. 92 below). From *A.C.*, xlvi, 36.

Mekely sheweth unto youre highnes, youre feithfull and true liegeman Thomas Stonore, Squier, that where it hath pleased youre noble and gode grace to appoynte him to be Sherief of youre Countes of Oxonford and Berkshire for the yere next comyng to be had and occupied, it is so that the seid Thomas Stonore in his accompt, the whiche he is to yelde or shall yelde to you in youre Eschekere of that office, is like to be charged of many and grete summes of money aswell of Vicountellez as of othere fermez and dettez, ammountyng to the summe of Centum li., the whiche cannot be leved by the seid Thomas or of whom to be leved to the seid Thomas Stonore it is unknowen, whereby and by the grete chargez and costez, the whiche he shall bere and have in that office, is like to be gretely hurte withoute your grace especiall be shewed unto him on this behalf. Please it therefor youre moost noble and habundaunt grace to graunte unto him youre graciouse letters patentez in due fourme to be made after the tenoure folowyng. And he shall pray God for the conservacion of youre moost roiall Estate.

Edwardus Dei gracia &c., omnibus ad quos &c., salutem. Sciatis quod nos considerantes bona et gratuita servicia nobis per dilectum et fidelem nostrum Thomam Stonore, armigerum, ante hec tempora impensa, ac certis aliis magnis consideracionibus nos specialiter moventibus de gracia nostra speciali ac ex certa sciencia et mero motu nostris concedimus prefato Thome centum libras habendas et percipiendas sibi de firmis, exitibus, proficuis, et revencionibus de Comitatu Oxon. et Comitatu Berks. provenientibus per manus Vicecomitis Comitatuum illorum pro tempore existentis. Volentes et concedentes quod tum ipse Thomas Stonore quam ipse Vicecomes pro tempore existens de eisdem Centum libris et qualibet inde parcella ad Scaccarium nostrum exonerentur, et acquietentur, et eorum quilibet exoneretur et acquietetur, aliquo statuto, actu, ordinacione, sive restrictione in contrarium inde facto, edito, seu promulgato non obstante.

79. STONOR v. FORTESCUE : ARTICLES

[? 1466]

These Articles seem to be the draft of a Chancery Bill, but there is no corresponding document amongst the extant Early Chancery Proceedings. They are clearly later than the Bill of Names—No. 72. Perhaps they may be a draft of some contemplated proceedings in 1466, when the complaint of John Frende was presented in Chancery—see No. 80. More is possibly Sir John More, the father of Sir Thomas More. For Reyny, who was a Devonshire lawyer, see No. 100. Exst is possibly the Thomas Hext of Nos. 263 and 284. From *Ch. Misc.*, 37, iii, 15.

Memorandum of divers Artycles ayenst Richard Fortescu.

First, where that ther was award made by More, Reyny, and Huddysfild, and in that award among othyr thynggis to be done the seyde Richard shuld relese all manere of accion personall to suche personys as shuld be deliveryd to the seyde Richard by byll by the bondys of Thomas Stonore : the seyde Thomas deliveryd to the seyde Rychard a bylle endentyd of certeyne namys, the wyche where never relest unto : and for defaute of suche reles many of the personys where sore amercyd and troubyld to the charge and coste of the seyde Thomas &c.

Also divers of my welwyllers have be causyd by *Supplicavit* and I-put to ther ffynabus, sum vj. s. viij. d., sum x. s., sum xiij. s. iiij. d., sum xl. d.

Also sithyn that award ther was award made by mouthe by Thomas Rogers of Greyysyn and Exst of the Tempyll, that I Sir Thomas Stonore shuld have had cf the seyde Richard a Aquitauns of all maner of accions, the wyche is nott yet done and that altho personys þat the seyde Richard had wrongfully take mony of for cause of me þat he shuld a restoryd ayen to hem in Ermyngton chyrche; the wiche is not yet don, and for lak of that doyng hyt is to my grete hurt and damage &c.

Also the seyde Sir Richard wrongfully occupyyth my severel grounde in occupyy[ng] of a wey thorowe the North park and in pasturyng of his bestis ther also.

Also where he fette dyvers fursis, feld and sold by myne officers, oute of Yarne Knolle to his use and there hurt, and woondyd John Ryt of Holbeton to my grete cost and charge &c.

Also where he suyth and avexyth divers pepill for love of me in Plympton Cort and ahs(?) Cort and Tremyngton Cort to my grete charge &c.

Also untruly by hym brougte up Frend by a *suppena* and the party not pryvy, and than withowte cause axyd Suryte of pees, the wyche was &c.

80. JOHN FRENDE v. RICHARD FORTESCUE

[1466]

Though these documents do not form part of the *Stonor Papers* they are important for the history of the dispute at Ermington. The date is fixed by the proceedings in the King's Bench, where it appears that the date of the assault on Frende was in December, 1465. The appearance of Stonor and Thomas Mulle (who no doubt represented Richard Drayton) shows that "plegii de prosequendo" were in some cases at all events genuine persons, although it has been argued that the pledges were usually fictitious persons (like John Doe and Richard Roe); the Richard Gryme and William Lyme of p. 79 below may be such a fictitious instance. From *Early Chancery Proceedings*, 31/34-36.

To the right reverend ffader in God, tharchebusshop of Yorke and Chaunceller of Engèlond.

Mekely besecheth and peteously complayneth your poor and continuell Oratour, John Frende, graciously to concydre that Richard Fortescu of Ermynton in the Counte of Devonshir. squyer, with other riotus persones to hym assembled to the nombre of iiij^{xx} persones and moo, ryotously arrayed in fourme of warre, that is to sey with Jackys, Bowes, Arrowes, Swerdes, Gleyves, and other defencible wepyns, the xij day of Decembre laste passed ayenste the pees of our sovereign lord the Kynge at Ermynton aforsaid ryotusly and ayenste the lawe come and tooke your seid Oratour oute of his hows as his prisoner, and hym ladd unto the hows of the seyd Richard Fortescue, and ther hym in pryson kepte by the space of iiij dayes unto the tyme your seid Oratour had payed for the delyveraunce and raunsom to the seid Richard Fortescue v. marc. And gracyous lord, your seid Oratour is in such poverte that he is not of power to sue for his remedy accordyng to the cours of the comone lawe of the londe, and so standyth as withowte remedy withowte your good grace be shewed to hym in this behalf. Wherfore, plese it your good lordeship gracyusly to concydre the premisses, and ther uppon to graunte a writte *sub pena* to be directed to the seid Richard Fortescue, commaundyng hym by the same to appere before the Kynge in Chauncerye at a certene day and under a certene peyne by you to be lymytyd ther to answer to the premisses, and to do and resceyve as concyence askyth and requyreth, and this for the love of god and in the wey of charyte.

Plegii de prosequendo ⎰ Thomas Stonour de London, armig. Thomas Mulle de London, gent.

This is the answere of Richard Fortescue to the bill putt ageynst hym by John Frende.

Fyrst, the seid Richard seith bi protestacion that the mater conteyned in the seid bill is mater determinable by the comon lawe of the land and noght in this Courte: bott for his answer and pleyn declaracion of the same he seith that he longe tyme before the seid arrest had a Wryte of *Supplicavit* oute of this Courte ageynst the seid John, directed to the Shyrryf of Devonshyr, the which Shyrryf made a Warraunte uppon the same Wryte to John Hillyour, John Saundre, William Screch, and Thomas Horne, jointly and severally to tak and arrest the seid John accordyng to the content of the seid Wryte: bi vertue of which Warraunte the seid John, John, William and Thomas arrestyd þe seid John in pesible wyse at Ermyngton, beyng oute of his hows, and hym from thens had toward the Kynges comon Jale by the howse of the seid Richard, and thair taried with hym bi the space of half an houre: and the same Jchn so beyng in the howse of the seid Richard, the same Richard fortunyd to come home fyndyng the seid John in his howse undre arrest as is afforseid, withoute that the seid Richard in riotous wyse or in such fourme tok and imprisonyd the seid John in

maner and fourme as he hath allegyd, and withoute that þe seid
Richard tok or made to be takyn the seid John or hym kepyd in prison
in house langer or in eny othere maner and fourme than the seid
Richard hath before rehersyd &c. Moreover, the seid Richard seith
that the seid John hath an accion of faux imprisonment hangyng
ageynst þe seid Richard in the Comon place,[1] bi reason the seid
arrest, which is ageynst all consciens he to be vexed here and in the
Comon place and all for on thyng. All which maters the seid Richard
is redy to profe as this Courte will reule hym, and prayeth þat he may
be dismissed out of this Courte with his costes and damages for his
wrongfull vexacion.

This is the Replicacion of John Frende unto the aunswere of Richard
Fortescu.

The seid John Frende by protestacion nat knowyng ony writte of
Supplicavit had ageyn hym nor ony warant made be the seid Shyryve to
John Saundre and other to arreste the seid John Frende in maner and
fourme as ys supposed by the seid aunswere : but for aunswere the said
John Frende seith in dede that he was arested and taken in riotous
wise by the said Richard Fortescu and other, and lad to the bous of
the same Richard and as a prisoner kept in maner and fourme specified
in the seid bill : and over that he seith that he was atte that tyme ther
putte in dures in to Stokkes and gretly manassed and thretenyd and
put in fere of bodily harme : and many tymes sithen the seid em-

---

[1] The record of this action appears in Hilary Term 1466, in *Placita de Banco*,
Roll, 818, m. 251 : Devon. Johannes Frende per attornatum suum optulit se iiijto
die versus Ricardum Fortescu de Ermyngton in comitatu predicto, gentilman,
Thomam Horne de Ermyngton in comitatu predicto, husbondman, Willelmum
Screche nuper de Ermyngton in comitatu predicto, grome, et Johannem Saunder de
Ermyngton in comitatu predicto, souter, de placito quare vi et armis in ipsum
Johannem Frende apud Ermyngton insultum fecerunt et ipsum verberaverunt,
vulneraverunt, imprisonaverunt et male tractaverunt, et'ipsum ibidem sic in prisona
contra legem et consuetudinem regni Regis Anglie diu detinuerunt, et alia enormia
&c., ad grave dampnum &c, et contra pacem Regis &c. Et ipsi non venerunt, et
preceptum fuit Vicecomiti quod attachiet eos &c. Et de prefato Ricardo mandat
Vicecomes quod attachiatus est per plegia Johannis Lok et Ricardi Cok. Ideo ipsi
in manu &c. Et distringatur quod sit hic a die Pasche in xv dies &c. Et de
prefatis Thoma, Willelmo, et Johanne Saunder mandat Vicecomes quod nichil
habent &c. Ideo capiantur quod sint hic ad prefatum terminum &c. Ad quem
diem Vicecomes non misit breve. Ideo tam predictus Ricardus sicut prius distringatur, quam predicti alii defendentes capiantur quod sint hic in crastino Sancti
Johannis Baptiste.

There appears to be no entry in the Roll for Trinity Term, and the proceedings
in the Common Pleas were presumably dropped.

prisonement the seid Richard Fortescu hath thretened the seid John Frend and putte hym in greate feere boith of his persone and losse of his goodis, so that he thurst nat attend his husbondrye, to his importable losse, hurte, and greff, havyng in his hand as moche land in ferme as he paiethe therfor xl. li ; withoute that atte the tyme of the seid takyng, arestynge or imprisonement of the seid John Frend ony warant from the seid Shirive to him was shewed : which mater the seid John Frend is redy to prove like as the Courte will award : and prayeth that the seid Richard for the seid riote may be commytted to ward, and that he may be compellid to yeld to the seid John Frend resonable damages for his seid grete hurtys and wrongefulle vexacion, and also the costys of his suyte.

81. JOHN YEME TO THOMAS STONOR

11 JUNE [? 1466]

Since Frende was still bailiff in Dec., 1465—see p. 79 below—the year is probably 1466. From the reference to Plympton and Trematon Courts it would seem likely to be of about the same date as the Articles—No. 79. Thomas Stonor was apparently in London in May, 1466—see pp. 79, 80 ; but the date may possibly be 1467. For Yeme as bailiff, see further No. 126. For Thomas Horne, see Nos. 64 and 82 ; and for Menwynnek, see No. 126. From *A.C.*, xlvi, 86.

Rygth Reverent Mayster, y recomand me unto yowe, desyryng to here of yower wellefare and prosperyte of body and sawle, besekyng Almy3thy Jhesu preservy hit unto his plesure and to yower worly worschyppe and herte ys desyre. Furdermore, as for the accion of sewryte of pese, the wycche Thomas Horne hathe ayenst me, y have aperyd therto and have y-putte yn iij seuryteys, John Kyrton ys on, John Frende of Seynte Jely's parysche ys the secunde, and a cosyn of myn ys the thirde. And y hadde myche labur to gete me a weye. Fudermore, Walter Frende recomandes hym to yower good maisterchyppe, and he wolle pray yowe to sende hym worde wher to Mylle of Ermyngton schall be y-koweryn with stone or strawe, and wher he schall ordeyne any haye ayenst yower comyng. Y wold have come home to your maisterchyppe, but y have y-taryd vij dayys yn London apon you : for the osteler tellyd me that ye wolde have y-be ther atte the begynnyng of the terme. All so y have y-hofte me a hors atte London, for y loste my hors ful falsly and untreuly apon the waye, as I tryste to Godde to enforme yower maysterchyppe and ever y may speke with yowe. And y have y-spende mycche mony to gete me awaye fro the Marschall ys warde: for y was comyttyd ynto his warde, but yette y thanke Godde and ffrende men for. All so Ric. Fortescu ffaryth ffowle with Walter Frende and me, and layyth his men yn awayte to murder me when y was laste atte Ermyngton atte Corte: and all ys for by cawse y wolde notte suffry hym to have his yntente at Plympton Corte: but y tryste he schal never have non yntente ayenste them that he sewyth ther. And as for the Corte of Tremeton, y have mycche laburr ther; but yette y have notte geffe no ple ther, for he ys asoynyd ij tymys a rewe yn his oune pleynte. And that sawe y never yn no place but ther: but that ys Menwynnycke, a felow of Corte of his, ys doyng, the whycche ys Steward ther. No more to yowe atte thys tyme. And Jhesu preservy yow yn his blessyd kepyng, Amen. Y-wrytyn atte London on Seynte Barnebe y Evyn yn all haste.

By yower pore servant John Yeme.

To my Reverent Mayster Thomas Stonor, Esquyer, thys letter be y-dylyveryd in all haste.

82. PROCEEDINGS IN THE SUIT OF STONOR VERSUS FORTESCUE

1466-68

The Stonor Manuscripts in *Chancery Miscellanea*, 37, iii, 44, include a copy, of the pleadings in the King's Bench in Trinity Term, 1467, reciting the proceedings in Chancery of the previous year. To complete the history of the case extracts are given from the Coram Rege Rolls down to Michaelmas, 1468, at which time Thomas Stonor's letter—No. 91—shows that Richard Fortescue was finally dismissed. The reason for the description of Thomas Stonor as a servant of the Archbishop of York is obscure—but see No. 97; he may have been steward of one of the archbishop's manors.

Placita apud Westm. coram domino Rege de termino sancte Trinitatis Anno Regni Regis Edwardi quarti post conquestum Anglie septimo.

Memorandum quod venerabilis in Christo pater G. archiepiscopus

Ebor., cancellarius domini Regis Anglie, per manus suas proprias liberavit hic in Curia tercio die Junii, isto eodem termino, recordum coram eo
in cancelaria habitum in hec verba :

Placita coram domino Rege in cancelaria sua apud Westm. a die
Pasche in unum mensem anno regni Regis Edwardi quarti post conquestum sexto.

Devon. Ricardus Fortescu de Ermyngton in comitatu predicto,
armiger, attachiatus fuit per corpus suum de respondendo Thome
Stonore, armigero, uni servientium venerabilis patris Georgii, Archiepiscopi Ebor., cancellarii domini Regis, de quadam transgressione eidem
Thome per prefatum Ricardum illata, ut dicitur. Et unde idem Thomas
per Christoforum Hamton, attornatum suum, queritur quod predictus
Ricardus, aggregatis sibi quampluribus malefactoribus eidem Thome
ignotis ad numerum quadraginta personarum, modo guerrino, scilicet
deploidibus [1] defensivis, salettis, glavis, et billis arraiatis, vi et armis,
videlicet gladiis, arcubus, et sagittis, decimo die Maii, Anno regni
domini Regis nunc secundo, in ipsum Thomam Stonore apud Ermyngton predictam insultum fecit, et ipsum verberavit, vulneravit et male
tractavit, et vicesimo die Decembris, anno regni dicti domini Regis nunc
quinto, in Johannem Frende, servientem ejusdem Thome Stonore, apud
Ermyngton predictam insultum fecit, et ipsum Johannem tunc ibidem
cepit, et imprisonavit, et in prisona detinuit contra legem et consuetudinem regni Regis Anglie, et eidem servienti tales et tantas minas de
vita sua et mutilacione membrorum suorum tunc ibidem affecit, quod
idem serviens circa servicium et negocia ipsius Thome, videlicet custodiam supervisionis messuagii sui ac averiorum, bonorum, et catallorum
suorum ibidem faciende, occasione imprisoniamenti predicti, et ob metum
mortis, per magnum tempus, videlicet a predicto vicesimo die per octo·
dies tunc proxime sequentes, palam incedere non audebat, sicque
negocia predicta per magnum tempus infecta remanserunt. Et idem
Thomas servicium servientis sui predicti amisit per idem tempus. Et
alia enormia ei intulit ad grave dampnum ipsius Thome et contra
pacem domini Regis nunc &c. Unde idem Thomas dicit quod deter-
ioratus est, et dampnum habet ad valenciam quadraginta librarum. Et
inde producit sectam &c. Plegii de prosequendo Ricardus [2] Gryme et
Willelmus Lyme.

Et super hoc sexto decimo die Maii, dicto anno sexto, Willelmus Eliot
de Assheperton, in comitatu Devon., Gentilman, et Henricus Brende de·
Lundon, Gentilman, coram domino Rege in cancelaria sua personaliter

---

[1] diplois, a doublet or jack.   [2] Radulphus, *Coram Rege.*

constituti manuceperunt, videlicet uterque corum sub pena viginti librarum, pro predicto Ricardo Fortescu, ac idem Ricardus tunc ibidem assumpsit pro seipso sub pena quadraginta librarum, quod ipse personaliter compareret coram dicto domino Rege in cancelaria sua predicta die Sabati tunc proximo futuro ubicunque tunc foret, et sic de die in diem usque in finem placiti, quam quidem summam viginti librarum [uterque manucaptorum predictorum, ac dictus Ricardus dictam summam quadraginta librarum][1] pro se concesserunt de terris et catallis ad opus dicti domini Regis levari, si predictus Ricardus ad diem predictum in forma predicta minime comparuerit. Super quod[2] predictus Ricardus Fortescu in propria persona sua venit et defendit vim et injuriam quando &c. Et quoad venire vi et armis, seu quicquid quod est contra pacem domini Regis, necnon totam transgressionem predictam preter dictum insultum, capcionem, et imprisonacionem predicti Johannis Frende ac in prisona detencionem ejusdem Johannis per spacium unius dimidie hore, dicit quod ipse in nulla est inde culpabilis, et ponit se super patriam, et predictus Thomas Stonore similiter. Et quoad insultum, capcionem, et imprisonacionem, et in prisona detencionem, illos idem Ricardus dicit quod predictus Thomas Stonore accionem suam predictam inde versus eum manutenere non debet. Quia dicit quod diu ante predictum tempus quo supponitur transgressionem predictam fieri, scilicet sextodecimo die Octobris, anno regni domini Regis nunc quinto, idem Ricardus Fortescu prosecutus fuit quoddam breve domini Regis de supplicavit extra curiam cancellarie domini Regis Vicecomiti Devon. directum Christoforo Wursley, armigero, nunc et tunc vicecomiti comitatus predicti existenti, ad capiendum predictum Johannem Frende, ac quosdam Willelmum Lusshe, Willelmum Willyng, Robertum Frende, et Thomam Martyn, necnon eos ad proximam gaolam domini Regis in comitatu predicto ducendos, quousque ipsi invenissent, et eorum quilibet invenisset eidem domino Regi sufficientem securitatem de pace gerenda erga dominum Regem et cunctum populum suum, et precipue erga ipsum Ricardum Fortescu. Quod quidem breve idem Ricardus Fortescu postea, scilicet octavo die Decembris, anno regni domini Regis nunc quinto, apud Exon. in comitatu predicto eidem Vicecomiti deliberavit. Pretextu cujus brevis idem nunc Vicecomes fecit quoddam warantum sigillo officii sui signatum, ballivo Hundr. de Ermyngton, ac quibusdam Hugoni Helier, Thome Horne, Johanni Helier, Johanni Holbeton, Johanni Sandre, et Willelmo

---

[1] The words in brackets, which are missing in *Chancery Misc.*, are supplied from the Roll.
[2] Subsequenter, *Chancery Misc.* But the scribe seems to have been doubtful.

Screche nuper directum et eorum cuilibet, et deliberatum apud Exon. prefato Thome Horne ad tunc infra warantum predictum in forma predicta nominatum nono[1] die Decembris tunc proximo sequente, ad capiendos prefatos Johannem Frende, Willelmum Luhsshe, Willelmum Willing, Robertum Frende, et Thomam Martyn, ac eos ad gaolam predictam ducendos quousque ipsi invenissent et eorum quilibet invenisset eidem domino Regi sufficientem securitatem de pace gerenda erga dominum Regem et cunctum populum suum, et precipue erga ipsum Ricardum Fortescu. Postmodumque, scilicet predicto tempore quo supponitur transgressionem predictam fieri, apud Ermyngton predictam idem Ricardus Fortescu venit cum eisdem Hugone Helier, Johanne Sandre, Thoma Horne, Johanne Helier, Johanne Holbeton, et Willelmo Screche ad monstrandum et ostendendum eis personam predicti Johannis Frende, et eundem Johannem Frende eisdem Hugoni, Johanni Sandre, Thome Horne, Johanni Helier, et Willelmo ad tunc et ibidem monstravit, eis requirendo ad ipsum Johannem Frende pretextu waranti predicti capiendum et proxime gaole domini Regis in comitatu predicto occasione premissa ducendum : pretextu quorum waranti et requisicionis idem Hugo, Johannes Sandre, Thomas Horne, Johannes Helier et Willelmus prefatum Johannem Frende, tempore quo supponitur transgressio predicta fieri, ceperunt et imprisonaverunt, et ipsum Johannem in custodia sua per spacium dicte dimidie unius hore ad eundem Johannem Frende ad gaolam domini Regis virtute waranti predicti ducendum ad tunc et ibidem custodierunt et detinuerunt ; que quidem capcio, imprisonacio, et in prisona detencio ejusdem Johannis Frende sunt idem insultus, capcio, et imprisonacio, et in prisona detencio predicti Johannis Frende per predictam unam dimidiam horam, unde predictus Thomas Stonor se modo queritur : et hic paratus est verificare prout Curia &c. ; unde petit judicium si idem Thomas accionem suam predictam in hoc casu versus eum habere seu manutenere debeat &c.

Et predictus Thomas Stonor quoad predictos insultum, capcionem, imprisonacionem dicti Johannis Frende, et ejusdem Johannis in prisona detencionem per predictum spacium unius dimidie hore, non cognoscendo aliqua per dictum Ricardum Fortescu in placito suo predicto allegata fore vera, pro placito dicit quod ipse per aliqua preallegata ab accione sua predicta inde habenda precludi non debet, quia dicit quod predictus Ricardus Fortescu, tempore transgressionis predicte facte, vi et armis, et de injuria sua propria in predictum Johannem Frende

---

[1] octavo, *Coram Rege Roll.* The scribe of *Chancery Misc.* first wrote "oc" and then erased it.

insultum fecit, et eundem Johannem cepit et imprisonavit, et ipsum in prisona detinuit, prout idem Thomas Stonore in narracione sua superius declaravit, et non ex causa per predictum Ricardum Fortescu superius placitando allegata. Et hoc idem Thomas petit quod inquiratur per patriam, et predictus Ricardus similiter &c.

Ideo dies datus est eis coram domino Rege in Octabas sancte Trinitatis ubicunque tunc fuerit in Anglia ad faciendum et recipiendum quod justum fuerit in premissis. Et ideo preceptum est Vicecomiti Devon. quod venire faciat coram eodem domino Rege ubicunque tunc fuerit in Anglia ad diem illum xxiiijor[1] tam milites quam alios probos et legales homines de visneto de Ermyngton, qui nec prefatum Thomam Stonore nec prefatum Ricardum Fortescu aliqua affinitate attingant, ad recognoscendum per eorum sacramentum super premissis plenius veritatem.

[*The* Coram Rege Roll, 825, *m.* 23, *then continues thus.*]

Ad quas quidem Octabas sancte Trinitatis coram domino Rege apud Westm. venerunt partes predicte in propriis personis suis, et Vicecomes retornavit nomina xxiiijor[2] Juratorum, quorum nullus &c. Ideo preceptum est Vicecomiti quod distringat eosdem juratores per omnes terras &c. Et quod de exit. &c. Et quod habeat corpora eorum coram domino Rege a die Sancti Michaelis in xv dies ubicunque &c., nisi Justiciarii domini Regis ad assisas in comitatu predicto capiendas assignati primo die Lune proximo post festum Sancti Jacobi apostoli apud Exon. per formam statuti &c. venerunt ad recognoscendum in forma predicta &c. Idem dies datus est partibus predictis &c., videlicet Ricardo Fortescu, qui manucepit quam prius &c. Ad quam quidem quindenam Sancti Michaelis coram domino Rege apud Westm. venit predictus Thomas Stonore per attornatum suum contra predictum Ricardum Fortescu in propria persona sua. Et prefati justiciarii coram quibus &c., miserunt hic recordum suum in hec verba :—

Postea die et loco infracontentato coram Waltero Moyle, milite, et Thoma Yonge, Justiciariis domini Regis ad assisas in comitatu Devon. capiendas assignatis per formam statuti &c., venit tam infranominatus Thomas Stonore quam infranominatus Ricardus Fortescu in propriis personis suis, et Juratores impanellati exacti similiter venerunt, qui ad veritatem de infracontentatis dicendam electi, triati et jurati dicunt super sacramentum suum quod predictus Ricardus Fortescu in nullo est culpabilis de infraspecificata verberacione et vulneracione predicti

---

[1] This seems to be an error for " xij ".
[2] This seems to be an error for " xij ".

Thome Stonore, necnon de imposicione infraspecificata minarum de vita et mutilacione membrorum infranominati Johannis Frende, prout idem Ricardus placitando allegavit. Et ulterius iidem juratores dicunt super sacramentum suum quod idem Ricardus culpabilis est de infraspecificato insultu in ipsum Thomam Stonore facto, prout idem Thomas per narracionem suam infraspecificatam versus eum queritur. Et assident dampna ipsius Thome occasione insultus illius ad viginti et quinque libras. Et ulterius iidem juratores dicunt super sacramentum suum quod predictus Ricardus Fortescu vi et armis et de injuria sua propria et non ex causa per eundem Ricardum interius placitando allegata. Et assident dampna ipsius Thome occasione transgressionis illius ad centum solidos. Et preterea iidem juratores assident dampna ipsius Thome pro misis et custagiis suis per ipsum circa sectam suam de et super omnibus et singulis premissis appositis ad quadraginta solidos. Ideo consideratum est quod predictus Thomas Stonore recuperet versus prefatum Ricardum Fortescu dampna predicta per juratores predictos in forma predicta assessa, que quidem dampna in toto se attingunt ad triginta et duas libras. Et predictus Ricardus Fortescu capiatur &c. Et predictus Thomas Stonore in misericordia pro falso clamore suo versus predictum Ricardum Fortescu de transgressione predicta, unde idem Ricardus superius acquietatus existit, et super hoc predictus Thomas Stonore, presens hic in Curia in propria persona sua gratis remisit prefato Ricardo Fortescu duodecim libras de dampnis predictis &c. Ideo idem Ricardus de duodecim libris illis sit quietus &c. Postea Ricardus Fortescu in propria persona sua venit et protulit hic in Curia predictas viginti libras prefato Thome Stonore in plenam satisfaccionem dampnorum predictorum deliberari &c., que quidem viginti libre in plenam satisfaccionem dampnorum predictorum prefato Thome deliberantur &c. Ideo consideratum est quod predictus Ricardus quoad eadem dampna est quietus &c.

[A precept was issued to the Sheriff of Devon to produce Richard Fortescue to answer for his trespass. The Sheriff returned that he was not to be found, and was thereupon, on 21 Nov., 1467, ordered to produce him within one month of Easter—*Coram Rege Roll*, 826, m. 175. In Easter Term, 1468, the sheriff again returned that Richard Fortescue was not to be found, and a writ of *exigi facias* was accordingly issued on 11 May for the appearance of Fortescue, Hugh Helier, William Saunder, John Robard and William Scryche on the octaves of St. Martin—"quod breve xxx⁰ die Maii deliberatum Johanni Gogh, vicecomitis deputato "—*Coram Rege Roll*, 828, mm. 72, 87. Nevertheless further proceedings occurred in Easter Term, 1468, as recorded in *Roll*, 828, m. 94, as follows :—]

Jurata xxiiij^{or} militum de visneto de Ermyngton ad convincendos xij juratores cujusdam prime inquisicionis venit recognoscendum si juratores, per quos quedam inquisicio nuper summonita coram domino Rege capta fuerit coram dilectis et fidelibus domini Regis Waltero Moille, militi, et Thoma Yonge, Justiciariis domini Regis ad assisas in comitatu predicto capiendas assignatis per breve domini Regis de Nisi prius apud Exon. inter Ricardum Fortescu de Ermyngton in comitatu predicto, armigerum, querentem, et Thomam Stonore, armigerum, unum servientium venerabilis patris Georgii, Archiepiscopi Ebor., nuper cancellarii domini Regis, de quadam transgressione eidem Thome Stonore per prefatum Ricardum Fortescu illata, ut dicebatur, falsum fecerunt sacramentum, sicut idem Ricardus domino Regi graviter conquerendo monstravit, necne. Et modo coram domino Rege apud Westm. ad hunc diem, scilicet a die Pasche in xv dies, venerunt tam predictus Ricardus Fortescu per Robertum Dene, attornatum suum, quam predictus Thomas Stonore per Johannem Snape, attornatum suum, et Hugo Champernoun, Robertus Hyllyng, et Willelmus Strecchelegh, tres juratores prime inquisicionis predicte in propriis personis suis similiter venerunt, et Willelmus Yeo, armiger, Johannes Speccote, Johannes Barnhouse, Willelmus Mileton, Robertus Wyllesford, Nicholaus Pyne, Rogerus Worthe, Ricardus Fokeray, et Ricardus Wyke de Wyke, novem juratores prime inquisicionis predicte residui, iiij^{to} die placiti solempniter exacti non venerunt. Et preceptum fuit Vicecomiti quod distringat eos &c. [The sheriff thereon reports distress.] Ideo jurata xxiiij^{or} militum predicta capiatur versus eos per defaltam &c. Et super hoc tam predictus Thomas Stonore quam predicti tres juratores prime inquisicionis predicte modo hic comparentes petunt auditum predicti brevis de attinctu. Et eis legitur &c. Petunt eciam auditum recordi, unde idem breve emanuit. Et eis legitur in hec verba :— [*The Record then follows down to* "duodecim libris sit quietus" *on p.* 83 *above*].

Quibus lectis et auditis, tam predictus Thomas Stonore quam predicti Hugo Champernoune, Robertus Hillyng, et Willelmus Strecchelegh, tres juratores prime inquisicionis predicte, modo hic comparentes petunt quod predictus Ricardus Fortescu assignet Curie hic suum sacramentum si quod &c. Et predictus Ricardus Fortescu dicit quod predicti tres juratores prime inquisicionis modo hic comparentes et predicti novem jnratores ejusdem prime inquisicionis residui modo non comparentes falsum fecerunt sacramentum in hoc quod dixerunt quod idem Ricardus Fortescu est culpabilis de predicto insultu in predictum Thomam facto, prout idem Thomas per narracionem suam predictam querebatur, quia idem Ricardus Fortescu dicit quod ipse in nullo est culpabilis de insultu illo in forma que idem Ricardus prius placitando allegavit. Item falsum fecere sacramentum in hoc quod assiderunt dampna ipsius Thome Stonore occasione insultus illius ad viginti et quinque libras, quia idem Ricardus Fortescu dicit quod predictus Thomas Stonore nulla sustinuit dampna occasione insultus illius eo quod idem Ricardus de insultu illo in nullo est culpabilis. Et ulterius idem Ricardus Fortescu dicit quod si per predictam juratam xxiiij^{or} militum comperiri poterit quod idem Ricardus culpabilis sit de insultu illo, tunc idem Ricardus Fortescu dicit quod predicti tres juratores prime inquisicionis predicte modo hic comparentes et predicti novem juratores ejusdem prime inquisicionis residui falsum fecere sacramentum in hoc quod assidere dampna predicti Thome Stonore ad viginti et quinque libras pro insultu predicto ubi idem Thomas Stonore non sustinuit dampna occasione illius ultra tres solidos et quattuor denarios. Item falsum fecere sacramentum in hoc quod dixere quod idem Ricardus Fortescu, vi et armis de injuria sua propria et non ex causa per ipsum Ricardum prius placitando allegata, in predictum Johannem Frende insultum fecit et eundem Johannem cepit, et imprisonavit, et ipsum Johannem in prisona contra legem et consuetudinem Regni Regis Anglie detinuit, prout predictus Thomas Stonore placitando allegavit, quia idem Ricardus Fortescu, ut prius, dicit quod durante predicto tempore quo supponitur transgressionem predictam fieri, scilicet predicto sexto decimo die Octobris, anno Regni dicti domini Regis nunc quinto, supradicto, prosecutus fuerit predictum breve dicti domini Regis de supplicavit extra dictam Curiam Cancellarii dicti domini Regis Vicecomiti dicti comitatus Devon. directum, Christoforo Worseley, armigero, tunc Vicecomiti comitatus predicti existenti, ad capiendum predictum Johannem Frende, et predictos Willelmum Lusse, Willelmum Willyng, Robertum Frende, et Thomam Martyn, necnon eos ad proximam gaolam dicti domini Regis in comitatu predicto ducendos, quouscue ipsi invenissent et quilibet eorum &c. [*as on pp.* 80-81 *above to* ad tunc et ibidem custodierunt et detinuerunt] in forma qua idem Ricardus prius placitando allegavit. Et hoc paratus est verificare per predictam juratam xxiiij^{or} militum. Et tam predictus Thomas Stonore quam predicti tres juratores prime inquisicionis predicte modo hic comparentes dicunt quod iidem tres juratores ac predicti novem juratores ejusdem prime inquisicionis residui bonum et legale fecere sacramentum in omnibus que dixerunt. Et de hoc ponunt &c. super predictam juratam xxiiij^or militum. Et predictus Ricardus Fortescu similiter. Ideo jurata xxiiij^or militum illa inde eos capiatur, set jurata illa remanet. capienda coram domino Rege usque in Octabas Sancte Trinitatis ubicunque &c., pro defectu juratorum ejusdem jurate xxiiij^or militum quia nullus &c. Ideo Vicecomes habeat corpora juratorum ejusdem jurate xxiiij^or militum. Idem dies datus est tam partibus predictis quam predictis tribus juratoribus prime inquisicionis predicte modo hic comparentibus &c.[1] Et super hoc breve domini Regis inde vicesimo sexto die Maii isto eodem termino liberatur hic in Curia Johanni Gogh deputato Vicecomitis comitatus predicti in forma juris exequendum periculo incumbente &c. Ad quas quidem Octabas Sancte Trinitatis coram domino Rege apud Westm. venerunt tam predictus Ricardus Fortescu quam predictus Thomas Stonore per attornatos suos, ac Hugo Champernoun, Robertus Hillyng, et Willelmus Strecchelegh, tres juratores prime inquisicionis predicte in propriis personis suis similiter venerunt. Et Vicecomes retornavit quod quilibet jurator predicte jurate xxiiij^or militum districtus est, unde exitus cujuslibet eorum xl. s., et manucaptus &c. ; qui quidem juratores exacti, quidam eorum venerunt, et quidam non venerunt prout patet in panell. &c. Quorum quidem juratorum modo non comparentium exitus et amerciamenta patent in rotulis de finibus et extractis de termino Sancte Trinitatis de anno regni domini Regis nunc octavo. Et super hoc predicta jurata - xxiiij^or militum .&c. remanet capienda pro defectu juratorum coram domino Rege usque in Octabas Sancti Michaelis ubicunque &c. Et preceptum est Vicecomiti sicut alias quod distringat predictos juratores predicte Jurate xxiiij^or militum &c. per omnes terras &c. Et quod exitus &c. Et ideo habeat corpora eorum coram domino Rege ad easdem Octabas Sancti Michaelis &c. ad recognoscendum in forma predicta &c. Idem dies datus est tam partibus predictis quam juratoribus predictis tribus jurate prime inquisicionis predicte modo hic comparentibus &c. Et sciendum est quod breve domini Regis inde x die Julii, anno regni domini Regis .nunc octavo, coram domino Rege apud Westm. deliberatum Johanni Gogh, deputato Vicecomitis comitatus predicti forma juris exequendum periculo incumbente &c.

[The *Coram Rege Roll*, 830, m. 20, for Michaelmas Term, 1468, ends the suit.]

Ricardus Fortescu de Ermyngton in comitatu predicto, qui tulit breve domini Regis de attinctu versus Thomam Stonore, armigerum, unum

---

[1] The original entry on the Roll ended here.

servientium venerabilis patris Georgii, Archiepiscopi Ebor., nuper cancellarii domini Regis Anglie, de placito jurate xxiiij^or militum ad convincendos xij juratores in placito transgressionis, breve illud non est
presentatus.   Ideo idem Ricardus capiatur, et plegii sui de prosequendo
sint in misericordia.

83. R[OBERT] MEDFORD TO THOMAS STONOR

1466

Clearly written in the year that Stonor was sheriff of Oxford and Berks,
i.e. in 1465-66.   Medford was presumably under-sheriff; he occurs in that
capacity between 1467 and 1472 (*Early Chancery Proceedings,* 46/307).
See also the reference to Robert Medford under date 1467 in vol. ii, p. 167.
From *A.C.,* xlvi, 59.

After due recommendacion unto your maistershipp be hadde : like
yow to wete þat y have be with my maisterys Langford and Roger as
for þe quenys gold.   Langford hathe promysed me to pay yow at
London þis same weke : and as for Roger, y sende yow v. marcs for
his parte : yff so be þat Langford make defaute þe ye most gete lenger
day of his parte, and þer for y sende yow þe writte white backed &c.
Also y sende yowe a noþer writte endosed ayenst my maister Restwold :
ye most sende unto hym for þe seid C. s.   Also y sende yowe a noþer
writte ayenst Dalamar.   As for þe *vendicioni exponas,* ye seye þat ye
have paid þe money : þer for y sende yowe the writte white, and sende
ye most sende Combes word.   Syr, y sende yow a *capias* þat Langford
delyvered me, as y rode homeward, which y coude nat serve for lac of
tyme, praying yowe to put hym yn to þe bondell amonges Berk.
writtes.   Syr, y wold have come to Walyngford as to morowe : but
þer shalle be a privy Session at Charlehamstre by Hungeford, and þer
will be Dalamar, and þer y may be suere to speke with hym for suche
writtes as byn ayenst hym &c.   On Sunday Dalamar was at Lytelcoote,
and þer was cominicasion as for þe child : but y hire seye they were
for a part.   To morowe at Hungeford at þe said Sessions I shalle
knowe more : for þer wilbe Syr George Darell, and Syr Ric. Darell
bothe.   Besekyng yowe to send forthe þes writtes to London, þat they
may be in court on Wennesday erly, and þat ye sende summe man to

Walyngford to awayte þer &c.   Wreten at Shaldebourne in hast þis same mornynge.

Your owne servaunt, R. Medford.

To my reverent Maister Thomas Stonor.

84. WRIT TO THOMAS STONOR AS SHERIFF

6 JULY, 1466

This is the only fifteenth-century example preserved amongst the Stonor Papers of the class of documents of which the shrievalty of Edmund de Stonor in 1377-78 supplied so many instances.   See p. 165.   From *Ch. Misc.*, 37, iii, 17.

Edwardus, dei gratia Rex Anglie et Francie et Dominus Hibernie, vice-comiti Oxon. et Berkes. salutem.   Precipimus tibi quod non omittas prop-ter aliquam libertatem quin eam ingredias et de bonis et catallis, terris et tenementis Cancellarii Universitatis Oxon., et Majoris ejusdem ville, qui pro tempore sint, in balliva tua fieri facias C. s., quos nobis debent de quadam firma C. s. per annum de custodia assise panis et cervisie in eadem villa et suburbiis ejusdem: Necnon de bonis et catallis, terris et tenementis Collegii Animarum Omnium Fidelium Defunctorum in Oxon. in dicta balliva tua fieri facias vij. s. vij. d. et ob., quos nobis debent tam de secunda medietate unius xᵐᵉ nobis a clero anno regni nostri tercio concesse, pro temporalibus taxatis sub nomine Prioris de Suthampton in Gussich in decanatu de Pymperne in archidiaconatu Dors., quam de prima medietate ejusdem decime pro eisdem tempora-libus ibidem.   Et de bonis et catallis, terris et tenementis Custodis et Collegii Animarum Omnium Fidelium Defunctorum in Oxon. in balliva tua fieri facias xv. d. q., quos nobis debent de prima medietate unius xᵐᵉ nobis a clero anno regni nostri secundo concesse, pro temporalibus taxatis sub nomine Abbatis de Insula Dei in parochia de Upchirche in diocesi Cantuar. ac jurisdiccione Archiepiscopi Cantuar. immedietate [*sic*]: ac de bonis et catallis, terris et tenementis Custodis et Scolarium de Excetre College in Oxon. in dicta balliva tua fieri facias xliij. s. iiij. d., quos nobis debent in duabus particulis tam de prima medietate unius xᵐᵉ nobis a clero anno secundo concesse, quam de prima medietate unius decime nobis a clero anno tercio concesse, pro sp iritualibus suis in archidiaconatu Berks, que quidem temporalia dicti Cu stos et Scolares tenent in proprios usus.   Ita quod denarios illos habeas ad Scaccarium nostrum apud Westm. in Crastino sancti Michaelis nobis tunc ibi solvendos. Et habeas ibi tunc hoc breve &c. T. R. Illingworth, milite, apud Westm. vj° die Julii anno regni nostri sexto, per Magnum Rotulum de anno iiij^{to} Regis nunc in Oxon. Berks., ac per peticionem Johannis Barantyne, armigeri, nuper vicecomitis comitatuum predictorum, computantis a festo sancti Michaelis anno quarto Regis nunc usque festum Sancti Michaelis tunc proxime sequens. fforde.

Endorsed : Thome Stonore, armigero, Vic.

85. PETITION FOR ALLOWANCES AS SHERIFF BY THOMAS STONOR

1466

For some references to Stonor's accounts as Sheriff, see L.T.R., *Memoranda Rolls*, 239—m. 1, Hilary Term, 1467, as to absence of accounts from Bishop of Salisbury, and Abbot of Westminster and other matters; and 240—Recorda, Trinity Term, 1467, m. 2, re John Love of Hungerford, and m. 5, re Sir Richard Harcourt and John Croston, executors of Sir John Lovell of Lovell. From *Ch. Misc.*, 37, iii, 22.

Oxon et Berks.

Peticiones Thome Stonore, armigeri, nuper vicecomitis de anno vj^{to} Regis E. iiij^{to}.

In primis petit exonerari de x. li. de firma de Godyngton in ij particulis &c.

Item de xiij. s. iiij. d. pro Roberto Broke de firma picagii &c. in novo mercato infra villam de Bircestr. de hoc anno vj^{to} et ejus arreragiis.

Item de xxvj. s. viij. d. pro custodia ducentarum acrarum bosci cum pertinenciis in Hurst in comitatu Wiltes et hundredo de Asherugge in eodem comitatu &c.

Respectuatur pro recog-nicione facienda pro [hoc anno].

Item de xx. marcis de custodia duarum parcium dominii sive manerii de Swalowfeld.

Respectuatur pro computo videndo et certificando.

Item de cxxvij li. xvj. s. vj. d. pro custodia maneriorum Regis de Wodestoke &c.

Item de xxv. li. de custodia assise panis et cervisie in villa Oxon. &c. per quinque annos.

Resp. vij. li. xij. s. j. d. pro vad. Sturmy pro acquietando de ser., et resp. residuum pro recognicione facienda

Item de xxj. li. de custodia manerii sive dominii de Hampsted Marshall &c.

Item de xj. li. xiij. s. iiij. d. pro custodia manerii de Denham Lovell cum pertinenciis.

Item de cxxxiij. li. vj. s. viij. d. pro custodia maneriorum Regis de Cokeham et Bray.

Resp. et fiat corpus cum causa vic. London, postea exoneretur.

Item de xx. li. pro Johanne Love de Hungerford in comitatu Berks, skynner.

Exoneretur xix. li. xvj. s. iiij. d. et stet onus de residuo.

Item de xx. li. pro Johanne Sawyer de Abyndon in eodem comitatu, yoman.

Exoneretur vicecomes et debeatur.

Item de xxxj. s. x. d. in ij particulis pro Roberto Harcourte, milite, de expensis suis forinsecis.

Item de xxx. s. iiij. d. pro dicto Roberto in xvj. particulis de expensis suis forinsecis.

Exoneretur lxv. li. xiij. s. iiij. d. et stet onus de residuo.

Item de lxvj. li. pro Johanne Lidyard de Glympton.

Exoneretur xj. li. xiij. s. iiij. d. et stet onus de residuo.

Item de xij. li. pro Willelmo Wykeham, nuper vicecomite, de pluribus debitis suis de anno xxviij. H. vj^{ti}.

Item de xliij. s. ob. pro custode et canonicis de Wyndesore de x$^{mis.}$

Exoneretur vic. et debeatur.

Item de xxxiiij. li. pro Willelmo Brocas, armigero, nuper vicecomite, de pluribus debitis suis.

Resp. et fiat breve Episcopo ad certificandum citra octabas animarum A⁰ vij⁰.

Item de xxxiij. s. iiij. d. pro collegio Regine in Oxon. pro ecclesia de Sparsholt.

Resp. pro tall. dimidii.

Item de vij. s. xj. d. ob. pro abbate de Redyng de pluribus debitis suis.

Exoneretur et per sequent. (?) rotulum fieri facias ibidem.

Item de vj. li. xiiij. s. vij. d. pro collegio voc. the Quenes college in Oxon. &c.

Exoneretur vic. et debeatur.

Item de xx. li. pro Thoma Burgh' et aliis de firma manerii de Shiplake de anno iij⁰ Regis hujus &c.

Item de xxxix. s. iiij. d. pro Decano et canonicis capelle Regis de Wyndesore &c.

Johannes dux Suff., et filius et heres Willelmi, nuper ducis Suff., et Alicia ducissa Suff. ut administratrix bonorum &c. Placitorum termino pasche ao secundo, Ro v ij. et lviij.

Item de xxiij. d. pro custode et scolaribus collegii voc. Seynt Mary college of Wynton.

Item de xxj. s. viij. d. pro Willelmo, Marchione Suff. de expensis suis forinsecis.

Item de lxix. s. vij. d. ob. pro Wynchestr. college in Oxon. de x^{mis} &c.

Item de lxix. s. vij. d. ob. pro Wynchestr. college in Oxon. de x^{mis} &c.

Item de l. s. et viij. d. in ij particulis pro Decano et canonicis capelle Regis de Wyndesore.

Item de C. marcis pro Johanne Colyngrygge de custodia manerii de Padworth &c.

Item de ix. li. x. s. iiij. d. pro custode et canonicis capelle Regis de Wyndesore &c.

Item de xxxiij. s. iiij. d. pro eisdem Decano et canonicis &c.

Item de xxiij. d. pro custode et scolaribus collegii voc. seynt Mary college of Wynch.

Resp. et fiat breve Episcopo ad certificandum citra octabas animarum Ac vijo.

Item de xl. s. pro collegio voc. Bailly College in Oxon. de x^{mis} &c.

Item de lvij. s. vj. d. in ij particulis pro collegio et scolaribus Animarum Omnium Fidelium defunctorum in Oxon. &c.

Item de viij. li. x. s. ob. pro custode et scolaribus collegii voc. Seynt Mary college of Wynchester in Oxon.

Item de xl. s. pro collegio Animarum Omnium Fidelium defunctorum in Oxon. &c., pro Lewkenor.

Item de iiij. li. xiij. s. iiij. d. in ij particulis pro magistro et scolaribus collegii voc. Seint Marie College of Wynchestre in Oxon.

Item de vj. li. iiij. s. vj. d. ob. in iiij particulis pro custode et canonicis capelle Regis de Wyndesore.

Item de xxiij. s. j. d. ob. pro custode et collegio Animarum Omnium Fidelium defunctorum in Oxon.

Item de xvij. s. viij. d. pro Ricardo episcopo Sar. de clameo suo de exitibus, finibus et amerciamentis diversis integri tenementi sui.

Item de xv. s. pro computo forinseco de Bloxham. Littera Patens irrotulata Trin. Rec. aº iiijᵗᵒ Rº tercio Thes.

Item de xiij. s. de exitibus ij. solar., unius selde, unius vac. placee, et ij. acr. prati in villa Oxon. per Originalia de aº vᵗᵒ Rº xvᵐᵒ pro Staveley et aliis.

Item de c. marcis per ipsum solutis Thome Stonore.

Item de lij. s. iiij. d. pro Waltero Devereux, milite, &c.

Item de xxiij. s. pro Johanne, comite Oxon.

[Item de xx. s. pro Johanne Chalers, nuper de Lyterum in comitatu Berks, milite &c.][1]

Summa peticionum predictarum   [2]

86. ACCOUNT OF WILLIAM COVENTRE

[? 1466]

Written on a sheet of paper —*Chancery Misc.*, 37, iii, 21—in two columns, ending near the top of the second. There are 26 items in all. The most interesting are given below. The mention of Sackville indicates a date not later than 1466. William Coventre was collector of rents at Watlyngton in that year (*Ministers Accounts*, 1122/21).

Expense facte per Willelmum Coventre &c.

In primis spende at Illysley when ye rode yn to Deveneshyre, ij. d. Itm., at Ermyngton for wosshyng of yowyr shertys and M. Wyllyams, iij. d. Itm., at Bedwyn, iij. d. Itm., when y rode to seke M. Sakvyle, spende at Abyndon, iij. d. Itm., yn makyng of M. Wyllyams gowne, vij. d. Itm., a lase for M. Wyll., j. d. ob. Itm., for ij chekons both at Wodestok for yowre hawkys, ij. d. Itm., yn yowre drynkyng when ye wente a hawkyng at Wodestoke, ij. d., Itm., when y rode yn yowre erand to areste Edmond Dyer at ij tymys for my expenses on my horse

---

[1] Entry erased.   [2] Left blank.

and me, vj. d.   Itm., for a payre hosyn for M. Mary, ij. d.   Itm., a payre hosyn for M. Isabell, j. d. ob.   Itm., a cappe for M. Isabell, ij. d. ob.   Summa, xxx. s. iiij. d. ob.

87. HUMPHREY FORSTER TO THOMAS STONOR

21 OCTOBER [1466]

This seems to have reference to the death of Thomas Sackvile of Falley or Fawley in 1466—see Nos. 88 and 89.   Sackvile's wife Isabel was a sister of Thomas Stonor and of Forster's wife.   Rokes was Sackvile's nephew and heir (see note on No. 89).   In *Ch. Misc.*, 37, ix, 38-39, there is the rough draft of a contract of marriage between Thomas, eldest son and heir-apparent of Thomas Rokes, and a daughter (unnamed) of Stonor.   If the said daughter died "before flesshly knowleche had" another daughter, if unmarried and of convenient age, was to take her place.   Rokes bargained to make a grant of the reversion of the lands which Isabel, late wife of Thomas Sakevyle, held for life, to the value of 20 marks a year, and of other lands to the value of 10 marks.   If Rokes' son at the age of fourteen and Stonor's daughter at the age of thirteen disagree the contract was to be void.   The marriage does not seem to have ever taken effect though it was still being discussed in 1477—see No. 179.   The marriage contract was probably drafted about the date of this letter.   From *A.C.*, xlvi, 47.

Ryght worshypfull and my goode kynde brother, in my most feythefull wyse I recommaunde me to yowe : and liketh yow to be remembrid to commune with the Eschetour of Bokyngham shire for the wrytte of *diem clausit extremum* of my brother Saquevile, whom God assoyle : and þat ye like to wryte unto me as ye fynde hym disposed : for I ensure yowe I have communed with your worshipfull and weldisposed Suster Saquevile as for suche estate as shulde be made unto your doughter and Rokes' sone, wherin I fynde her as well disposed as ye wold desire your self, so þat her husbondes wille be not broken ne she hurte duryng her lyff.   Brother, I dowte not ye shall have worship of her grete sadnesse and þe vertuous disposicion þat she is of &c. : hit were to grete pite to put hir to trowble or charge to cause her to change from þe disposision þat she is fully astablisshed to.   My goode brother, yef it please yowe ferthermore to remembre of þe letter my lord wrote unto yowe, Marmyon and me, as for þe matter betwene Fowler and Heynes, whiche Heynes hath be with me and is bounde in an Obligacion of ij. c. li. to abide þe rewle of alle þe matter betwene Fowler and hym of yow, Ric. Quatermaynez, William Marmyon and me. And Fowler to appoynte suche season as ye and other may atende; and þe souner þe lever to Haynes. I have wryten to Fowler in semblable wyse in this matter: whether my lettre be come to hym or no, I wete ner. I pray you to put hym in knowlache, and to understonde of hym whether my wrytyng be come to hym or no, and to move hym by your wysdom after my lordes wryting, as ye understonde hym. And so I pray yow to sende me worde in wrytyng, for I have sent diverse tymes to Fowler place, and he hath at alle tymes be owte &c. My goode brother remembre of þe woman ye wote of &c. And God preserve yow. Wreten þe xxj day of Octobre.

Your trewe brother Humfrey Forster.

To my ryght worshipful Brother Thomas Stonore þis be delivered.

88. INDENTURE BY THOMAS ROKES

22 JUNE, 1467

From *Ancient Deeds*, C. 1288. There is only a trace of the seal.

Be hyt remembred that Thomas Stonore, squyer, bathe resceyved of Thomas Rokes, squyer, yn the name of Isabell, late the wyfe of Thomas Sakevyle, squyer, executrice of the testament of the same Thomas Sakevyle, ffoureskore pound yn money yn full payment of all soche sommes of money as the seyd Thomas Rokes shuld content and pay by the last wulle of the seyd Thomas Sakevyle to his executors for havyng of the revercyon of hys maners, landes and tenements after the discese of the seyd Isabell as hit apperith by the seyd laste wulle. In wytnes wherof the seyd Thomas Stonore and the seyd Thomas Rokes to these presentes enterchaungeably have put ther seell the xxij day of June the seventh yere of the reign of Kynge Edward the ffourthe.

(*Signed*) Thomas Rokes.

89. THOMAS ROKES TO THOMAS STONOR

[1 OCTOBER, 1467]

Sir Thomas Sakeville of Falley or Fawley, Bucks, had a son Thomas, and a daughter Maud who married N. Kentwood. The second Thomas Sakeville had a son Thomas and a daughter Margery. The third Thomas is probably the husband of Isabel, sister of Thomas Stonor (d. 1474). Margery married Thomas Rokes, no doubt the Thomas Rokes the elder of Ascot and Wing who died in 1457, and mentions in his will Margery his wife, and his sons John Rokes and Robert Rufford.[1] He was presumably the father of Thomas Rokes the writer of this letter, who calls Isabel Sackville his aunt, for in an inquisition held in 1487 it was found that Thomas Rokes son of Margery Sakeville inherited property granted to N. Kentwood as heir of Sir Thomas Sakeville. Thomas Rokes the younger calls Thomas Stonor his brother, and must therefore have been married to his sister or half-sister; from No. 182 it appears that his wife's name was Alice, and since Alice daughter of the elder Thomas Stonor was married to Humphrey Forster, it is probable that Alice Rokes was a daughter of Alice and Richard Drayton (Wrottesley, *Pedigrees from the Plea Rolls*, pp. 438, 441, 458; *Cal. Inq.*, Henry VII, i, 317; *P.C.C.*, 12 Stokton, will of T. Rokes, 1457; *Sede Vacante Wills*, Kent Records, will of T. Rokes, 1500). A pedigree in *Harley MS.*, 1139, f. 45, makes the second Thomas Rokes of Falley marry a daughter of Fowler of Ricote, and his son, a third Thomas, marry a daughter of Sir William Stonor; the last statement is certainly incorrect. See p. 93 above. From *A.C.*, xlvi, 70.

Rygth worshypfull Syr, and my rygth Good Brodyr, aftyr all dew recommendasyon had, I recomawnd me unto yow, to my Mastres, my dowter, and to all my young Cosyngs, the weche I pray God to preserve and kepe for his mersy: and I ame sory that my horse servyd yow no better: and yf he mowghth have plesyd yow for a yoman to have redyn on, I wold have holdyn me rygth well content and ye had kepyd hyme styll: but I trust in God I schall purvey yow of a lytyll hors, soche as ye schall com and thanke for. And I send yow yowr hors by the brynger of thys letter, yowr servant: he wyll not be in pleyte as I wold have hyme, but he ys both herty and hoole: God save hyme. And hyt lyke yow, ye send me word how my Nawnte is dysposyd, now the dettes be payd, to performe my Nonkilles wyll, hoys sowle God pardon. I beseche you as for my Nowntes surte and myn, that ye wyll comyn hyt with sum leryd body for the surte of us both

---

[1] For a lawsuit by his executors see *Placita de Banco*, 818, m. 41.

acordyng to his wyll. And I schall old me rygth well content: for I trust yow as myche as I do eny man alyve: and I schall do to plese you as mych, yf that I cane. I wold pray yow, yf ye come in to the Contre, that ye woll se my pore howse for yowr logyng; and ye schall be as welcome to me as eny man alyve. I have a lytyll besynes yet in my hervyst: as sone as I cane ryd that, I schall se both yow and my Nawnt with Godes Grase, whome evyr preserve yow and yowrs for his mersy. Wretyn at Ascot on Satyrday next aftyr Mykaellmes day

By yowr Brodyr Thomas Rokes.

To my Rygth Worschypfull Syr, and Rygth good Brodyr, Thomas Stonor.

90. ACCOUNT OF T. SAY WITH THOMAS MULL ON BEHALF OF RICHARD DRAYTON

1468

The account runs from 21 July, 1466, to 12 July, 1468. Mull was executor for Drayton. From *Ch. Misc.*, 37, iii, 23.

Soluciones facte per T. Say ex mandato Thome Mull pro Ricardo Drayton xxj die Julii A° vj^{to} E. iiij^{ti} et deinceps.

In primis paid to John of Devenshire proctor of the fraternite of Seynt Elen in Abendon for makyng of the seid Richard brother there, xl. d. Item, paid to William Atkyn for v^c lxxv fote stone at ij. d. the fote, iiij. li. xv. s. x. d. Item, paid for carriage of vj^c fote stone, xxx. s. Item, paid to Richard Fylpott for makyng of vj^c and xx^{ti} fote of Creste stone at ij. d. the fote, Summa, v. li. iij. s. iiij. d. Item paid to the said Richard for xiiij[1] dais werke and di., layng the seid Creste, viij. s. Item, paid to a laborer servyng hym the seid xviij dais and di., vj. s. ij. d. Item, paid for ij lodes lyme, xiiij. s. iiij. d. Item, paid for xiiij lodes sonde, xxij. d. Summa, xiij. li. ij. s. x. d. Inde recepi die et anno supradictis per manus dicti T. Mull xij. li. So rest due to the said T. Say, xxij. s. x. d. Item, the seid T. Mull borowed of the seid T. Say the xij. day of Julii a° E. iiij.^{ti} viij°, v. li. x. s. And the seid T. Mull bought of the seid T. Say iiij. yerdes Russet for iiij. s. the yerd. Summa, xvj. s. Item, ij yerdes and iij quarters Russet for v. s. þe yerde, Summa, xiij. s. ix. d. Summa totalis due to the seid T. Say by the seid T. Mull, viij. li. ij. s. vij. d.

---

[1] Apparently an error for "xviij".

91. THOMAS STONOR TO JANE STONOR

8 OCTOBER, 1468

This was clearly written by Thomas Stonor to his wife, on the occasion of the death of his mother and her second husband, Richard Drayton, in October, 1468; it shows that Alice died on 1st October and Richard on 3rd October. "My adversary of Devonshire" is of course Richard Fortescue (see No. 82), where it appears that the lawsuit finally ended in Michaelmas Term, 1468. The "xliij gentylmen" were presumably the panel for the jury of twenty-four who were summoned to appear on the octaves of Michaelmas. From *A.C.* xlvi, 243.

Myne oone good Jane, as hertely as I can I recumaunde me to yow. Like yow to wyt that my ffadyr is gone to God also: and the there was a sone wytyng: and my modyr on Saterday by the morne, and my ffadyr on Munday by [d]ayrove. And I pray yow that William is chyld may cum with hym, and a amblyng hors for me in hand led. I saw (?) yow a letter as this that was wrytyn yestyrday. And let them cum with William that I wroote ffor, and they shull have her clothe of blak to make hem gounys with. And where William hathe wrytyn a letter unto me for his parsonage, whan he comyth let hym tell me tale of trouthe and hit shall be remedyyd, with mercy of God. And myne owne Jane, I thanke God myne adversari of Devenshere hathe had no wurshyp: ffor ther aperyd xliij gentlymen as this day, and he is shamyd and nonsuyd in the cort to his great shame. And Lemman, charge Wykys to gete as myche money as eney be had: ffor I shull spende myche money. And goode swete Lemman, be ye myry and of goode comfort for to cumfort me when I cum. I can not cum to youe as sone as I wuld: ffor I most set sum direccion in Horton or I goo. Let William cum in all hast. And the blessyd Trinite kepe yow. I-wrytyn at Lundon the Saterday afore seynt Edward is day.

                                                    By your ovne Stonor.

To my Cosyn Jane Stonor, in hast.

92. JOHN CROOCKER TO THOMAS STONOR

18 OCTOBER, [1468]

In Michaelmas Term, 1457, a writ was issued to the Sheriff of Devon to bring up William Saunder, Hugh Helyer, John Roberd and William Skryche of Ermyngton on the morrow of St. Andrew (1 Dec.) to show cause why they should not pay 10*l.* damages which Richard Drayton had lately recovered against them for trespass. They failed to appear, and were cited for Hilary Term, when it was ordered that Drayton should have execution. In Trinity Term, 1468, a writ of *exigi facias* was issued to the Sheriff against them. (*Coram Rege Rolls*, 826, m. 41, and 829, m. 105 ; see also p. 83 above.) Thus the date of this letter is 18 Oct., 1468, a fortnight after Drayton's death. Lyneham is in Yealmpton, not far from Ermington. The writer is no doubt the John Crocker who was knighted in 1471 and died in 1508-9, and is commemorated on a brass in Yealmpton Church. From *A.C.*, xlvi, 40.

Ryght worshipful cosyn and frende, I commawnde me unto you. The cause that y write unto you at this tyme ys to pray you for to do for me in þat I woll desyre you as ever ye will that y shall do for you. Ther as on Hewgh Helyer is at exegent at your father Drayton ys sute with William Saunder, John Robard, and William Skryche, and as for John Robert ye have utterly promyseyd me that he shall not be hurt in no wise, and as for Scryche my broder Predyax telleth me that ye and he be agreyd for hym, but in especiall y pray you to save Hewgh Helyer that he be not hurt, for he came into my service now at Michel- masse and ys my plowghman, to thentent that y shulde make an ende betwyxt hym and you. And yf evere ye woll have my good will and service, favereth hym at this tyme. Be the same token that ye were with me the Fryday before that ye departeyd from Ermyngton, and that y promiseyd you to have be with you at Ermyngton the Sonday than next folowyng : the cause that I cam not yt ys nat unknowne to you : my will ys trewe unto you, as God knoweth. Also here y sende you halfe a ryall to token that at the next tyme that ye and y mete y shall make an ende for my servaunt Hewgh Helyer, as y am trewe gentyl- man &c. And God have you in his kepyng, Amen. I-wryten at Lynham on seynt Lukes day,

Be your owne John Croocker.

Unto my Ryʒt Tresty and wel beloveyd Cosyn Thomas Stoner, Squyer, this letter be delyvered.

93. ACCOUNTS BY NICHOLAS WENDOVER

1468-72

Wendover may possibly have been in the service of Thomas Stonor. The account is on a single sheet of paper folded bookwise, and contains entries made at various dates. The first is the most interesting as a year's account with a servant. From *Ch. Misc.* 37, iii, 24.

Md. That Thomas Pratt hath made comenant to serve Nicholas Wendover fro Michaell masse the yere of the regne of Kyng Edward the iiijthe the viij yere by a whole yere, takyng for his labur xiij. s. iiij. d., and a goune cloth : and therof he hath receyved in price of half a bote lether vij. d., also of my wyff iiij. d. ; also in price of a peyre hosyn, ix. d. ; also for a peyre shon vj. d. ; also in money, j. d. ; also to pay for cloutyng of his shon j d. ; for offering, j d. ; to bie wyth a peyre shon, vj. d. ; to bye wyth a bowe xij. d. ; also payed to Welyam Onyat for a peyre hosen, ix. d. ; also to Richard Taylour for makyng of his doubelett, vj. d. ; Item for a peyre of shon at Weteringes opon seynt Laurence eve, vj. d. ; Item, for an apron bought at Wycombe ij. d. ob. ; payed in money wen he went to Nettelbed viij. d. ; also to paye fore his hosyn at Rysburgh xvij. d. ; Item to make his botes viij. d. ; Item to John James for mendyng of his doubelett j d. ob. ; to bye wyth arowe hedes ij. d. ; for drinkyng money geve by our parson, ij. d. ; Item payed to hymself to bye wyth a peyre shon viij. d. ; and payed for lether ij. d. ; Item at his departyng ij. s. Et ultra nunc [1] debetur T. Pratt xvj. d. et pro servicio suo a festo Michaelis usque festum.

Another account is with Jobane Laurence who served for a year from St. Martin's Day, 1468, for 10s. and "a goune cloth". She had in money "for lynyng of her goune" 2s. 8d., and "to goe to Richard Tayler's weddyng iiij. d. " with some other small sums.

Other memoranda are of sale of stock, the last being : Delyverd to John Ive at Astwyke the Monday nexte aftyr Seynte Barnabyes day the xij yere off the Reyne off Kyng Edward the iiij[th] xlix olde shepe and xxij lambys.

94. RICHARD QUATERMAYNS TO THOMAS STONOR AND HUMPHREY FORSTER

[? 1467 or 1468]

In the absence of any clue to the commission referred to, and of any certainty as to the feast intended by St. Thomas Day, it is difficult to fix the

---

[1] *The reading is doubtful, perhaps* ultimo.

date of this letter. But Richard Croft, Stonor and Forster were not on the commission of peace for Oxfordshire or the town of Oxford in the reign of Henry VI. Quatermayns, William Marmyon and Croft appear on a special commission in the county in 1463 (*C.P.R.*, Edw. IV, i, 278), but I have not found any commission relating to the town. Since Stonor was not sheriff, 1465-66 is impossible. If St. Thomas Day means 7 July (Translation of St. Thomas the Martyr) the year is probably 1467, when 7 July was a Tuesday ; if it means 21 Dec. (St. Thomas the Apostle) the year is probably 1468, when 21 Dec. was on a Wednesday. There were sessions of Parliament in June, 1467, and in May, 1468. The subsidy voted on the latter occasion was being collected in Nov.-Dec. following (*Rot. Parl.*, vi, 233). From *A.C.*, xlvi, 66.

Worshipfull Sirs, with all recommendacion due hadde, wille ye wete that it is so that I was at Oxonford as uppon Fryday next byfore seint Thomas day for diverse maters by the Kynges commaundement for the seid Towne of Oxonford: and at my commyng thethyr ther was the Shiriffe and also William Marmyon : and ther the Shireff shewyd ij comyssions of this graunt as well of the lordes as of the comyns, with certeyn ynstruccions conteynyng ij papyr leves. And whan the seid Shiryff hadde shewyd the seid commissions and the ynstruccions to William Marmyon and to me, he wolde not resseyve them ayen, but willyd and desyred that William Marmyon and I shuld send and write on to yow on the Kynges behalf that all the commissioners yn the commissions expressid shuld assemble and mete togeders at Oxonford as uppon Monday next, for to take a dyrection what is to be done yn the premisses, at whiche day Richard Croft, Thomas Croft, William Marmyon to be ther the same Monday. And they prayd and desyred me to write unto yow to attende ther the same day, and I graunt them that I so wold doo : that moveth me to write to yow at this tyme, prayng you that ye write to me of youre commynge, yea or nay, that I may sende them worde &c. Writyn yn hast uppon Satirday next, befor the seid seint Thomas day.

Your Cosyn and Unkle Rich. Quat'.

To my right trusty and well-beloved Cosyns, Thomas Stoner and Humfrey Forster, and to everych of them first seyng this letter, be this delivered in hast.

95. A WEAVER'S BILL FOR CLOTH TO MISTRESS STONOR

21 Dec., 1468

From *Ch. Misc.*, 37, iii, 25.

Item to my Mastres Stonor xvj erdys of brode clothe, wyte, ij. d.
Item also vj erdys of fyne clothe, j. d. ob.
Item also xvj. erdys of roset of fyne brode, ij. d. ob.
Item also vij. erdys of kersey þat was made of þe same roset, j. d.
Item also xiiij erdys of cors roset brode, ij. d.
Item also xij. erdys of fyne   re blew, v. d.
Item also xij ellis of roset kersey, j. d.
Summe xvij. s. x. d.[1]

Althyng rekekynnyd betwene Willm. Demnyst wever of Watlyngton for wevyng of all maner clothe, [sa]vyng a white pece the wyche is at fuller.   And this rekenygge unto Seynt Thomas nexte afore crystemas in the viiij yere of Kyng Edward the iiij[th] payyd.

96. ACCOUNTS AT HORTON

October, 1468, to July, 1469

Household accounts, apparently kept by a son or son-in-law of Alice Drayton (cf. the reference to "my brother Mull"). The date is from Alice Drayton's death on 1 Oct., 1468, to Ascension Day, 1469—11 May, with a supplementary account to 5 July. Thomas Stonor was at Horton from 17 to 24 June. The account is on two sheets of paper stitched together. *Ch. Misc.*, 37, iii, 26, 27.

(1) *A long slip : items include :* for the showyng of xij oxyne, v. s. ; for a peyre of plcwellys xiiij. d. ; for a servys of Trenchers, iiij. d. ; for ij salte, xiiij. d. ; for ij dossyne of candelle, xv. d. ; for fflessche (*several entries,* 18s. 7d. *in all*) ; for ij pygkys, viij. d.   Total, iiij. li. ij. s. j. d.

(2) *Items include :* a shert for Richard, viij. d. ; to peyre of shone,

---

[1] The total does not agree with the particulars ; possibly an item has been lost at the beginning.

xij. d. ; for half a foote of cloutyng ledyr, iiij. d. ; a playys, iij. d. ; saltefyhs, and saltesamon, vij. d. ; iij quart. of resyn, x. s. ; for the shepherd v. s. ; for a carpenteris wagis for makyng of a cort a plovis, for v dayys and a di.. xxij. d. ; to Raulyn Clerke for the eryng of xij akyrs londe in lityll Derrabut fyld, xij. s. iiij. d. Receyved of my Mayster at iij tymes, iij. li. xv. s. ; at a nothyr tyme at London, ix. s. ; Receyvyd of the korne mill for terme of the Annunciacion of oure lady xxxvj. s. viij. d. ; of my Brother Mull, iij. li. vj. s. viij. d. ; of Barrey, iij. li. ; of the Couper, vj. s. ; of marke silver, v. s. x. d. Summa of the Receyte viij. li. xiij. s. vj. d.[1]

" This Rekenyng is from the dethe of my modyr unto the Assencion day next folovyng by this bylle and a nothyr of the clerkys hande in a longe bill.[2] Summa x. li. xiij. s. vij. d.

In dorso. Expenses for five weeks " after Assencion day, in catis " (*total* 10s. 8d.) ; the vj^e weke while my mayster was there (*total,* 6s. 5d.) ; the vij^{the} weke (*total* 8s. 5d.) ; for midsummyr Candyll, iij. d. ; for wedyng in the whete, iij. s. j. d. ; unto Richard mason for crosenpynnyng in the hey bern, xij. d. ; *with other items.* Summa xlix. s. ij. d.

Hereof received. (*Rents, etc., and payments from* my mayster, *the last being* 20s. the Wednesday afore Seynt Thomas day.) Summa, iij. li. xv. s. vj. d.

97. THOMAS STONOR TO WILLIAM STONOR

[1468 or 1469]

Since the Archbishop of York must be George Neville, who was in prison from April, 1472, till late in 1475, the date of this letter cannot be later than 1471. In 1471 St. Peter's Day was on a Saturday, and in 1470 on a Friday ; therefore neither of those years are probable. As the letter is written to William Stonor the date is not likely to be earlier than 1468 or 1469. Thomas Stonor is styled " one of the servants of George, Archbishop of York " in No. 82. From *A.C.*, xlvi, 123.

Willm. Stonore, I sende yow Goddes blessyng and myne. And I wulle that ye bespeke for a gentylman of my lord Archebyhsshopis of York a doseyn Brode arovys of Kyng, ffletcher : let them be wele fedyrd

---

[1] Apparently some item has been omitted.
[2] Clearly the first slip attached hereto.

with Styffew and short fedyr, and let the shaftys be no bygger than Edmond sletyth ; let hem be longer.   And let not hit be wete tymbyr in hond.   I must have these redy in hast, and that hit be not ffaylyd as my trust is in yow.   I can no more, but the blessyd trynite kepe yow.   I-wrytyn at London the ffryday aftyr seint Petyr is day.

By your ffadyr Stonor.

To Willm. Stonor.

98. H—— S—— TO THOMAS STONOR

[c. 1469]

The writer of this and the next letter was the husband of one of Thomas Stonor's sisters, and had property at Stockbridge, Hants ; but I cannot discover his name.   The reference to William Bourchier, Lord Fitzwarren (d. 1471) and to his brother, the Earl of Essex, indicates that the date was between 1462 and 1470.   This letter is at least eleven months earlier than No. 99 ; but the two letters are most conveniently put together.   From A.C., xlvi, 71.

Right worshipfull brother, I recomaunde me to you : ffor as much as I understonde by my lorde ffitz Wareyn þat he bathe diverse thynges to doo with you for certein matiers touchyng bothe his worship and profite, wher in ye maye greatly please and also put you in suerte to have in tyme to come, if you neded, right good lordship as well of my lorde of Essex, to whom I am moste bounde, as of other my lordes his brethern : for trouth my lorde of Essex, and he also, specyally desired me to write to you. thynkyng þat ye shulde be þe better willed for my sake, the which I wyll veryly trust ye will doo.   Also I understonde þat þe title of Jobury is by his owne Counsell wayved and taken for nought. My wife, your suster, recomandeth hir to you as to hire unkynde brother, for þat ye wer so longe in toune and wulde not see heer.   No mor to you nowe, but Jhesu kepe you.   Wreten at London þe xj day of Marche.

H. S.

To my worshipfull brother, Thomas Stonor, esquyer, be this letter delivered.

99. H—— S—— TO THOMAS STONOR

[*c.* 1469]

As to the writer see note on the previous letter. Since Thomas Stonor's mother is dead, the date cannot be earlier than 1469. From *A.C.*, xlvi, 72.

My Ryht worschypfull broþer, as hertely as I can I recomawnde me wnto ȝow. Brothyr, I conseyve by ȝowr wryttyng that my wyffe, ȝowr suster that wasse, hose sowle I beseche Jhesu have mersy apon, scholde have astate of the maner of Porterys in Stockbryg to ȝow. Brothyr, I wose nevyr prevy that sche havy sowche astate, yff so be that I had not gevyt nor sche hyt, withowte I hade done aȝenste my ffadyr ys wyll, the wyche I purpose with the myht of Gode nevyr to do. Brothyr, thow I do make my wyffe þe joyntur of my taylend I dyseryte nat my heyres : wer ffor yn my reson I offend nat. Brothyr, consideryng the seyd premyssys I woll hertely pray ȝow to onsele hyt ; and yff so be that ȝowr conscyense do groge ther at, that ȝe wod do make astate wnto me, my brothyr Clopton, John Grene, and Tomas Hyhcham, gentylmen. Syr, I thynke nat dyseryt hym of one fote of land. ȝe be remembryd that I bound yn xx (?) markes to make ȝowr suster, my wyffe, soer of xl. li. joyntur after my dyscese, the wych oblygacyon I hade of ȝowr modyr, hosse sowle Gode have mersy, the wyche evyr have ȝow yn hys cepyng. I-wrytyn the vj day of Febyrer.

ȝour brothyr H. S.

To my most Worschypffull brothyr Tomas Stonor.

100. THOMAS MULL TO THOMAS STONOR

[1469]

The reference to "my moder and your" shows that this was written to Thomas Stonor. Mull had presumably married a daughter of Alice Drayton by her second husband. The date is probably some time early in 1469, or at all events within a year of Alice Drayton's death ; it is clearly earlier than that of No. 111. "Rayne of Devonshire" is perhaps the lawyer Reyny, who was an arbitrator in the suit of Stonor *v.* Fortescue, see No. 79. From *A.C.*, xlvi, 106.

Right worshipfull Master and Brother, I recommaund me unto you: prayng you to conceyve that or Robert Barre come I had borowed iij. li. to content and paye Rayne of Devonshir for your offis upon the *diem clausit extremum* after the dethe of my good Mastres and Moder and your, whos sowle God assoyle, which I have payd hym.   And syr, I conceyve by Robert ye wold I shold make up the offis accordyng to suche instruccion as ye sent by hym to my cosyn Willyam in a bille, which I dar not take uppon me, for I conceyve it not a right: wherefor I pray you to come your self and to bryng with you the cope of all thos dedes: or ell, and ye be not disposid to come here this terme, send us a pleyn cope of al your dedes made seth the dethe of your ffader with a more playne instruccion, and ye shall have my service: and I woll call to me sum good master or felowe: and I will geve him for his labor, and spede your mater as well as we can.   And as for the mater of my lord of Caunterbury, thowgh ye come not this terme, I truste to God to kepe me from al hurtes in that behalf.   And syr, as for this mone whiche ye have sente me, before God I have leyd oute for you therof, which I borowed, ij. li.: and so with me abydeth therof no more but xl. s.: and I shold have resceyvid of you at this tyme x. li. and v. nobles, which I must paye and dispose or Wennesday nexte cummyng, or ellys I must be untrewe to God and to them that be dede, and fals of my promys, which God defend me fro.   Wherfor I praye and beseche you, as my servis may and shalbe redy to you at al tymes, that I may have my mone her uppon Tewesday nexte commyng: and I shal be redy to your plesyr with Goddes grace, which preserve you and yours.

T. M^{ll} (Mull).

To my master Stonor.

101. ACCOUNTS OF JOHN FORDE OR FORTHE, BAILIFF AT HORTON KIRBY

1469-71

There are eight papers of accounts rendered to Thomas Stonor between 20 October, 1469, and 19 October, 1471, besides two undated accounts. The greater part of the fourth account is given below, together with extracts from four other accounts. The three last accounts are for 14 April to 4 May,

15 August to 29 Sept., and 29 Sept. to 19 October, 1471.   For later references to John Ford as farmer at Horton in 1472 and 1482, see Nos. 124⁻ and 322.   The originals are *Ch. Misc.*, 37, iii, 28-33 and 37-43.

(*a*) In expensis et costis don be John Forthe, servaunt with my mayster Stoner fro the ffriday next after Sent Edward day, the ix^the 3ere of Kyng Edward the iiij^the.

First in flessh and ffissh bought the next weke folwyng, ij. s. ij. d. (*Eleven other weeks*.)   Summa xxv. s. xj. d.

Item, paid for a peyre of plough wheles ıj. s. ıııj. d.   Item, paid to my lord of Cauntterbury baly for quiet rent goyng oute of the maner of Horton, ij. s.   Item, paid to the Castell of Eynesforth for Kyrkebys, ij. s.   Item, paid to Baker, smyth, for iren work and shoyng, xx. s.   Item, for shoyng of xj oxen, iiij. s. vij. d.   Item, paid to a thetcher thetchyng on the berne be xiij dayes takyng a day iij. d., iij. s. iij. d.   Item, for a man to serve hem vij daies, xiiij. d.   Summa, xxxv. s. iiij. d.

Other payments : for men to plough, for candles (15*d. the dozen*), "a potell of tarre iiij. d., for fettyng of Aunsell horse fro London, viij d." &c.   *Total* 39s. 9d.

Whereof receyved of John Lyndesey for ferme of the corne mylle for Mich. terme, xxxvj. s. viiij d.   Item., rec. of the seid John fore Cristemas terme, xxxiij. s. iiij. d.   Item., rec. of the fermour of the ffullyng mylle, iiij. s. iiij. d.   Item of John Stonestrete, xj. d. ob.   Item., of William Custamice, v. s.   Item, of Thomas Wylshire, vij. s.   Item., of John Miller of Pynden, ij. s. vj. d.   Item, of William Alfold, ij. s. iiij. d.   Summa, iiij. li. xij. s. ob.

(*b*) [1470.   13th Jan. to 2nd March.]   *A similar account.*   For flesh, fish "and other acatys," 20s.   *Various other items :* "ij dogges of Iren for the corne mylle," 16*d.* ; "for C and vj li. of Iren, iiij. s. v. d, for the wharfage, j. d., for bringyng of the seid stuffe to Derteford, vj. d. "; "for ij bottys of Sak clothe," 11*s.*   *Total*, £5. 2ᵗ5.   "Whereof I receyved of my Maister whan he was last at Horton, l. s.   Item, re. of hym at London, xl. s.   Item, re. for vj Stone of Wulle, x. s.   Item., re. of William Lyndesey for rent of Gillez, xxiiij. s. iiij. d. ".   *Further account of expenses for repairs and labour, total,* £5. 8. 2½, *with receipts* £6. 16. 0.

(*c*) [1470.   20th May to 9th June.]   *Similar account : payments,* 16*s.* 11*d.*   *Other payments* " to the sexteyne of the churche for Michelmas quarter, iij d. ; to the clerke for his wagis of Crystmas and Ester termys, ij. s. "; "for sheryng of xij^xx ix shepe xxij. d. and of viij^xx lambis

THE STONOR LETTERS AND PAPERS

and viij, vj d. ob." *Total*, 9s. 8d. *Total receipts*, 23s. 7d. "Remembyrd on Wytsun Eve in the x^the yere of Kyng Edward the iiij^the, althyng rekynnyd as hit aperyth by viij billys bothe of the charge and receyte betwene Thomas Stonore and John Forde, the seyde Thomas ovyth to the seyde John xvij. s. iij. d. And the seyde Thomas payde to the seyde John forthewith the seyde xvij. s. iij. d. the seyde day and yer."

(*d*) [1470. 7th July to 14th Dec.] *Similar account. Begins with expenses for seven weeks from* 7th July (£5. 10. 5); and *eight weeks from the* "fest of Sent. Barth, the xth ʒere of Kyng Edward the iiij^the " *The reckoning was made* "the ffriday afore the Imbryng dayys afore Crystemas in the xlix^te yere of Kyng Harry the vj^te."

(*e*) [1470. 15th Dec. to 22nd Feb., 1471.] *Similar account.* "A peyre of shoyn for Maister Edmund, vj. d."

102. R. RESTWOLD TO THOMAS STONOR

[1470 or earlier]

Richard Restwold of Lee and Sonning, Berks, who died in 1475 (*Cal. Inq. p.m.*, iv, 369), had a long association with the Stonor family. The letter may perhaps imply that Stonor had been present in the Parliament; the second Thomas Stonor was M.P. for Oxfordshire in 1447 and 1449, but the reference to his wife makes the first of these years unlikely; it may, however, belong to 1449. There are, however, no Returns of Members of Parliament for 1455, 1461, 1463 and 1470, and Stonor may have sat in one of these Parliaments. But Richard Restwold was a party to the deed of 1 Dec., 1432—No. 56—and the letter may have been addressed to the first Thomas Stonor, who sat in the Parliaments of 1429 and 1431. From *A.C.*, xlvi, 68.

Right worshipfull and reuerent Cosyn, I commaunde to you and I thank you hertyly for your writyng and your tythyngs and for the Actes of the Parlement. And yf ther be eny thyng I may do for you, hit schall be redy with all my hert. As for tythynges I have none, but I pray you to yef credence to K. the brynger of this: and God have you in blessid kepyng. Wretyn in hast at Lee. I pray you commaunde me to my Cosyn your wyffe &c.

R. Restwold, Esquier.

To my right worshipfull Cosyn, Thomas Stonore, Esquiere.

103. THOMAS PRATT TO THOMAS STONOR

[*c.* 1470]

The date is uncertain. No. 105 is not later than 1473. It is convenient to place this and the next two documents together. The writer is probably the Thomas Prat of Henley mentioned in No. 272. From *A.C.*, xlvi, 64.

Ryʒt reverent and wurchypfull master, I have ben with Richard Golborne and he may nat helpe me of xx. s., þat ye wrote to hym for, wherefor I beseche ʒow as my trust ys unto ʒowr gode máysterchep that ʒe wull sende me xx. s. be my sone, for and ye helpe me nat now I can nat ryde to þe feyr, and then I have loste vj. s. viij. d., þat I have leyde yn ernyste off a geldyng. Wherfore yf hyt plese ʒow that ʒe will ʒeve me leave, I wull make money off my oxyn to kepe with my promys. No mor to ʒow at þys tyme, but God have ʒow yn his kepyng, Amen. Be ʒowr awne bedeman and servant,

Thomas Pratt.

To my Ryʒt wurchipfull Master, Thomas Stonor, thys lre. be delyvered.

104. AN ACCOUNT FOR THOMAS STONOR

[*c.* 1470]

For Golborne and Pratt see No. 103. From *Ch. Misc.*, 37, iv, 5.

Be it remembyrde that Richerd Golborne delyverd to my master Stonor at Thomas Prattes in the presens of Richerd Balaam and Tho. Pratt, vj. s. viij. d. It., delyverd to John Bucher be the commandment off my seyde mayster ffor freche watyr ffysche for my lorde off Lyncolne, llj. s. vllj. d. It., delyverd to my seyde master at Nettylbede in the presens off Sawnder Blakhall and other moo, llj. s. llj. d. It., payed when my seyde master and mastresse went to Cawyrsame for drynkyng at watter syde, iij. d.

Summa istius bille xiij. s. xj. d.

105. THOMAS PRATT TO THOMAS STONOR

[c. 1470]

Some indication of the date is given by the reference to William Marmyon, who probably died about the end of 1473, see No. 135. Pratt may possibly have been employed at Stonor and wrote this letter thence. But there is nothing to show what "town" or "court" he refers to. From *A.C.*, xlvi, 65.

Jhesus.

Ry3t reverent and moste wurchypffull Master, I recommend me unto 3ow, desyryng to here of 3owr welfare. My Mastres, yowr wyffe, recommend her to 3ow, and sche faryth well and all 3owr howsolde, blyssyd be God. Furthermore, I have spokyn with my Master Wyllyam Marmyun, and he hath spokyn with the Warden and with John Denyun, and as for the nexte corte they bathe founde a wey þat ther schull no thyng be do, yn so myche as ye be absent, and therffor ye schull nat dowt as for the nexte corte, and my master wyll enduse them whan that they come that they schull put all maner of maturs uppon xij wurchypfull men of the same towne. And my Mastres hath sent yow yowr iij botelles be the brynger of thys letter. No more to 3ow at thys tyme, but God have 3ow, body and sowle, yn hys kepyng, Amen.

Be 3our servant and the Bedeman
Thomas Pratt.

To my Ry3ht reverent Master, Thomas Stonor,
thys lre. be delyvered yn hast.

106. JANE STONOR TO [THOMAS] STONOR

[c. 1470]

In spite of the address this would seem to be written by Jane Stonor to her husband. Lord Morley was William Lovell (uncle of Francis, Viscount Lovell) who married Alianore Morley before 1466, and was summoned to Parliament in her right from 10 August, 1469, to 15 October, 1471. The reference to "the chelder" would suggest a rather earlier date than 1470, and William Lovell probably used the title from the time of his marriage; he is styled "Willelmus Lovell, dominus Morley" ap. *Placita de Banco*, Roll 820, m. 64, in Trinity Term, 1466. From *A.C.*, xlvi, 249.

Syr, I recommande me unto yow as lowly as I cane : pleseyt yow to wyte I have ressevyde a byle frome yow wherby I undyrstonde My lorde Morlay dissyrres to sugiorne with yow : what answere þat ye have ȝevyn hym I cannot undyrstond be your bylle : I soposse your mynid was apon sum odyr materys when þat ye wrotyt, bot and ye have not granttyde, I beseke yow to aschusyt and to contend your litylle abyddynge at home, and allso þe joberde of yowr chelder and of all your howys at your hasty goyng in to Devenscheyr : for and your abyddyng at home be no nodyrwyse þan yt ys, þat wolle be [non]e profete unto yow and bertes ese unto me : raythere breke up housallde þan take sugiornantes, for servantes be not so delygent as þei were wonto bee. Now farewelle, goode syr, and Gode ȝeve yow goode nyghte and brynge yow welle home and in schorte tyme. Wrytyn at Stonor apon Sante Symon and Judes daye at eve.

Be your awne Jayn Stonor.

[*In dorso*] Ples yt yow to be remembyrde apon genciayn, ruberbe, bays, cappys, pouttys, cheverellaseys, a nounce of flayt selke, lasses, tryacyl.

To my brodyr Stonor in hast, at þe Swerde in Fletestrete.

107. OLIVER WITTONSTALL TO THOMAS STONOR

[*before* 1470]

This is clearly a little earlier than the next letter. The draft Award—No. 109—shows that the matter in dispute related to the estate of Wittonstall's stepson, John Cottesmore, who was a ward of Thomas Stonor, and married one of his guardian's daughters, probably in 1470—see Nos. 110 and 137. The date of this and the next two documents may possibly be a few years earlier, but it is convenient to place them immediately before No. 110. From *A.C.*, xlvi, 83.

Ryght worshypfull syr, y recomaunde me unto, thankyng you for the good scher that y hadd with you ever at suche tyme that y was with you. Please you to remembre the pointement by you and me, that ys to sey we scholde me to g[eder] at Henley the first Thorsday in clene lenton, or that y schold sende you worde. Y have comynet with my wyfe, and sche sayes with good wel, so that her brother Barantyne be on of thame with Mayster Rede, and sche to be ther at the awarde whene it is yoven: and at Ester sche and y schull be with and not fayle in no wyse. Forthermore, take credens to the berer hereof: and God preserve you worship, whom [do he ha] [1] you in hys kepyng.

By your own Olyuer Wittonstall.

To the ryght worschipfull Thomas Stonor, be thys letter delyved.

108. OLIVER WITTONSTALL TO THOMAS STONOR

[*before* 1470]

See the note on the previous letter. From *A.C.*, xlvi, 84.

Ryght reverent and worshypful Syr, y recomaund me unto you: and for as [mych] as ye desire to know how y wilbe desposet as tochyng your land for titil thereof, for certen my wyf and y welbe with you uppon Ester to see yf ye and we cane agre within our self: and we, and yf we can not agre, desyre your frendes and oures to see a dereccyon betwene you and us: yf thay can not fynde the menes theryn, thene ye and we in Pach. terme to take our evidens with us to London, and by the avyce of a juge take a lerned man or ij endyfferrently, and to abyde the rule of thaym in all suche thyngges as we schewe and declare. Yf yt please you it be soo, and thys y promyte you schalbe performet on oure behalfe; and affor any rent taken or to be taken; yf it be youre ryght ye schalbe truly content, for y halde it be necessare that we be wel avyset how we dele theryn. Wryten yn London the ij Monday of clene.

By your own Olyuer Wittonstall.

To the ryght reverent worshypful Thomas Stoner, be thys bill delyveret at Stoner in Oxforshyre.

---

[1] These three words are only faintly legible, and so are bracketed.

109. STONOR v. WITTONSTALL

[*before* 1470]

From *Ch. Misc.*, 37, iii, 18. A draft only, without date.

ABSTRACT. Draft of the award made by Sir Edmond Rede on
"dyvers contravercyes and variaunces . . . had and moved betwen
Thomas Stonor of Stonor in the Counte of Oxon, esquyer, garden . .
of all the manors, landes, and tenementes of John Cotesmore, son and
heyre of John Cotesmore, duryng the nounage of the seid John Cotesmore on the oon party, and Olyver Whitonstall and Margaret, his wyff,
late the wyff of John Cotesmore, the fader of the seid John, on the
other parte," touching the possession and profits of all the manors etc.
of the said John Cotesmore in the Isle of Wight, and in the counties of
Oxford, Berks, and Bucks. First: "the same Olyver and Margaret
shall have and pesibely possede and resceyve all the issues, profites,
and revenues of the Manor of Dourton in the Counte Buks" and 4*l.*
yearly rent from Holcome, Oxon, during the nonage of John Cotesmore.
Thomas Stonor is to let to farm to them all manors etc. in the Isle of
Wight during the nonage of John Cotesmore; they paying to Stonor,
or his executors, 38*l.* 13*s.* 4*d.* Stonor is to have the issues of all other
lands, the Manor of Mylton, Oxfordshire, excepted.

110. SIR RICHARD HARCOURT TO THOMAS STONOR

1 FEB. [? 1470] .

The chief subject of this letter was clearly the marriage of Thomas
Stonor's ward, John Cottesmore, to one of his daughters—probably Joan—
see Nos. 128 and·136. I cannot explain why Harcourt addresses Stonor as
"my ffadyr". The letter would naturally imply that Harcourt was married
to a daughter of Thomas Stonor, and that a son or daughter of his by a
former wife was going to marry a daughter or son of Thomas Stonor. But
Richard Harcourt is said to have married (1) Edith, daughter of Thomas
Sencler or St. Clere, by whom he had a son Christopher and a daughter
Anne ; (2) Eleanor, daughter of Sir Roger Lewknor, by whom he had a son
John, who married Margaret, daughter of William Bray ; and (3) Katherine,

daughter of Sir Thomas de la Pole, and widow of Sir Miles Stapleton, by whom he had a son William. Christopher Harcourt married Joan, younger daughter of Sir Miles and Katherine Stapleton. Anne Harcourt married Henry Fiennes, Lord Say. In his will Harcourt mentions two other daughters, Isabell, and Alice, wife of William Besillys. He mentions his two wives, Edith and Katherine, but there is no reference to Eleanor nor to her alleged son John. (See Collins' *Peerage*, iv, 436-7, ed. Brydges ; *Harcourt Papers*, i, 73-6 ; Blomefield, *History of Norfolk*, ix, 320-21 ; *P.C.C.*, 27 Logge.) It would be a simple solution to the difficulty if we could suppose that the Richard Harcourt of this letter was a different person to the well-known knight. But the writer of No. 145 was certainly Sir Richard Harcourt, and the signatures of both letters are in the same hand, and have paraphs of identical design. Moreover, Sir Richard Harcourt and Thomas Stonor were co-feoffees for Katherine Arundel (see No. 125). The pretended relationship must therefore remain a mystery. In his letter to William Stonor (No. 145) Harcourt signs himself as "your loving cosyn," but in this letter refers to "my brother William Stonor". If there had been a child-marriage between children of Harcourt and Stonor it would explain "my daughter and yours" ; but even of this there is no evidence, though if one of the parties had died young that would be not unnatural.

As to the date of the letter the reference to Harcourt's business about the King's matters would suggest 1467, when he was sheriff of Oxon and Berks. But since Sir Miles Stapleton only died in October, 1466, Harcourt is not very likely to have married his widow before 1 Feb., 1467. Moreover, the marriage of Cottesmore to Thomas Stonor's daughter was some time later than October, 1468—see No. 137. This letter is therefore probably not later than 1 Feb., 1470. Dame Katherine Harcourt was niece by marriage to Alice, Duchess of Suffolk, which makes the reference to "our own good lady" natural. This letter may just possibly be holograph ; but probably is signed only, like No. 145. From *A.C.*, xlvi, 57.

My Ryght worshepfull fadyr, I recumaund me to ȝow as hertely as I can : and it leke ȝow to wete, acordyng to ȝowr wrytyng I send Cottys-more to London to have his aray made ther after ȝowr desyer, a long goune of cremesyn clothe and a nothyr long goune of blew clothe : and I prey ȝow þat my servaunt may know wher þe clothe schal be bowth for my dowter and yours, þat Cottysmore may have of the same clothe, and a frend of myn schal pay þerfor tyl þat I come to London, as for hys part. And as for þe day of mariage I wold ryght fayne a be ther in goode feythe, and I myght an had leysyr : ffor ye know wele þe besy-nesse þat I have aboute þe Kynges maters atte þis tyme. Never þe lesse, ffader, I prey ȝow that ȝe wyl atte þe day of mariage to ley downe upon þe boke xl. s. and I schal content ȝow ageyne. And þat is I-now for a ȝong man, as me semeth &c. Morover, ffadyr, I prey yow þat ȝe wold be atte London, whan I am þer, for dyverse matters longyng to Cottysmore, and I pı ey ȝow þat þis wrytyng may recomaund me and my wyfe unto my modyr, ȝowr wyfe, and to my brothyr Wylleam Stonor &c. Forthermore, my wyfe send ȝow a ryng be my servaunt atte þis tyme for my dowter and ȝowrs to be weddyd þer with. And preyth God to graunt them bothe moche Joy togeder, and have ȝow and al ȝowris ever in hys most mercyful kepẏng. Wretyn in hast un Candelmesse Evyn. And, fader, I prey ȝow to recomaund my wyfe and me to owr owne good lady, my lady of Suffold: and we be ful glad þat we her sey be ȝow servaunt þat my seyd lady is in good hele, blessid be God.

Your sone Ric. Havrecourt.

To my ryght worshepfull fader, Thos. Stonor, Esquyer.

111. THOMAS MULL TO THOMAS STONOR

[1470?]

The date is probably early in 1470, since it was more than a year after the deaths of Richard and Alice Drayton, and Christmas was past. The goblets, etc., appear to have been valued at £6 16s. 8d., and were presumably family plate purchased by Stonor from Mull. From A.C., xlvi, 60.

Right worshipfull Master and Brother, I recommaund me unto you: and wher it lykid you to send me iij li. by Robert Barre, sendyng me by your letter word that yt was for no duete of my ffader, yf it lyke you to call to remembraunce, ther was by you due for my ffader ys dette, whos sowle God assoyle, at Alhalowyntyde x. li., of which I have resceyvid by the bandes of Robert Barre, before thes iij li., vij li., and so nowe the full x. li. is content: and when ye wer in Kente and in my pore hows ye payed me x. li. for my wyfes duete, and ther lefte v nobles behynd.&c of her duete unpayed. Also, and ye be not ther with displesid, when ye bought in London the goblettes and flat pees coverid, with spones &c, that sume drewe to viiij li. x. s, wherof at Cristmes ye sente me by my Cosen Willyam x marcs, and so ther restyth behynd unpayed therof v nobbles iij s. iiij d. And as for the summez in your letter, parte of the smethes sume, a xxxiij s., I understand well: for xij moneth passid I had a bill therof of Balam after the moneth mynde of my ffader Drayton. As for the sum of the carpenter for the lok, I remembre well what sum of mone was by my mene assigned therto &c. I shall comyn with you, when I may mete nexte with you, which with Goddis [grace][1] shall not be long &c. And I trust to God that ye woll conceyve your self, that as for the carpenteris wages ther may by no reson be no mone due to hym therof, but yf it so wer that the mone to hym assigned wer not payed, for he had it in grete for that his labour, and a warrant made to Harre Dogett to pay yt. I wot well it woll come to your remembraunce &c. Notwithstandyng I ame as much behold to you for the iij li. nowe to me sente, as though ye had lente it or geve it me. For sumwhat I had endangerid me for the sowles past to God more than I had mone to. And as for shepe I bought of you at the xij month mynd vj shepe at the pris of xxij. d. a pes, which is in dute therfor to you xj. s. &c., Syr, I am yours as ferre as my pore power may strech : and as for your mater of inquisicion, I trust to God it be to your plesyr and profyte, but your Councell in no wyse wold not agre to have the said way found, after they conceyvid that it was over your ground for other mennes ease: for though of old ther wer a toll payable to you ther for, and long seth it was payed, yet and it wer found your Maner were charged for ever ther with : and as for your toll, never the nerrer for the fyndyng : and the right of your toll never the ferther fro you, though it be not founde &c. I sende by the berer herof the dede of lees to my Moder, and the cope of all your dedes, and the cope of the Inquisicion. And Jhesu preserve you to your plesyr.

Your Thomas Mull.

To my maister and Brother Stonor.

112. LETTERS OF PRIVY SEAL TO THOMAS STONOR

3 APRIL, 1470

From *A.C.*, xlvi, 42. Printed in *Archæologia*, xvi, 1-2.

By the King.
Edw.
Trusty and welebeloved We grete you wele ; Letting you wit þat our Traitours and Rebelles þe Duc of Clarence and Therl of Warrewik,

[1] grace, *om*. MS.

which daily labour þe weyes moyens at þeir power of our final destruc-
cion, and þe subversion of this owre Realme and þe comon wele of þe
same, been fledde westwardes : Whome we wol folowe and pursue with
our Ooste with al diligence possible, and let and represse þeir fals and
traiteroux purpose and entent with Goddes grace.   Wherfore we wol
and straitely charge you þat immediatly after þe sight of þies owre
lettres ye arredie you, with such a fellasship on horssebak in defensible
arraye as ye goodly can make, to come unto us wheresoever ye shal
undrestande þat we þen shalbee, to aide and assiste us to thentent
aforesaid, without failling as ye love and tendre the wele of us and of
owre said Realme, and uppon the feith and liegeaunce that ye owe unto
us.   Yoven undre owre Signet at owre Citie of Coventre, þe iij^{de} day of
Aprill.

To our trusty and welebeloved Thomas Stoner of Stoner.

113. WADEHILL TO THOMAS STONOR

17 JANUARY [1471 ?]

This letter from a servant of John de la Pole, Duke of Suffolk, was clearly
written after the birth of the Duke's eldest son, John, who was probably born
in 1464, and before the death of his mother, the Duchess Alice, in May, 1475.
The only intervening years in which 17th January fell on a Thursday were 1465
and 1471.   The former seems precluded by the mention of "the young
ladies," since Suffolk's daughters were probably younger children ; though
the fact that an adjourned Parliament met in 1465 on 21st January would
make this date otherwise suitable.   The date 1471 is difficult, since it
involves a reference to an otherwise unknown meeting of the Parliament of
the Lancastrian Restoration.   The Chancellor in both years was George
Neville, Archbishop of York, with whom the Stonors had friendly relations.
Suffolk, who was married to a sister of Edward IV., would naturally desire
to keep away from Court in 1471.   From *A.C.*, xlvi, 85.

Worshipfull and my right good maister, I recommende me to youre
good maistership : and like you wete þat my lord, and my lady his
Moder also, have commaunded me to wryte unto you þat þey bothe
hertily desire and prey you, yef ye may in eny wyse or your
goyng to London, ye wole take þe laboure as to come hider to speke

with my seid lord and lady for diverse grete matters and causes þat þey wolde speke unto you of. And yef ye may not come hider, þan þat ye wole find þe meane to my lord Chaunceler as to excuse my lord of his comyng not to London at þis time, like as my seid lord was wreten unto by a pryve seal whiche was delivered to him on Munday last passed at vj of þe clokke withynne night at Ewelme, which as your maystership knoweth well was right shorte warnyng, remembring þat þe more parte of my lordes servauntes were sente into Suffolk to þe houshold þere ayens Crystemasse, and þe remenaunt of his servauntes, þat were here awaytyng, your maystership knoweth well been forthe with my lady, my lordes wyf, into Suffolk to bringe her þider: ffor God knoweth she thought full lenge from þe yonge lorde and yonge ladies here childerne, þat been þere. And so my lord might not come at London himself at þis time to his worship, and his servauntes from him : flor I dare sey he hath here at þis day awayting uppon his lordship not a dosen persones. Nethelese with Goddes grace my seid lord purposeth and woll be and attend at þe Parlement as oþer lordes shall, ffor by þat time his seid servauntes þat be nowe absent woll be with my seid lord ayen here. Wreten in haste þis Thursday xvij day of Januare.

Youre servaunt Wadehill.

To my right worshipfull master, Thomas Stonor.

114. LETTERS OF ATTORNEY BY THOMAS STONOR THE YOUNGER AND SIBILL BREKNOK

2 APRIL, 1471

ABSTRACT. Letters of Attorney by Thomas Stonor of Stonor, the younger, esquire, and Sibill Breknok, daughter of David Breknok, son of John Breknok, appointing Thomas Wode to receive in their name from John Breknok, seisin of all the lands, tenements, rents, reversions and services in Hadnam, Bucks, called Pennys, which John Breknok lately had by grant and feoffment from William Chapman, in accordance with a charter granted to them by John Breknok. "Datum secundo die mensis Aprilis, anno ab inchoatione regni Henrici sexti quadragesimo nono et readempcionis sue regie potestatis anno primo." From *Ancient Deeds*, C. 1106. The seals are gone. In C. 5014 there is the draft of a bond by Thomas Stonor of Stonor the younger and

Thomas Stonor the elder, to Richard Quatermayns and Richard Fowler in 40*l*., for the protection of Quatermayns under a release made by him, on 8 April, 1472, to Thomas Stonor the elder to the use of Thomas Stonor the younger relating to "Penis lond in Hadnam".

115. HUMPHREY FORSTER TO THOMAS STONOR

[? 5 APRIL, 1471]

Sir William Norys had a pardon by word of mouth from the King on 8 April, 1471 (*Cal. Pat. Rolls*, Edward IV, ii, 241). This may possibly fix the date of the letter, as "this same Friday" will then be 5th April, which would suit well enough. Humphrey Forster of Harpsdon, Berks, married Alice, sister of Thomas Stonor. Pury is probably John Pury, squire, of Oxford and Berks, and Dalamar, Delamere of Aldermaston. From *A.C.*, xlvi, 48.

My goode kynde brother, I recommaunde me to yowe in my most [1] feythefull wyse: and lyketh yow to wete þat it pleased you to speke unto me for my ladies ferme of þe ho., þat Grey myght have it stille, yef he cowde entrete Fryghthe, þat I have made the graunt unto &c. My good brother, it is so þat þe seid Fryghthe hath be with me this same Friday and enformed me howe þat my nevewes Willm. Stonor and Emond came unto hym to his plowe and wold have entretid hym to have departe his graunte. And he seid he wold not. And þen my nevewe seid he shuld departe from it maugre his hede, and had unto þe pore man manasyng wordes, as he seythe. So þat þe pore man stode in grete fere. And my nevewe made hym ayenste his wille to take viij. s. My goode brother, this dealyng and demeanyng is not to my pore honestie; for, as I understond, Grey hath seid he wolle have it maugre my hede, which shall not be by my wille. My goode brother, in your wysdome reformeth this matter, trustyng to you þat Grey shalle not be supported to my rebuke &c. My goode brother, this same nyght passed Syr Willm. Norys laye at Walyngford to London ward to þe Kyng; and Dalamar and Pury ladde hym, and he shall have his grace. My goode brother, I sende yowe þe viij. s., þat my Nevewe made the pore man

---

[1] *In the original* my most *is repeated.*

take for fere.   I prey you latt þe pore man no more be so entretid.
Jhesu preserve you and alle yours.

Your trew brother Humfrey fforster.

To my goode kynde brother Thomas Stonore.

116. RICHARD QUATERMAYNS TO THOMAS STONOR

[? 12 APRIL, 1471]

There is no clear indication of the date.   Quatermayns had a lawsuit with
John Barantyne as to the manors of Chalgrove and Haseley, of which he was
feoffee under the will of Barantyne's father ; this was between 1467 and
1472 ; during the same time John Parys was parson of Haseley (*Early
Chancery Proceedings*, 31/440 and 39/246-8).   Barantyne also had a dispute
with Thomas Mylle or Mull as executor of Richard Drayton, with reference
to a bond in surety for an annuity on the manor of Churchill ; this was not
earlier than 1469 (*id.* 45/98)   This letter may belong to the same year as
No. 118 ; if so it may probably be dated in 1471, when Good Friday was
12th April.   From *A.C.*, xlvi, 67.

My right worshipfull Cosyn, with all dewe recommendacion had, I
wol ye wete that I have resseyvyd your letter send unto me by your
servaunt, berer herof : and, Cosyn, all the contenus of your writynge I
have wel understand, and where yn the seid contenu of your letter
that such promys and speche as hath be betwene yow and me att
dyverse tymes, that tho shuld be holdyn, Cosyn, I asserteyne yow that
such speche as hath be betwene yow and me I shall in my parte vary,
with the helpe of Jhesu, nether for cosyn Barentyne nether for parson
Parys, for they both shall not make me ayenst yow, and that ye shall
right wel knowe, for I truste to Jhesu that I have not be varyant of my
promys in tyme passyd : and they shall not make me brake it.   How-
beit, cosyn, the seid parson Parys was with me at Ricoote appon our
Lady evyn last past, and brought with hym grete writyng under the
Seal of the deane of the Arches under my lord of Caunterbury, mak-
ynge mension of Innybucions and other mucche maters, and of appar-
aunce in the seid Arches at such days as in his Innybucions it is
conteynyd.   And, cosyn, when he had shewyd me this, he willyd to
be aydyd by me.   I aunsweryng hym that I wold not in no wise, but I

chargyd hym to kepe the peas, and seid hym that I had conspromytted, and that I wold not breke with the helpe of Jhesu, whom kepe yow. Wretyn in hast half crasyd appon goode Fryday.

Your cosyn, Ric. Quat'.

To my right worshipfull Cosyn, Thomas Stoner, be this letter deliveryd.

117. FEES OF THOMAS STONOR

Sept. 1471

From *Ch. Misc.*, 37, iv, 6.

Th. Stonore, Ar., Michaelis Archangeli, A° xlix° Regis Henrici vj[ti]. Rec. per H. Dogett de maneriis subscriptis.

Sotwell. De Johanne Pope, collectore et firmario ibidem, de parte officii sui, iiij. li. De quibus in expensis iij d. Et rem. lxxix s. ix. d. Summa, lxxix. s. ix. d.

Retherfeld. De ten. in Rethirfeld Pippard, ut patet per bullam huic sedule annexam, viij. li. xiij. s. x. d. De quibus in expensis, xxij. d. Et rem. viij. li. xij. s. Summa, viij. li. xij. s.

Penyton. De firmario et collectore de Penyton et Shipton (lxvj. s. vilj. d.),[1] xij. li. x. s. viij. d. De quibus in expensis iiij. s. iiij. d. Et rem. xij. li. vj. s. iiij. d. Summa, xij. li. vj. s. iiij. d.

Hembury. De Johanne Bondy, collectore de Hembury, viij. li. viij. s. vj. d. De quibus in expensis, ij. s. v. d. Et rem. viij. li. vj. s. j. d. Summa, viij. li. vj. s. j. d.

Burton et Cundycote. De collectore et firmario de Burton et Cundycote, Cij. s. ob. De quibus in expensis unacum regard. collectoris, iij. s. vij. d. Et rem. iiij. li. xviij. s. v. d. ob. Summa, iiij. li. xviij. s. v. d ob.

Receptus forinsece. De feodo magistri Th. Stonore pro domina ducissa Suff., ultra vj. s. viij. d. de prima resolucione coll. redditus de Ewelme, ix. li. xiij. s. iiij. d. Summa ix. li. xiij. s. iiij. d.

Summa totalis, xlvij. li. xv. s. xj. d. ob. De quibus in denariis liberatis Roberto Oxslade pro frumento, vj. li. xiij. s. iiij. d. Et domine Isabell Saquevyle, x. li. Et magistro per manus Will. Thornhyll xxiij. li. Et in feodis &c. liij. s. iiij. d. Et rem. Cix. s. iij. d. ob.

[1] Written above the line; apparently the receipts for Shipton.

118. WILLIAM STONOR TO THOMAS STONOR

24 OCT. [? 1471]

There is no sure indication of the date, though it cannot be later than 1473, and in view of William Stonor's age is not likely to be earlier than 1470. This letter may belong to the same year as No. 116, which is probably not later than 1472. It cannot well belong to the same year as No. 106, at the date of which letter Thomas Stonor was himself in London ; but the date of No. 106 is itself uncertain. The date is perhaps rather more likely to be 1471 than 1472. From *A.C.*, xlvi, 77.

My ryght reverent and wurshypfull fadyr, I recomaund me unto yowur good fadyrhod, mekely besechyng of yowur dayly blessyng : plesyth yowur good fadyrhod to wytt that Barentyne complaynyd to my lord, and he bathe made many ontru surmysse, the wyche I kannot yt undyrstond them, but to morow I must be with my lord by vij a kloke at my answere : and Barentyne desyryd a wryte of ryat a pon te statud [1] ayen yowur ffadyrhod, and ayen me and the pryst : and my lord will do noyn delyver ayen yow, but only ayenste the pryst, the wyche wrytt ys owte all redy : where for I beseche yowur fadyrhode that the pryst may abbesente hym that he be not a-tachytt, and that sum odyr pryst may sey servys for a sesun. I am myche bounde to Molynerse, Nedam, Malyverer and many odyr jentelmen and be the tyme my lord bathe herde me I trust to good he wylle be my good lorde, ho have yow, my good modyr, and alle yowrs yn hys one fyfull kepeyng, Amen. I-writtyn yn Flete strete the xxiiij day of Octobur.

By yowur chyld Willm. Stonore.

To my ryght reverent and worshypful ffadyr, my fadyr Stonere, yn hast.

---

[1] Probably meaning a writ of " Testatum Capias " for execution by the sheriff.

119. E[DWARD] LANGFORD TO THOMAS STONOR

[? 1472]

The date must be not later than 1474. In 1474, 2nd February was on a Wednesday, and in 1473 on a Tuesday; so the year is probably not later than 1472. Edward Langford was on the Commission of Peace in Berkshire from 1471 to 1473 (*Cal. Pat. Rolls*, Edw. IV, ii, 608; cf. *id.* i, 492 and ii, 406). From *A.C.*, xlvi, 82.

Ryght worshipfull syr, I recommende me unto you, praying you that by this writyng I may be recommendid to my Maistres, your wyf. Syr, it ys so that Robert Goldriche, a tenaunt and an old servaunt of myn, bought, at Michaelmas was iij yere, of Watkyn Bolter ix quarters of barley, of William Surman vj quarters barley, and of Willm. Bowyer iiij quarters of barley; which shuld have byn delyveryd to þe seide Robert Goldriche at Bradfeld at þe puryficacion of our lady þat tyme next folowyng: and as yet they have non delyverid of the corn afore rehersyd. Howe be it they be boundyn by obligacion unto my saide servaunt in þe sum of x. li., þe whiche summe is forfet. Syr, I understond þe iij personys afore rehersyd byn your tenauntes: wherefore my servaunt neythir woolle ne dare take accion agaynst them unto þe tyme that he have leve of you. Syr, I pray you that it may pleas you to write or send to your tenauntes afore rehersid in suche wise that they delyver my servaunt his corn, which he hath bought and payd for; and ellys þat yf they so do not, ye wolle yf[1] my servaunt leve to take his accion. And all myghty Jhesu have you and all yourys in his blessud kepyng. Written þe Thursday next afore þe purificacion of our lady.

Your old ffellawe E. Langfford.

To the Ryght Worshipfull Thomas Stonor, Squyer.

120. [JANE STONOR (?) TO HER DAUGHTER]

c. 1472 (?)

It seems most likely that the writer of this letter is Jane Stonor, in which case the date is probably between 1470 and 1473, since her husband is alive ·

[1] *Sic:* meaning " yefe " (= give).

the Queen is then Elizabeth Woodville, and possibly the daughter is with the Duchess of Suffolk (see No. 172).   The end of the letter with the signature has been destroyed, and there s no endorsement.   From *A.C.*, xlvi, 244.

Welebylovyd doughter, I grete yow wele: and I understond ye wold have knowlech how ye shuld be demenyd.   Doughter, ye wot wele ye ar there as it plesyd þe quene to put yow, and what tyme þat ye cam fyrst fro myn: albeit myn husbonde and I wold have had . . . wherwith þe quene was ryght gretly displisyd with us both: hall be it we knowe ryght wele it cam nat of her selfe.   Also me thynk þay sshuld nat be so wery of yow, þat dyd so gret labour and diligence to have yow: and wher as ye thynk I sshuld be unkynde to yow, verrely þat am I nat, for and ye be as I left yow, as I trust verrely þat ye be, I am and wyll be to yow as a moder sshuld be, and if so be þay be wery of yow, ye sshall cum to me, and ye wille your selfe: so þat my housbond or I may have writyng fro þe quene with her awn hand, and ells he nor I neyther dar nor wyll take upon us to reseyve yow, seyng þe quenys displesyr afore: for myn housbond seyth he hath nat wyllyngly disobeyde her comaundment here afore, nor he wyll nat begynne nowe.   Also I understond .

No endorsement.

121. THOMAS MULL TO THOMAS STONOR

[MAY, 1472]

Margery, daughter of Sir Thomas Etchingham, married William, son of Walter Blount, Lord Mountjoy, who was killed at Barnet on 14 April, 1471. Margery subsequently married Sir John Elrington and died in 1481; she was buried at St. Leonard, Shoreditch (Stow, *Survey*, ii, 75).   Cicely, widow of Sir Thomas Kyriel, died on 19 April, 1472 (*Chancery Inq. p.m.*, Edward IV, file 42).   Since Lady Kyriel was lately dead, and since this letter was probably not much earlier than the next, the date must have been quite early in May, 1472.   Sir John Fogge was Treasurer of the Household to Edward IV.   From *A.C.*, xlvi, 62.

Right worshipfull Brother, I recommaund me unto you: lykith you to wete that my Cosen Willyam hath ben with a full goodly Gentil-woman, and comynde with her after love's lore: and for certein I knowe

that ych of them ys verely well content of other. Shee was late wyf
unto the son of my lorde Montjoy : and for the certente what my cosen
shall have with her, yf God provide for them that they shall go throwe
in mariage, suer yt is that of her ffader's enheritaunce she hath in possession C. marks of lande, and after the deth of her ffader shee shall
have over that the half of al the residue of al the lande of her ffader,
and of my lorde Mountjoyes lande shee hath iiij^{xx} marcs of annuite fe
by dede endentid, for wher the lande was in value C. marcs shee hath
layn it ayen to my seid lord for yelding her yerly iiij$_{xx}$ marcs.   Thes
certentees I have by my bedfelow Thomas Powtrell, which ys of councell
with my seid lorde, and was of councell at the mariage makyng, when
my seid mastres was maried to the son of my seid lord ; and as I
understond by my seid bedfelowe the hole value of syr Thomas Ichyng-
ham is londe, as it was at the tyme of the seid mariage makyng shewyd
in writyng, was betwen CCC. and CCCC. marcs, not fully CCCC. and
better then CCC., but how much it ys oute of the remembraunce of my
seid bedefelowe.   And for certeine shee is well named, and of worshipfull disposicion.   I have ben with my Cosen Willyam there, and seyn
my seid Mastres, and comynde with her.   And I fele by them both that
and ye woll, with mercy of our lorde the mater shall take gode ende.
I know verely my Cosen woll in no wise in this cas doo but as your good
ffaderhode woll he doo.   Wherfor in the name of God beth in this cas
and in al other good ffader to my Cosen in councelyng, helping, and
preferring after your hertes plesyr : for and I sholde mary I wolde he
sholde chese for me.   I wot well ye woll lyke my Mastres right well
when ye se her, and better when ye comyn with her.   Nowe ys al in
you ; in which and in al other God be your guyde.   Syr, as for the
manor of Clyf, I have comynd with Webley, þat is of my lorde Cobham
is councell : I hope the mater shall take goode ende by trete, of which
I shall have worde þis halidayes.   Notwithstanding þer is an attourne
recordid for syr John Fog and his felowes, in hap that we accorde not.
Jhesu preserve you and my gode Suster to your hertes plesyr.   Sir, as
it is seid, ther is of late fallyn to my Mastres ffader, syr Thomas Yching
ham, CCC. marcs more after the deth of my lady Kyriell.

T. Mull.

To my right worshipfull Brother, Thomas Stonor.

122. WILLIAM STONOR TO THOMAS STONOR

[? 14 MAY, 1472]

This seems to relate to the projected marriage with Margery Blount, who we know from No. 123 to have spent some time with William Stonor in London. From the previous letter it seems likely that this was written in 1472, and so we get the day 14th May. Barrey is no doubt the Robert Barre of No. 111. From *A.C.*, xlvi, 75.

My ryght reverent and wurshypfull good fadyr, I recomaund me unto youre good fadyrhod, mekely besechyng yow of yowre dayly blessyng, and my good modyr also : lykith yowre good fadyrhod to wytt that I truste weryly to alle myty Jhesu and to youre good fadyrhod that I shalle spede well of my mater, for I have comfortabul demenure of my mastresse, but as to the wery purpose, but yt I hope well : my good fadyr, Barrey shalle tel yow of the demenure, and what they be that laburyn to the jentylwoman. I beseche yow, fadyr, that Barrey may be with me here alle thys halydayys, for the jentyllwoman wyll not departe tyll the weke after Wytsuntyd, and ere that I trust to alle myty Jhesu to know more to my hertes ese than I do now, bom I beseche to preserve youre good fadyrhod and my good modyr, and have yow yn hys mersy-full kepyng, Amen. I-wrytyn I-Lundun, the Thursday next afore Whytsunday.

By yowre chyld Wyllm. Stonore.

Address undecipherable.

123. THOMAS MULL TO WILLIAM STONOR

[1472]

This letter seems to be preliminary to No. 124, and as probably some little time later than Nos. 121 and 122 may be referred to the latter part of 1472. From *A.C.*, xlvi, 105.

Cosen, I recommaunde me to you. And wher as I fele by your letter and wrytyng that my Mastres hath not that good wyll of you as sume tyme ye ought her, Syr, ye may owe her right good will, how be

yt that it be not in so herty wyse as ye dyde before.   But and I understode þat she had seyd to you þes wordes : "Syr, I wold not have you,
but yt so bee þat I may have C. li. or CC. marcs with you in joyntur" :
Syr, then it had ben a mater by which ye myght conceyve þat shee þen
had loved your londe better þen your self.   But I understond that ther
wer no such wordes, but I conceyve the wordes wer þees : "Syr, I may
have CCC. marcs in joyntur, and I to take þe lesse when I may have
þe more, my ffrendes wold þenke me not wyse &c. : and howe be yt,
your ffader wol not geve me, yet lette hym do well to you."   In which
wordes I understond noon utter nay.   But and ye in your mynde conceyve þat shee hath yoven you an utter nay, then shall ye by myn assent
never speke more of the mater, but lette yt goo : but yf it be so þat ye
your self brake the mater for þat shee seid, "I may have CCC. marcs
in joyntur," þen shee hath geven no cause in her parte of an utter
breche : for it ys not oon to sey, I may have wiþ a man CC. marcs, and
þes wordes, I woll not have you but it so be I may have CC. marcs in
joyntur wiþ you.   But for al thys resonyng I wold knowe þis of you :
and the case wer so þat shee wolde ben agreable to have you with xl.
li. or iiij^{xx} marcs joyntur, wolde your herte þen love as ye have doon
before þys seson ?   Þis question wolde I knowe of you, for and I knowe
your disposicion in this behalf, I trowe to God al þis love and mater of
love wolde be revyvyd ayen in short seson : ffor and it so be þat ye
brake þis mater for a lytyl hastynes of your self, þen wolde I not we left
so : but and shee wer þe cause of brech, þen woll I not stere ne avise
you after þis neþer to write nor sende to her.   But oon thyng I dar safly
sey in my conceyte, that shee on her parte sithe your departier hath
ben vexed and trowbelyd with þe þrowes of love more fervently in her
mynde þen ye have ben syth vexid wiþ her seyinges.   And þis my cause
so to sey and deme, I know oonys for certeyn shee loved you as a par-
fyte lover, and þat right late never better þen þe last seson þat shee was
in London.   Trewe it ys love oones parfytide, þough þer hap sum
daungerus speche or countenaunce, yet ys not þe hole ffyr of love
quenchyd, but when þat þe person, þat was moste daungerus in speche
or countenaunte, by her self allow : wher as shee may revolve at her
lyberte wiþoute controllyng every þyng þat longeth to loves daunce,
þough þe fflame of the ffyre of love may not breke oute so þat it may be
seyn, yet the hete of love in yt self is never þe les, but rather hootter in
yt self.   Wherfor I sey þis for certayne, I dare depose for her þat the
sharpe and unwar chaunges from thought to þought, and ofte remembrance of the trowbely wawes of love have so possid her to and fro in

her owne mynde, þat shee desyreth as sore after relief, as fer as shee may for shame, as þe man in the water desyreth to be releved frome drownyng in þe perill of þe see : but daunger and shame woll not suffir her to speke yt with oute it be so þat þer be sume newe mocyon made to her &c. : the menes wherof I have compassid in my mynde, which by þe mercy of Gode I woll attempte yf it so be ye kan be plesid þat way, and þat in shorte tyme. Syr, if I may, I woll be with you on Saturday or Sonday &c. I wot well ye remember what your ffader by his last letter assureþe you in joyntur : and syr, þat ys feyr : and as for oþer thynges touchyng your self, I shall enfourme you at our next metynge to your hertes plesyr, with the mercy of Jhesu, which preserve you.

Thomas Mull.

To William Stonor of Horton in Kent, be this letter delivered in haste.

124. THOMAS MULL TO THOMAS STONOR

[1472]

As the negotiations for the match with Mistress Blounte are still going on this letter probably belongs to 1472 : on the whole it seems to be later than No. 123, and to detail the "menes" which Mull had "compassid in his mynde". John Forde was farmer at Horton, see No. 101. From *A.C.*, xlvi, 63.

Right worshipfull Brother, I recomaund me to you. And in as muche as that my Cosen Willyam cumeth home to you hymself, therfore I wrytt not to you of the demyng &c., ne of the communicacion betwen my seid Cosen and my Mastres Blounte : but this direccion have I taken in the mater, I have thorowly comyned with the preste þat I spoke to you of, and tolde hym my conceyte howe he shal be demened in brekynge with my seid Mastres : and that he shall not breke to much at oones to her, but ever when he spekyth in the mater to her and fele here, and certenly to marke her wordes unto the tyme that he be verily assured in hymself, as nygh as he kan, of her disposicion. And over þat I have appoynted with hym that withyn iiij dayes after þat he is come to my seide mastres I shal send hym a letter directe to her fro me and in my name: and he hath promysid me that every letter þat I sende here shal be brekyn or he departe from her.   And the man þat shal ber the letter shal be namede, Cosen, to þe said prest, so þat he shal abide þer in the howse.   And, if it so be þe preste fele her veryly applyable, þe messenger shall [speke] with her hymself.   John Foorde shal do the message, and abide ther ij or iij dayes.   Furste I was disposid to have sente to þe [Norce] to have felte my seid Mastres: but me thought after, þat it had not bene beste, for paraventur the Norce wolde feer to breke fer wiþe her, and also shee myght not contynue and abide uppon the communicacion.   This preste may alwey have liberte and lesyr to speke with her.   And I have lefte with him a remembrance in writyng how I wol he shal do, wherein I am verily assured he wol do his parte &c.   Syr, as for my Cosen Willyam, for God is sake callyth hym forth with you when he is at home with you, and let him walke with you, and gevyth wordes of good comforte, and beth good ffader unto hym, as I certenly knowe ye be, and so letyth hym veryly understond and know.   For, Syr, he is disposid to be a musyr and a studyer, which remembreth and breketh that as much as ye may.   And Syr, but if þis mater sum dele come of her own hert, she shal not otherwyse be labored to for certen.   Also, yf it kan be, the preste promysith me that she shall sende me worde in writyng of her dysposicion, if her disposicion be to us warde: which letter I shall sende you and my seid Cosyn.   And veryly, if she be appliable, it is to be remembred her of her joyntur of the lorde Montjoy, and also of her own ffader, for he taketh the profite of a grete parte: and also in what case lorde Montjoy is land standeth it is good to be remembred to her.   And I beseche Jhesu spede and directe this mater to his plesyr, and to preserve you and yours &c.

Thomas Mull.

To my Right worshipfull Brother, Thomas Stonor.

125. DAME KATHERINE ARUNDELL TO THOMAS STONOR

27 JAN. [? 1473]

Katherine Arundell, daughter of Sir John Chiddiock, was wife of Sir John Arundell of Lanherne, Cornwall, and on his death married—after Feb., 1475

—Sir Roger Lewknor (*d.* 1478); she died on 9 April, 1479 (*Chancery Inq. p.m.*, Edward IV, file 71). Sir Richard Harcourt, Edward Grymston, and Thomas Stonor were feoffees of Lanherne, "Wynyenton," Kenell and other manors, to the use of John and Katherine Arundell and their heirs. After Stonor's death, and the death of Sir John Arundell, Katherine filed a petition in Chancery showing that Harcourt had refused to make an estate to her; "William Menwynnek de Lostwythyell, gentilman," was then one of her sureties (*Early Chancery Proceedings*, 66/140, P.R.O.). "Wynyanton" or Winnington is in the parish of Gunwalloe, and Kennall in the parish of Stithians; for deeds relating thereto, see *Ancient Deeds*, A. 10303, A. 10409. In 1481 Sir James Tyrell and Anne his wife brought an action against Sir Richard Harcourt for the manors of Nansladron, Carmynowe, Kenell and Wynyanton; Harcourt in his reply stated that Kenell and Wynyanton were held by Richard Tomyowe; Edward Grymston was then dead (*Placita de Banco*, Roll 876, m. 458). The date of this letter is of course later than 1465, when Harcourt was knighted, and cannot be later than 1474. Possibly it may belong to the same year as No. 127, in which case the year will be 1473. From *A.C.*, xlvi, 38.

Ryght trusty Cosyn, I comaunde me to you: and where as hit was agreed by you and my councell at your beyng at Dorchester byfore Crystmasse that Richard Tomyowe, consyderyng the gode service that he hath don for my husbonde and me in dayes passed and the charges that he must do for me here after, shulde be made sure of landes and tenementez to the yerely value of xx^ti marke. And he ys agreed to take too lytill Manours in Corunwall, one called Wynnyanton and the other called Kenell, of the value by the yere of xij. li.: of the whiche I pray you, Cosyn, to speke to my cosyn Syr Richard Harecourte and Edward Grymston that betweene you to sealle hym a dede that William Menwynnek other Richard Reynolds shall brynge you of the said Maners terme of his lyve: for he woll not procede no furder in my maters in to the tyme he be made sure of the same, whiche were to me a grete hurt, as ye understonde. And that this be done as my speciall trust is in you: and our lorde have you in his blessed kepyng. Wrytten at Excestre the xxvij^th day off Janyver.

By your Cosyn Dame Kateryne Arundell.

To my ryght worshipfull Cosyn, Thomas Stoner, Esquyer.

126. THOMAS MATHEW TO THOMAS STONOR

[? 1473]

This seems to be somewhat earlier in date than the next letter, so may be placed early in 1473. Thomas Mathew was bailiff at Ermington ; he certainly held that position some time between 1474 and 1476 (see No. 174), and is referred to as a former bailiff in 1480 (see No. 270). John Yeme was bailiff about 1466 (see No. 81). Orchard and John Gybbes were servants of Selenger (see No. 183, which apparently has to do with the conclusion of this dispute). For John Rytte, see No. 174. From *A.C.*, xlvi, 58.

My Ryght worschepful Mayster, y recomande me onto you : desyryng to here of youre prosperyte and gode hele, the whech y pray almyȝty God longe to contynue you theryn. Furthermore youre water of Erme ys y-stoppyd at Flutedamerel ɩby the offycers there that ther may no ffyssch com ɩup : wherfore the gentelmen that holdyth the water may not paye ther rente, and as thay havyth y-warnyd Water Frende. Wherapon y went to Willyam Fowel, as ȝe commandyt me, to wete what aunswer he had of Johne Gybbes : and he sayde, yff ȝe cowde schew youre tytel gode of olde tyme, as ȝe sayde to hym that ȝe haddé, yf he myȝt have understondyng therof by you or by youre councell that hyt myȝt be schewyd to Syr Phylyp Courtenay and to Orchard, that he wolde doo hys goode wyll theryn to fulfylle youre intent. Also y was wyth Mayster Courtenay, and tolde hym of the sam mater : and he sayde, that my lady wolde that ye scholde have youre ryȝt, yf ȝe cowde schew that hyt were youre tytel of olde tyme. Also y mevyd John Huchyn for the ward of N . . . yayn : and he aunsweryd me, yf ȝe myȝt reken eny part of the londe, he wolde entrete youre Maysterschep therfor. And y spake to Willyam Fowel of the sam mater : and he sayde, yf the londys were y-ffeffyd to that yntente to dissayve you, that hyt was collucyon and ȝe myȝt reken by the lawe. Also the parson of Bykebure hath y-chargyd hys tenents that they schol noȝt pay no ale wytys to me : and Johne Yeme toke a dystresse, whane he was Baylee, and put hyt yn warde, and the parson delyveryd the dystresse ayen, by what delyvere y can noȝt understaunde : wherfor y pray you that ȝe wol sende worde to youre councel how hyt schalbe demenyd. And as for the comyssyon, the commyssyoners havyth y-made a rule to sytte in every hundryd, and y tryst yn God by the rule of youre councel ȝe schalbe savyd harmeles, y

tryst yn God. Also John Ry3t promysyd me that he wolde bere thys
letter : y pray you that 3e sende wrytyng by hym after youre intent how
al materys schalbe doo by ycure avyce. No more, but the holy Trynyte
have you yn hys blessyd kepyng.

T. Mathu.

Thys letter be delyveryd unto Mayster Thomas Stonore in hast.

127. WILLIAM STONOR TO THOMAS STONOR

[? 20 APRIL, 1473]

The most probable year is 1473. In 1471 St. George's Day was on a
Thursday, so that year is out of the question. In April-May, 1472, William
Stonor seems to have been at Horton and in London (see Nos. 121 and 122);
in this letter he proposes to come home by Henbury. The letter has to do
with the dispute about the water of Erme, of which we hear first in the previous letter, and get the conclusion in No. 184. Selenger is probably
Thomas St. Leger, who was on the commission of peace for Devonshire. As
to Lady Arundell, see No. 125. From *A.C.*, xlvi, 74.

My ryght reverent and wurshypfull fadyr, I recomaund me unto your
good fadyrhod in the most umbylle wyse that I kan or may, mekely
besechyng your good fadyrhod of your dayly blessyng : lykyth your good
fadyrhod to wytt that I have spokyn with master Selenger for your dute
of your water sondage and sute of the Flete Damerell, and I am
answeryd that I shuld be at Holbyntun at the corte, the wyche shalle be
at holy rode tyde nexte comyng, and there to show evydens and recorde
by mouth how hyt hath byn usyd yn tymys past : and as after Selenger
seyyng in to my ladys counsell and hys that my lady wold not nother he
but that your tytyll shuld be krowyn and no maner of fraude by them
leyd to abatryt, and yff yt were tryyd with your fadyrhod so to be recorded and you to yn-joyye : and I found Gybbys welle disposyd to
your fadyrhod, but Orcherd and Columb made many resuns ayen the
water and eke ayen the sondage, the wold ye shuld have a wey to your
grounde, but they wold ye shuld nat cum and send that wey. And yt
lyke your fadyrhod I spoke to master Selenger acordyng to your comaundment for my brother Tomas mater, and enfourmyd hym hov they had

resseyvyd the rent, and hov your fadyrhod had don acordyng to hys desyre, and they entend nat : and he hath wrytyn unto the party to de-lyver the mon[ey] ayen : the wyche letter I send unto your fadyrhod that ytt myte be delyveryd unto the seyde party.   Master Selenger de-syryth your fadyrhod to forbere your sute ayen them thys terme, and that the trety go forth yff yt may be, or ellys your fadyrhod to take your a-wantage the nexte terme : but he ys dysplesyd sore with them for the reseyvyng of the money, and seyth they shall pay yt ayen.   Also fadyr, master Selenger hath comaundyd alle my ladys counsell that non of my ladyse tenantes shuld fysche yn your water, and that the tenantes be so warnyd.   Fadyr, and yt lyke yov, Umfrey Salman ys ded, and he hath a may chyd of x yere old to hys eyyr, the wyche ys ward unto your fadyrhod, and I trust to sesen yt unto the behofe of your fadyrhod, thov I tary a day or to the lengger.   And also, fadyr, Frynd kannat yt delyver me, but he seyth unto me that your fadyrhod shalle be plesyd, and that I shalle have alle maner of dutys with me, both the old and eke the nev : corte day shalle be at Ermyngtun on a Sunday on senyte, and I caste me to departe on the morrov after, with the grace of Jhesu : for erst I kannat be delyveryd the lond of the ward wych [1] dravyth to rent by yere xx marke : and I porpose fadyr to cum hom ward by Henbery, and so forth, as I dyd the laste tyme.   No more to your good fadyrhod at thys tyme : but I mekely beseche your good fadyrhod that thys my bylle may recomaund me unto my good modyr yn my most umbyl vyse, mekely besechyng my good modyr of hir dayly blessyng &c., mekely besechyng your fadyrhod in lyke vyse, and I mekely besechyng alle myty Jhesu to preserve your good fadyrhod and your [wyf, my] modyrs good modyrhod, amen.   I-wrytyn in Exeter the Thursday next afore seynt Jorgeys day.   My lady Arundell prayyth your fadyrhod to be good cosyn unto her yn suche maters as her servant shall move your fadyrhod of.

By your chyld Wylliam Stonor.

To my ryght reverent and worshypfull fadyr, my fadyr Stonor.

[1] wych, *om.* MS.

128. WILLIAM STONOR TO THOMAS STONOR

[? 1473]

The reference to the birth of "my suster Cotymore's" son shows that this is earlier, though probably not much earlier, than No. 136. John Cotysmore was a ward of Thomas Stonor and married one of his daughters, perhaps in 1470 (see No. 110). It would have been quite usual for him to have been thus married as a boy, so that the birth of his son might well be some years later. From *A.C.*, xlvi, 76.

My ryght reverent and wurschypfull fadyr, I recomaund me unto your good fadyrhod yn the most umbyll wyse that I kan or may, mekely besechyng your fadyrhod of your dayly blessyng: lykyth your fadyrhod to wyt that my modyr ys in good hele, and alle my brethern and susters, blessyd be alle myty Jhesu : and I beseche your good fadyrhod not to be dysplesyd with me for Feyrmers mater, for I never medyld odyrs wise but told Sawnder, that that dede that he shewyd me shulde be to the womans tytyl after my conseytt: and by my trowth, fadyr, that that ys feld was don ere I knowyt : but fadyr, there is nothyng caryd, nether shalle nat be with the grace of alle myty Jhesu, hom I mekely beseche to preserve your good fadyrhod, Amen.   I-wrytyn

By your chyld Wyllm. Stonor.

Also, fadyr, my Suster Cotymore ys delyveryd of a feyre sun, and both don welle, blessyd be Jhesu.

To my ryght reverent and wurschipful fadyr, my fadyr Stonore.

129. A BAILIFF AT BRIDPORT TO HIS MASTER, TOGETHER WITH AN AGREEMENT BETWEEN CRISTINE AND ROBERT BATTESCOMB

8 DEC., 1473

Ancient Correspondence, xlvi, 88, is a sheet of paper containing copies of three documents which do not appear to belong properly to the *Stonor Papers*.

The first is a copy of the Latin Letters of Presentation addressed on 20 July, 1473, by William Olyver and John Hille, bailiffs of the town of Bridport, to Richard Beauchamp, Bishop of Salisbury, on behalf of John Wikes, chaplain, for his admission to the Chantry of St. Katherine in the parish church of Bridport, in their presentation and now vacant through the resignation of John Lugge. The second is a letter written apparently by a bailiff to his master, of which there are two drafts written on the back of the paper; the date of this is 8 Dec., 1473. The third document consists of Memoranda written on the same side as the Letters of Presentation; they are probably of about the same date as the other two. These latter documents seem to have sufficient interest of their own to justify their inclusion.

Right reverent and my most Worschipfull Master, I recommaunde me to you: letyng you to understonde þat y hafe dylyvered to Thomas Baylegh of Brydeport iiij. li. v. s. for the quarter rent at Mis[somer] last passed by vertu of your letter þat ye sent to me by hym.

Notwithstondyng ye ·send me long before a letter by Nicholas your servant, þat he scholbe your generall reseyvour fro þat y come yn to your prebende, and for fawte of payment to distrayne &c.: the same Nicholas reseyved of me your Missomer quarter rent þe moryw apon þe Nat. of seynt John Bapt. before þe Vicar of Nytherby and oþer, so y ow you no money afore Cristismasse. Y pray your gode masterschip þat y may be kept harmles ayenst þe same Nicholas þat he distrayne me nat for þis money þat y dylyvered: and þat y may hafe very knowlych fro you to whom y schall dylyver your money: and y to be discharged. Also' ye send me word, and charged me by your letter þat y schold dylyver to Thomas Baylegh wode and tymber: y dar not do hit, nor not so moche to fille for to content ꞁ. Amylle is covenant, for þer be so many wayters and controllers; and y schold any thyng do, þey wold accuse you and me to þe Chapiter of Sarum; þer for y and wyff be right heve and sory and alwey schalbe unto tyme we mowe speke with you or som comfort fro you &c. Ye mos make rywhell for your Courtes to be holde. Scribeled &c. the day of Conception of our lady, aº E. iiijti xiijº

The earlier draft which was erased concluded :—

Also I hafe do certayn reparacions apon þe were of þe mille and oþer longyng to your reparacion. Y wote well ye woll alowe me þerof. Also ye send to me your letter þat y schold dylyver to Thomas Baylegh wode and tymber: y dare nat do hit, neyther to fylle ne sille þat ye gafe me in commaundment as moche as come to xls. to serve John Amylle: for þer beth so many wayters, yf y schold any thyng fille þey wold accuse you and me to þe Dene and Chapiter Sarum, which myȝth turne you and me to grete harme. Also ye send me in writyng that þer schuld no court be hold into your comyng oþer sendyng of your writyng to do hit, which is a grete grefe as well to you as to me : in lasse ye make another ordinaunce þerfor, your housyng of your tenentre wolbe lost.

On the other side are written the following Memoranda :—

Remembrance of covenants bytwyxt C. Battescomb and Rob. Battescomb.   First þat þe same Cristine hath grauntED to þe same Robt. all her part of her lond in Veriswatton, excepte as hit folwys, terme of hys lyffe, beryng þerfor yerly to þe same C. xlvjs. viijd. quarterly to be payed, in fawte of payment by a moneth arearige &c. : excep' the grete chamber with fre goyng therto, and easement of þe Parllour, Kechyn, bakhouse, buntyng hous, and a lytell appell hous over þe ovene, and esyment of þe stabel yf any frend of myne come to me, with a chamber for þem, and the pantery &c.   Item þe lytell orchard, reservyng hole to me with vj appel trees in þe grete orchard, with a lytell plat of hemp lond, and also suche ffuell as me nedeth : and he to repayre al maner tynges þat ought to be repayred as well in housyng as in clausure &c. : and also to nyw make a prevy to þe grete chamber for me, and also a lyte mywe to set in goos, capun, and chekyn and other &c.

In another hand :—

Y-spend for J. Danyell for wyne to þe Dene of Sarum xijd.

And y delyvered to Syr J. stockfisch xx, wherof he brouȝth me ayen and he for to wayte apon þe Dene of Sarum, and so he dyde vij dayes.

130. THOMAS GATE TO THOMAS STONOR

[*before* 1474]

Thomas Gate of Brutewel (i.e. Britwell, between Farnham and Hitcham), Bucks, *alias* of Wycombe, was escheator of the counties of Beds and Bucks before 1467 (*Cal. Pat. Rolls,* Edw. IV, ii, 390 ; cf. *Lists and Indexes,* xi, 268, P.R.O.).   A pedigree of Ramsey, ap. *Harley MS.,* 1533, f. 57, gives the descent of Thomas Ramsey from Richard Nernute.   According to this pedigree Nernute had a son Myles, whose daughter Isabel married Reginald Beauchamp ; the Beauchamp line of descent was Myles, Myles, John, Richard, Myles of Hicham, and Robert ; Robert's daughter Isabel married Thomas Ramsey, father of the Thomas Ramsey who married Isabel Hampden, half-sister of the first Thomas Stonor. The early part of this pedigree seems to be un-trustworthy. Miles de Beauchamp held Hucham or Hitcham at his death in 1336 (*Cal. Inq.*, viii, 149). He was probably the husband of the daughter of Richard Nernute (or Noirnute). His heir was his grandson Miles (son of his son Richard), who held Hucham in 1346 (*Feudal Aids*, i, 116). This Miles was probably the father of Robert de Beauchamp, who was great-grandfather of the Thomas Ramsey of 1474 and brother of Elizabeth, the ancestress of Thomas Gate. In 1382 Isabella (or Elizabeth) de Beauchamp held Hucham as heiress of Miles de Neirnut (*Cal. Pat. Rolls*, Richard II, ii, 193). Thomas Worley occurs as a servant of Edward IV in 1465 (*Cal. Pat. Rolls*, Edw. IV, i, 437). The date of this letter must be earlier than 1474 and later than 1460. From *A.C.*, xlvi, 52.

Right wurshipfull and my especiall good master, y recomaunde me unto you : prayng you hertly to shue me your favour after my deservynge, and not without cause resonable to be of oþer disposicion, as my verry trust is in you most syngulerly of all your blode and my knowlege. Howe be it ye and oþer wurshipful haven lete be moved ayenst me by Thomas Ramsey, your kynnesman and y his, wherof to me-werd he makith gret straungenese : y merveile why : our faders, of whos sowlez God have mercy, dyd nat so, for their moders weren cosyns germaynez descended of Sir Milys Beauchamp, knyght, late lorde of the manor of Hucham, litill Merlowe, Crowelton and Illesley, entailled to hym and his wif and to ther heires generall,[1] doughter to Sir Ric. Noirnute, knyght, donor of the seid entaile, which Milys had issu Robert Beau-champ, Bessayle of your kynnesman aforseid, and dame Elizabeth, my Bealaylez, maried to John du Brutewell, myn auncestor : the denyer of these premissez is oon of the causez of my writtyng to your mastership : blame me nat of this, for it is resonable a gentilman to know his pedegre and his possibilyte : seynt Poule foryete nat to write to the Romayns of what lynage he was descended, Ad Romanos xj⁰. Also I merveile of this unkyndnes of your seid kynnesman to me warde and my frends in seying, writtyng and doyng, and hath in me found no cause nor occa-cion, but alwey to my power tru lovyng and kynde, unto nowe late he wrote to me a letter of unkyndnes, y trowe in hast, and so it was answerd, wherof me repented. Howe be it myn entent was y wold nat have the taile aforseid lost ne foryetten by hym, for y have seyn it in his bandes and red it, as y can remember hym well : for what cause therfor our letterz of unkyndnes were made, and for that it pleassed hym to take partie with straungers as to his blode both ayenst me and my

---

[1] "entailled . . . generall" has been inserted.

allye Thomas Worley, a servant of the kynges, as for the right of my cosyn Kateryn his wif, havyng no resonable consideracion to my understandyng. Natherthelesse y shall abyde such direccion for my partie as shall plese you to ordeyne or awise betwen us most convenyent to leve and love in peas to the confort of our neyghbors and lovers, to God and our selfes gret pleasure, which lorde preserve you and yours. Written at Brutewell, the vth day of October in hast.

Your servaunt, Th. Gate.

To the right wurshipfull Thomas Stonor, Esquier, this be delivered in hast.

131. WILLIAM SWAN TO THOMAS STONOR

[before 1474]

The year is not later than 1473, and probably not many years earlier. There was a dispute between Stonor and Lord Cobham as to the Manor of Cliffe in 1472—see No. 121. In 1473 SS. Simon and Jude's Day—28th Oct. —was on a Thursday; this perhaps suggests that 1471 or 1472 were more likely dates. From *A.C.*, xlv., 79.

Ryght reverent and worshypfull mayster, I recommande me unto your mastershyp, hertyly desyryng to here of your welfare and of all yourys, the whiche y beseche God to continue: fforþermore y sent my man to Clyve yestyrday on an erande of myn, and þer hit was told him hov þat my lady of Cobham on Satyrday last sent hir men, and havyn fette awey my susterys corn and catell and stuff, all þat that she left in þe plase, and havyn broke up every dore and locke, and set hem wyde opyn for every thyng to go in, and also have fett aweye a cowe of herys, þat was with novyn: of oþer thyngs he herd noon. As y here I shall sende word. Also all þe tenauntes havyn left up here land, and wyll no lenger ocupye: of the whyche y shall do my part to helpe remedie hit after my power. Y wryte no more &c.: but y praye God kepe you and all yourys. Wrytyn at Southflete, on seint Simon daye and Jude in hast.

By your servaunt W. Swan.

Unto my worshypfull mayster, Thomas Stonore, be this bylle delyveryd.

132. THOMAS TALYOUR TO THOMAS STONOR

[*before* 1474]

From *A.C.*, xlvi, 80.

Most Reverent Wurschypfull Mayster, I recummande me unto your Maysterschyp, desyryng your prosperyte and helth, wych all myghthy Jhesu preserve to his plesur and your hertes ese.   Besekyng yow as I schall be your pore Bedman to have ʒevyn me lysens to have goyn bom to my cuntre to have spokyn with my ffader, sendyng for me under thys forme : yff y wolde have his blessyng or any thyng þat schulde be my forthurans þat I schulde speke with hym in all þe hast þat I kolde. Besekyng yow to have grantt me thys, and to have sende sum mone for my spendyng : and as long as I am from you I. schall serve after my terme, iff hit be plesur to your Maysterchyp &c.   Allmygthy Jhesu preserve yow.

Your pore Servaunt in that I kan or may Thomas Talyour.

Unto my most Reverent and Wurschypfull Mayster, Mayster Thomas Stonor, Esquier.

133. JEFFERAY DOYLY TO JOHN HANKOKE

[*before* 1474]

A Geoffrey Doyle of Dover, gentleman *alias* esquire, had a pardon on 11 June, 1463 (*Cal. Pat. Rolls*, Edw. IV, i, 267).   He may be the writer of this letter.   The Doylys held at one time the Manor of Pishill Napp.   The Stonors owned the manor of Pishill Venables from 1335 (see vol. i, p. xii). From *A.C.*, xlvi, 258.

Rygthe welebelovede, y grete you well : letynge you wett that I have solde the maner of Pussull unto my Cossyen Thomas Stonar : werffor y pray you to be at the lyvery of the state þat chall be delyverede to hym by the vertwe of the letteres of attornaye that y sende to you, and att suche tymes as my sayde Cossyen woll call on you, and that ʒe ffayll notte, as my very tryste is in you &c.

Jefferay Doyly.

Wreten in London on Sayent Peters Day.

To John Hankoke thes be taken.

134. N. PALMER TO [THOMAS] HAMPTON

[*before* 1474]

Though this is not strictly a Stonor letter, and is now detached from the Collection, it may probably have been sent to Master Stonor by Hampton, and so have formed part of the Stonor Papers. Hampton is Thomas Hampton of Kimble (cf. No. 236), and "master Stonner" is more likely to be Thomas than William. Thus the probable date is before 1474. The letter seems to have been written by a fellow-prisoner of Mistress Palmer. Mistress Palmer may be a relative of the Palmer referred to in No. 76, which was written by Hampton of Kimble. From *A.C.*, lx, 2.

Worshypfull and reverent Syr, I recommawnd me unto ʒow with all myn hart : doyng ʒow to undyrstond that the manne, þat shuld ffeche all my evydens that þat þe ffrerre spake to ʒow off, bathe ben herre thys xiiij days and weytyþe every day after ʒow and master Stonner. And bott ʒe com now he woll go hens and byd no lengger. And þer ffor y pray how þat (ʒe)[1] well be her in all hast possybyll, ffor but ʒe com now y can not have my evydens at the begynnyng off the next terme, ffor master Skott ys my good master and bad þat y schuld send ffor ʒow in all hast, and affter master Stonner, for Wellys woll be here at the begynnyng off the nexte terme to ffynysshe all maner matterres. And I pray ʒow that ʒe send a letter to master Stonner that he com in all hast by þe berrer her off. Y-wryʒt yn hast at þe fflett. And the wrytter her off comawnd hym on to ʒow, and he trustyþe to God, how be hyt þat (he)[1] ys in prisson to performe all Covenauntes þat he mad per n. p.

Per ʒowr Bedewoman N. Palmer.

To Master Hampton at Olde Stoke þys letter be delyvered.

135. WILLIAM HARLESTON TO THOMAS STONOR

[1474 *or earlier*]

As to Harleston, see No. 260, and for his nephew Sulyard, No. 276. Harleston's wife was Stonor's sister. The date cannot be later than 28 Jan. 1474. Neither letter nor signature are autograph. From *A.C.*, xlvi, 246.

[1] Omitted in MS.

My right trusty and well enprovyd Brothyr, y recommend me unto yow : desiryng to here of your well fare. The cause of my wrytyng unto yow at this tyme is for this cause, mervelyng me gretly þat ye send me nat my monay, for I have wretyn unto yow sondry tymys and I have nevyr non answer aȝeyn þerof ; wherfor y besech yow, good brothyr, þat ye will delyver the seid mony unto my neve Sulyard now at this terme, and he xal endente with yow therfor. And, good Brothyr, fayle me nat now in my gret necessyte, for y had nevyr so mych nede therof in my lyve ; for in good feyth, brothyr, I moste pay gret somme of mony now at this lenton tyme on our lady day : and þerfor I besech yow fayll me nat now, as ye wyll have eny good turne of me anothyr day. No more to yow at this tyme, but God have yow in his kepyng. Wretyn at Eye Abey the xxviij day of Janyver.

By your good enprovyd brothyr
Wyllm. Harleston.

To my right reverent and Wyrchypfull my good Brothyr Stoner in hast.

136. WILLIAM STONOR TO THOMAS STONOR

[? 6 FEBRUARY, 1474]

The most prominent Marmyon in Oxfordshire at this time is William, who was on the Commission of Peace from 1461 to Dec., 1473, but does not appear in the Commission of Feb., 1474 (*Cal. Pat. Rolls*, Edw. IV, i, 570 ; ii, 625). If, as is possible, William Marmyon is here referred to the date must be 1474. William Stonor's own age makes an earlier date than 1470 unlikely, and since in 1472, 2nd Feb. was on a Monday and in 1473 on a Tuesday, these years are less likely. From *A.C.*, xlvi, 277.

My ryght reverent and wurshypfull fadyr, I recomaund me unto your good fadyrhod in the most umbull vyse that I kan or may, mekely besechyng your fadyrhod of your dayly blessyng : lykyth your fadyrhod to wyt that my modyr ys in good hele, blessyede be alle myty Jhesu, my brethern and my susters and my nevue Cottysmore. I beseche your good fadyrhod that yt wylle plese yov to speke with the Abbot of Dorchester that I may have suche fe as Marmyun had with hym with every thyng acordyng as he had : for I trust thorov your good fadyrhod that I may have hyt. And I beseche your fadyrhod to wryte for me to the pryor of Wychyswyde for such fe as he had there : and I trust thorov your fadyrhcde to spede with hym : for I have sente unto hym, and he hath answeryd that he wyll do to the pleasyre of your fadyrhod what he kan do : for he seyth he knovyth your fadyrhod, but he knovyth not me. And I mekely beseche your fadyrhod to wryte to the pryor of Byssam : and I trust to spede ther in lyke wyse thorov the helpe of your gode fadyrhod with the grace of Jhesu, hom I mekely beseche to spede yov yn alle your maters, and to preserve your fadyrhod yn alle maner of weyys, Amen. I- wrytyn þat Stonore the Sunday nexte after Kandelmas day

By your chyld Wyllm. Stonor.

To my Ryght reverent and wurshipfull fadyr, my fadyr Stonor.

137. WILL OF THOMAS STONOR

1474

This is an imperfect draft or copy of the Will. The date must be later than 8 October, 1468, since Richard Drayton is dead. Apparently all Stonor's daughetrs were unmarried, so the date must be before the marriage of one of them to John Cottesmore (see Nos. 110 and 128). The date of that marriage was therefore probably not before 1470. The will may be compared with the Arbitrament betweer William Stonor and his mother, No. 157. See further vol. ii., p. 184. From *Ch. Misc.*, 37, ix, 22.

of Stonore. And also I wyll that the issues and profetes except wode   off my maneres of Henbury in Saltmerche with the appurtenauncis, Harnell, Dughton with the appurtenauncis, Burton and Cundecote with the appurtenauncis in the Counte of Glouc., Wattcombe with the appurtenauncis, with all other londes and tenementes with their appurtenauncis in the townes of Watlyngton, Cuxham, Standell, Clayer, Tame, Ricote and all other londes and tenementes I-called Tettesworthlond, Saddelereslond,. and Lyncolneslond in the pariche of Watlyngton, and the ij partes of the maner of Bryghtwell sumtyme Parkes maner, with all there appurtenauncis in the Counte of Oxford, Penyton Meysey with the appurtenauncis in the Counte of Shuthhampton, londes and tenementes in Redyng, Tylehurst, Benesheves, Burughfeld, Erle, Whytle, Shenefeld in the Counte of Barkeshyre, be receyved by the bandes of myne execcutours to the contentacion and payment of my dettes, and after my dettes payed the issues and profetes of the seyd maneres to be receyved by the seyd excecutours for the mariage of my doghters that is to sey for Jane CC. mark, Mare CC. mark, and Elizabeth CC. mark, and yf eny of them dye, as God defend, afore her maryage than the payment of her that is dede to sese.   Also hyf eny of my seyde doghters wulle be Relygius than I wull that she that so wull be have a C. markes and her habites accordyng.   And aftyr this done I wulle that my ffeffees make astate to William my sunne and heyre, or els stonde ffeffees to his use in maner as I shalle declare, in my Maner of Stonor.   And as for the advowsons that long to the maneres above seyde I wulle that William Stonore have the nomynacion of the chapileyn and he to be presentyd by the ffeffees.   Also I wulle that the issues and profetes of my maneres of Rotherfeld Pipard and Bluntis with their appurtenauncis be receyvyd of myne excecutours for the contentacion and payment of the det that I ove to my ffadyr Drayton excecutours, that is to seye yn iij obligacions vj.xx markes and every obligacion xl. markes, and ij obligacions of xl. li. eche of them in xx. li. : the Remenaunt of the seyde Maners over the payment to my ffadyr Drayton is excecutours be for the contentacion of my dettys : and aftyr my dettes payyd I wulle that my ffeffees of the seyd maner of Ritherfeld Pippard and Bluntes make astate of the seyd Ritherfeld Pippard and Bluntes with the avowson of the churche of Ritherfeld Pippard to Thomas my son and to his heyres of the masculine gender of his body lawfully begoten, and for defaute of suche issue remayne therof to William my son and his heyres and to the issu of hys body lawfully begoten, and for defaute of suche issue remayne ther to Edmond my son and to the issue of his body lawfully begoten, and for defaute of suche issue to the ryght heyres of me the seyd Thomas Stonore, with this that the seyd Thomas my son cleym not nor demaund as by the wey of mater of record eny lond in Cleve in the Counte of Kent.   Also I wulle that my ffeffees of my maneres of Mychell Court and Paynell Court in Burwardescote make astate to Edmond Stonore my son by dede indented of the seid Maneres of Mychell Court and Paynell Court in Burwardescote with the afowson of the churche there to hym and to hys heyres of masculine gender lawfully begoten, and for defaute of suche issu the seid Maneres with the afowson to William my son and heyr and to the issu of hys body lawfully begoten, and for defaute of suche issu to Thomas my son and to the issu of hys body lawfully begoten, and for defaute of suche issu to myn heyres.   Also I wyll that my ffeffees of my Maneres of Stonore with the appurtenauncis in the Counte of Oxon., Ermyngton in the Counte of Devonshyre with the afowson of the churche ther, the hundered of Ermyngton with all the appurtenauncis within the seyd shyre, the Maner of Horton with the Chauntery with all the appurtenauncis longing ther to, Mortemer place with the appurtenauncis, londes in Cleve in the Counte of Kent, the Mote at Westm. with all the londes that longeth ther to with all other londes and tenementes, rentes, services, medowes, lesues, and pastures in Westm. and in the paryche of Seynt James and in the Counte of Midd. &c.

138. [THE FUNERAL OF THOMAS STONOR]

[1474]

This Memorandum—*Ch. Misc.*, 37, iv, 9—was most probably drawn up for the funeral of the second Thomas Stonor, though there is no positive indication of the date. At this time Stonor was in Pyrton parish. In *Ancient Correspondence*, xlvi, 228, amongst several papers relating to the decease of Thomas Stonor there is a brief Memorandum of a similar kind :—

Md. to send for the cover with ornamentes of the Auter : and the herses to be hadde over. Itm. a blakke cloth for the house . . . and blakke. Itm. sug. cuppes . . . pottis.

From No. 157 we learn that the funeral of Thomas Stonor cost £74 2s. 5d.

In Pirton Churche.

First vj auters. Item, the hie autre with blakke ornamentes therto. Item, candelstikkes, sensers, hasens, silver therto. Item, rectores chore seutes of vestmentes blakke and white &c. Item, ornamentes for the herse and for the beriell, blakke cloth to the ground with a white cloth of gold. Item, a crosse with a fote on the herse, silver and gilt. Item, iiij tapers aboute the herse. Item, ij tapers aboute the beriell. Item, blakke hangyng aboute the chauncell and chirche. Item, lightis for the hie auter and odir auters beside. Item, syngyng wyne, syngyng brede.

Mete for pouer men at deriges. Item, after deriges brede and chese for the seid pouer men. Item for [prestes ?] and gentilmen, sew purtenaunces of lambis, and vele, rosted moton, ij chekyns in a dysch.

On the morow to brekkffastes. For prestes and odir honest men. Item calvis hedis and sode beeff.

At the dyner on the morow.

For pouer men : item, vmbils to potage, sode beeff, rosted wele in a dische to geder, and rosted porkke.

The ffirst course for prestes &c. First to potage, browes of capons or,[1] &c., capons, motons, ges,[2] custard. The second course. The second potage. Jussell, capons, lambe, pigge, vele, peiouns rosted, baken rabettes; ffesauntis, venison, gelie &c.[3] Item, vovtys.

Item, Spisis. Furst a pound of Saunders, a unce of saferon, iij li. Pepir, half a pound Clowes, half a pound Masis, a loff Sugre,[4] iij li. resons corauns, iij li. datys, half a pound gynger, j pound Synamon. Item, in turnsole, iiij. d. Item, in greynys j li. Item, in Almondis, iiij li.

Item, treen vessell for pouer men. Item, sittyng plasis for the pouer men. Item, peuter vessell for gentilmen. Item, a rome for them acordyng. Item, sponys of silver, salt selers of silver for the most worshipfull men &c. Item, borde clothis for gentilmen and pouermen. Item, Salt &c. Item, a convenient rome for the ij botries for gentilmen and pouermen. Item, a convenient place for the Kechyn. Item, Cokis. Item, Botilers. Item, a man to overse the sadde purveiaunce of the chirche. Item, a porter. Item, Odir servauntes to serve &c. Item, vessell for ale. Item, cuppis and bollis and pottis. Item, spitis, caundrens, pottes, rakkis, and odir necessaries for Cokis. Item, wode and colis.

Written in dorso are some further memoranda, scarcely legible ; amongst them are :—

It., chesis for pouer men and moer gees.

It., remembre milke, pulters, egges.

It., wyne for grene geese.

It., remembre pygges.

---

[1] Originally " frumenty or " was written; " frumenty " was struck out and " browes of capons " inserted.

[2] Originally " sode beeff and moton, pigge and vele ".

[3] Originally " venison, grene geesse &c."   [4] Originally " iiij li."

139. EXPENSES OF AN INQUISITION POST MORTEM

[? 1474]

This most probably relates to the Inquisition for the second Thomas Stonor in 1474. The names of Twenyo (Twynho) and Sir John Butteler point to the reign of Edward IV. See Nos. 215 and 294 (note). Nos. 229-232 in *Ancient Correspondence*, xlvi. contain the oaths of the Jurors in the Inquisitions held on that occasion in Kent and Hampshire together with the names of the Jurors. The Inquisitions were held in October, 1474 ; it was found that Thomas Stonor held no land in either county, that he died on 23rd April last, and that William, his son and heir, was aged 24 and more. The nine documents numbered *A.C.*, xlvi, 225 to 233, were found stitched together ; for the others see Nos. 138, 143, 144, 152. From *Ch. Misc.*, 37, iv, 10.

Of þe scher of Glowceter.

Item. yn primo receyvyd of þe fermer of Harnyll iiij. li. It., of þe fermer of Dowton, xxij. s. iiij. d. It. of Henbery, vij li. Summa, xij. li. iij. s. iiij. d. Glowseter schere. It., for þe writte ix. s. ij. d. It. y hafe payt to þe escheter, xl. s. It., to Syr John Butteler, xxvij. s. It., to Twenyo, xiij. s. iiij. d. It., for þe rewarde to þe Jur., xxij. s. viij. d. It., yn expences for Bryan and John Yoman, vj. s. v. d. It., yn reward for eschetters clerke, v. s. It., for þe bayleys retourne, xx. d. Et remaneth Summa vj. li. v. s. i. d.

Oxonford scher and Barkescher for þe ofyce.

It., for ij wryttes, xviij. s. iiij. d. It., to þe exchater, iij. li. x. s. It., to þe schreyve xxxiij. s. iiij. d. It., for þe questes and dyner, vj. s. viij. d. It., for hors mete, vij. d. ob. Summa, vj. li. viij. s. xj. d. ob.

140. HEIRLOOMS IN THE CHAPEL AND HOUSE AT STONOR

[1474 ?]

The reference to Mistress Jane suggests that this document was drawn up after the death of Thomas Stonor in 1474. The mother of Thomas Stonor (*d.* 1431) was also called Joan or Jane, but she had married again and died long before 1431, and is hardly likely to have been referred to as " Mastres Jane Stonor ". On the alabaster tables, see *English Mediæval Alabaster Work* (Society of Antiquaries, 1913), p. 35, and Plates V and XIX ; retables dealing with the Passion seem to have been characteristic of the period 1420 to 1460. The original is stained with dirt and in places difficult to decipher. From *Ch. Misc.*, 37, iv, 11.

Thys be the stuffe of þe chapelle of Stonor þe wyche must be left fro Eyur unto Eyur wythyn þe maner of Stonor.

First the vestments of purpulle velvet lynud with grene sarsnet wyth awbe, stole, vanone,[1] and amyce þerto. Item [another vestment] of Bawdkyn lynud wyth tawney sarsenett, ij awbs of Raynus, and ij amyces þerto to þe [vestment of] purpull velvet. Item, . . . carpets for the sacrament wyth a canape of reede tartarne. Item ij copus of purpulle velvett lynud wyth tawney sarsenet. Item j fygure of þe trynite of alebasture. Item j tabulle of alebasture þe storyus of þe passyon of owr lord, þe wych Tabulle Mastres Jane Stonor has yeft unto þe chapelle of Stonor wyth many oþer þynges þerto belongyng. Item, vj labells of purpulle velvet wyth crossus. Item j olde fruntelle of purpulle velvett losenchyd with gold. Item, j olde vestement of Blwe Bawdkyn, with awbe, stole, vanone, and amyce. Item j corperas of Rayns and þe case þerfor of whyte and blwe velvett y-browdred with j trayle of yvi, with j barr of reed velvett. Item, j crucifyxe of sylver y-gylt yn a tabelett of tree. Item, j chales of sylver with þe patent. Item, j peyr cruettes of sylver y-gylt. Item, j pelowe y-keverd wyth tartarne for þe sepulture. Item j seler and j testur of whyte lynone for þe sepulture. Item, j kerchew of umpull for þe sacurment. Item, ij narowe karchews of lawne for þe sepulture. Item iij cloþus for to kover þe ymagis yn lent. Item j steynud cloþe for þe rode wyth j crucyfixe and drops. Item, j hangyng for þe awter y-steynud with j crucyfixe, þe ymages of owre lady and seynt John. Item, ij curteyns and a noþer beneþe þe awter of þe same wrke wyth iij ymages. Item, j hangyng for þe chapelle of olde wurstyd. Item, ij awter cloþis for þe awter and j her. Item, j superaltare for þe awter. Item, j peyre canstyckes of laton for þe awter. Item, ij Masse Bokes, one of þem ys at Pyrton, ij portews, and j Grayle. Item, j halywhatur stocke of laten, wyth j spryngelle of þe same. Item, j sacryngbelle. Item j old fruntelle of purpulle sarsenett.

[*In dorso.*] Also þes byth þe standderdus of Stonore þat schalle abyde yn þe Manor of Stonore from Eyur unto Eyur.

---

[1] I.e. fanon, a maniple.

Furst j stondyng Cuppe of sylver y-gylt wyth a keveryng and ij ymages yn þe bottume. Item, þe macch of þe same cuppe, y-gylt wyth owte a ffote. Item, a grete Bolle of sylver with þe armys of Stonore and Kyrkeby yn þe bottume.

Also þis is þe stuffe þat ys lefte wyth yn þe manor of Stonore þat schalle rest yn the seyd Manor ffro Eyur unto Eyur. Furst yn the halle a peyer of coburnes left þer for standderdes. Item þe seyd halle y-hangyd wyth blacke saye. Item, þe lyttulle chamburr ennyxid unto þe parlowre, þe hangyng þer of ys palud cloþ purpulle and grene. Item, iij chamburs byth hangyd wyth palud saye, reede and grene, wyth a Bedde of þe same. Item, þe chambur at neþer ȝend of þe halle ys hangud wyth grene worstyd, and þe hangy[ng] for a Bedde of whyte. Item, to þe Bedde yn þe parlour chambur ij peyer of blankettes, a peyre of þe schetes, and a rede coverlet wyth grene chapelettes. Item, a ffedur Bedde, þe wych þe seyd Jane Stonor lefyth þer yn lone to þe seyd chambur. Item, a grene coverlett wyth pottes and Estrych ffeþurs, yn þe same chambur; a peyr of schetes, j peyr of blankettes, and a matres for þe truckle bedde yn þe same chambur. Item a awnedyrone for þe same chambur, and a tynone bason. Item, j ffyer forke for þe halle. Item, a chaffur of laten. Item, ij playn cheynes. Item, j turnyd cheyne, ij cusschyuns y-keverd wyth grey skyns. Item, ij cuschyns y-keverd wyth redde worstyd. Item, ij cuschyns of tappestri wurke wyth nottes. Item, yn þe Botry ys left j bason and a ewer of laten. Item, j bason and ewer of tynne. Item, a chaffyng dysche of laten. Item, v canustyrs of laten. Item, ij borde cloþes of dyaper. Item, a long borde cloþe and a schorte. Item, a coberde cloþe wyth iij towellys, and j trencher knyfe, and iij leþer pottes, and ij saltes of tynne. Item, yn þe Kechyn ij grete pottes, j medulle potte, j possenet, ij hangyng rackes for pottes, ij coterellys, ij rackes for to reste [them] upon, ij grete greders, ij olde pans, ij ffrying pannys, j stone morter, j brode grate, j grete broche, j medulle broche, j byrde broche, ij dressyng knyfus, j fflesshe axe, j wode axe, j flesshehoke, j skymmer of laton, a scale of tree . . . . . ., j garnysshe of pewter veselle. Item, yn þe Backehousse þer ys lefft j meshyng vatte, j ȝeel vatte, vij kevers, ix barells, j grete caudren, : trevett, ij bultyng pypes, j cabulle, j axe, j weegge of yron.

Item, v jackus, iij salettes, ij gleyfes, and a borespere.

141. W[ALTER] ELMES TO WILLIAM STONOR

[? 1474]

The dispute may have arisen through some question as to Cottesmore's affairs after the death of Thomas Stonor. The month-mind at Pyrton Church was no doubt in commemoration of Thomas Stonor. Strictly speaking, therefore the date should be in May, 1474; but "month-mynd" may possibly be used loosely for "twelvemonth-mind". "Katermayns" means Richard Quatermayns. From *A.C.*, xlvi, 94.

Jhesus Christoforus.

My rygth wurshupfull Cosyn, I recommaund me unto yow with all my herte : plesyth hit yow to undyrstond that I have spokyn with my cosyn Cottismore, and aftyre the effect that ye and I comynyd, that is to sey that ye and he to stond and abyde the direction of eny ij wurshupfull in your contre : to the wych he is agreable, so ye name soch as ye afore named, that is to sey Master Fowlere, M. Katermayns, M. Rede, and if hit plese yow to name M. Harcort : I suppose he wull be with yow at Pyrton.   And the mene seson that no rent be levyd till such direction be had by such as ye afore rehersyd me of : which shall cawse grete amyte and the sonner the better : I suppose yf hit wulle be at the month mynd, at wych seson I suppose some of the afore rehersyd will be ther : and I suppose ye shall fynd hym a good and kynd brothyr. No mor to yow at this tyme, but Almyghty God preserve you fro all adversyte.

W. Elmes.

To my ry3th wurshipful Cosyn, Wyllyam Stonor.

142. THOMAS STONOR TO HIS BROTHER, WILLIAM STONOR

[1474]

This letter seems to be written before William Stonor's first marriage, probably therefore in 1474 ; or if it refers to Elizabeth Ryche, Stonor's first wife, perhaps early in 1475. From *A.C.*, xlvi, 125.

Broder Stonar, after all dewe forme of recomendacion hadde, plesse hyt yow to hunderstonde þat I never longed so sore to speke with you as I do now, marvellyng grettly þat ye be longe hense, remembryng how grettely in consette ye stonde in London with a gentylwoman, and the grette labore þat hys made for here agynes you : and grettely hyt hys nossed and hasse bene tolde me with many persons þat but ye be ware she shall be take from you. I here muche and sey no thyng : befor the laste tyme þat ye where abowte suche a mater my speche and presens with you hurte you, and awelde you not : whérfore orlt ye to me a sewrte. I wolle in thys mater honsware no man, and yette I am grettely question with for you of divers persons thynkyng þat I shulde ken muche of your delyng : for I wolde not for my horsse and harnes and all my oder goode þat in thys mater ye toke a rebuke : wherefore remember you shortely for the pass[ion] of Gode, for syth I cam to London xx men haffe questioned with me in thys mater, iffe ye shall be at your comyng, wheche I beseche Jhesu be not longe, who have you ever in kepyng.

Your fethefull broder Th. S.

Thys letter be delyvered to my broder Willm. Stonar in hast.

143. HENRY DOGETT TO [? WILLIAM STONOR]

[? 1474]

There is nothing to show the date, but since it was found stitched to *A.C.*, xlvi, 227-33—see Nos. 138, 139, 144—it may probably be assigned to 1474. From *A.C.*, xlvi, 225.

Ryght Worshepfull maister, I recomaund me to yow with all my service. Plesith yow to wete that I have herkened to understond off your Audite : I woll attence at suche tyme as shall please yow ; and I pray yow that ye like to remembre the letter that my maister Courtnay sent to yow, that my maister Ric. Fowler may by yow undistond the tenor þerof, as my parfete trust is in yow. And I trust to your maister-shep that ye woll se þat I kept harmeles for the money that Ric. Pygot, my servaunt, delivered yow at Tacham &c. Syr, a bedde þat I pro[mysed] your maistershep shall be redy, and my servaunt, with Godes mercy, who ever preserve yow, my good maister.   Wreton at Aston in hast.

Your servaunt H. Dogett.

I am sumwhat crased, or elles I wold have seyn your maistershep.
No endorsement.

144. THOMAS RAMSEY TO [WILLIAM STONOR]

[12 NOVEMBER, 1474]

This was clearly written to William Stonor shortly before the next letter. It was presumably earlier than the bond of 9 May, 1475 (No. 150) and therefore we get 1474 for the year. Ramsey was first cousin to Thomas Stonor—see p. xix—and one of his executors. . From *A.C.*, xlvi, 227.

My worschipfull Cosyn, I recomaund me to yow : pleasith yow I have spoken with Harper like as ye willid me : and as for your mater, he seith hit is ferre in the law and wolbe sued to the utterest acordyng to your title : wherfor he desired that my Cosyn Hampden and Harry Doget may have knowlage that they do no thyng contrarie to your title.   I have taken Hanyngton vij nobils, and to Syr Ric. Harcourt xx marcs : the seid Syr Ric. desyryng to know the weys and days how he shalbe content of his C. li., beyng verray hasty therafter.   I seid to hym, whan he and ye mete ye wold appoynt with hym that shold please hym.   Sith I cam to towne I have be bothe at phisikke and surgery : I thank God of amendement : my purs therby gretly appeyrid.   I pray God be with yow in all your doynges.   At Lundon, the Saturday after Seynt Martyn day.

Thomas Ramsey.

No endorsement.

145. SIR RICHARD HARCOURT TO WILLIAM STONOR

[25 NOVEMBER, 1474]

Like the previous letter this must be earlier than No. 150.   St. Clement's Day is 23rd Nov., so the date of this letter is 25th Nov.   Richard Brodoke was in the service of Alice, Duchess of Suffolk (*Ancient Deeds*, A. 10956). Since the letter was written after the death of Thomas Stonor, and during the life of the Duchess, 1474 is the only possible date. As to Katherine Arundell see No. 125. The signature alone is autograph. From *A.C.*, xlvi, 99.

Cosyn Stonor, I recommaund me unto you : and for asmoch as ye have wreton unto me desiring me to yeve you ij dayes of payment for the C. li. which ye owne me, I marvell gretly that ye woll soe desire, considering what grete costes and charges that I am ate by divers menys, and also as yet can have no payment of dame Kateryn Arundell, and now most yeve grete good to the Kyng : wherfore I pray you to make purveance of l. li. at this time, for I may no lenger forbere : and that it may be delivered to Syr Richard Brodoke, Tresorer of my lady's howse, without any delay : and as for the oder l. li., I woll that the payment therof be respitet at this time : nerthelesse ye myght have made full payment to me of the seid C. li. of Estir and Michelmas rent of Cottismor is lyvelode, which hade be more reson that I hadde be content of them : it shuld a goo to the contentacion of my cosyn, your fader, dettes, on whos soule Jhesu have merci. And owr blessud lord have yow in his most mercifull keping. Wrete at London, on Fryday next after St. Clementes day,

Your lovyng Cosyn, R. Harcourt.

To the worshipful and right enterly welbeloved Cosyn, Willm. Stonor.

146. JOHN MATHEWE'S ACCOUNT

DEC., 1474—MAY, 1475

These accounts are written in the same hand on three long slips of paper. The receipts, which begin the first slip, are given in full ; of the expenses only such items as seemed to be of interest. From *Ch. Misc.*, 37, iv, 12-14.

Md. þat y John Mathewe receyved of my mastur Wyllm. Stonore on Sunday nexst afore Seynt Thomas day in þe xiiij yere of þe reigne of Kyng E. þe iiijth yn þe halle of Stonor v. s. Item, y receyvid of my mastur yn þe seyd yer on þe morne after seynt powles day, xl. s. It., y receyvid þe same tyme of þe parson of Thynchest [1] vj. s. viij. d. It.,

---

[1] ? Fingest, Bucks., near Stonor.

y receyvid of my master on goode freday in þe xv yere of þe reyngne of Kyng E. þe iiijth xl. s.   It., y receyvid of my mastur yn þe seyd yere on Wennsday nexst a fore st. Phylippus day and Jacobbe, v. li.   Summa recept. ix. li. xj. s. viij. d.

Expenses include : On seynt Thomas yeve for rede heryng, iiij. d. ; for þe stelyng of a axe for þe Kechynne, ij. d. ; on Crystemas Eve y toke Mylis for þe makyng of tapurs for yowr Chapell, iij. d. ; þe freday nexst afore seynt powles day yn eysturs, ij. d. ; þe same tyme for syngyng brede, ob.   Summa (*to St. Paul's Day*, 25 Jan., 1475) v. s. ix. d. ob.

On seynt powles day y payd to þe smyth of Assynden, xx. s. ; þe same day for beefe, xvij. d. ; þe same day to Harry Chowne for lath nayle and tyle pinnes for þe dofe howse (*amount missing*) ; on freday nexst afore Candelmas day for packenedull and threde, j. d. ; þe same day for þe caryage of a barelle of heryng and a cade, xj. d. ; to þe porters of Henley, ij. d. ; for holy candulle, ij. d. ; for ij lockes and ij nawgers, x. d. ; to Crystmas for heggyng, ij. d. ; to þe seyd Crystmas on seynt Mathewes for þe hegyng of þe rowde crofte, ij. d. ; Summa (*to Good Friday*, 24 March) xlvj. s. iij. d.

Payde to Byrde on goode fryday for his wages, vj. s. viij. d. ; to More, vj. s. x. d. ; to Joye, iij. s. vj. d. ; to Fryth, iij. s. ; to Cocke, ij. s. vj. d. ; to Thomas More, iij. s. iiij. d. ; to Berde of Falley for makyng of harnes, ij. s. ; for syngyng brede and wyne, iiij. d. ; on freday nexst after Estur for eysturs and elys, iiij. d. ; to a man of Netylbed for lyme, xij. d. Summa (*to Hoke Tuesday*, 4 April) xxxiij. s.

On Phylippes day and Jacobbe payed to Symmys for plowyng ij. s. ; for ale at Redyng feyr, iij. s. iiij. d. ; to Byrd for myssomer quarter wages, vj. s. viij. d. ; for vannyng unto þe throssars at þer furst comyng for þer labur, ij. s. ; on Wyttson yeve for egges, ij. d.   Summa (*to Whitsunday*, 14 May) iij. li. x. s.   Summa totalis, vij. li. xv. s. ob.   Summa debit. xxxvj. s. viij. d.

147. EXPENSES FOR SERVANTS

c. 1475

The reference to John Blakehall shows that the date cannot be later than 1475 or 1476. St. Leonard's Dav is 6th Nov. From *Ch. Misc.*, 37, iv, 16-17.

Jhesus. ·

(1) A remembrans made the morne after synt leonarde ys day, when þat my Master Stonor come to Master Marmyun for expensys off hys men þat ys to sey for Thomas a Wode, and Tayleboyse and Elysaundur Blakehall and othyr, vj. d., and for a chekyn for þe hawke, j. d.

It., for ij styltys for Roger, ij. d. It., for John Blakehall, xvj. s. viij. d. ; for Roger ys borde and hys bedde, xxj wekes, xv. s. ix. d. Also ffor a bay geldyng, vj. s. viij. d. It., for a chert and a breche for Roger, xj. d. It., for a peyr schone, v. d. Summa, xlj. s. vj. d.

Also for þe barbur to make clene hys hed, xv. d. For a cappe, iij. d. For makyng off hys gowne and hys doblet, xvj. d. For lynyn cloth to hys doblet, iiij. d. Summa, ij. s. viij. d. Kyrstemes.

Also the saterday at nyȝt and þe sonday yn þe mornyng to ffor, for expenses off my mayster and hys horse, iij. s. And for byrdys home with hym, j. d.

Also for expensys of Harre Parsone and John Blakehall þe monday after þe twelffe day when þey comyn (?) to Harpeden togeder, ffor her dyner, ij. d. Also ffor horse met, j. d. when ȝe wer with Marmyun. Also for þe geldyng, j. d., when þat John dydde schoy hym.

(2) Md. that Will Bordeney delyvered for Richard . . . a payr close hosyn of russet karyssey, price, xvj. d. It., by the commaundement off yow the parson off Thyngest fett for Alson Dell, ij ȝerde off medley russett, price, ij. s. viij. d. It., a payre off hossen for D . . . off russet keryssey the price, ij. s. It., a payr off hosse for the chyld off the stabull off russet karyssey, price, xvj. d. It., a ȝerde off blake russet karyssey to make Richert Baron a dublet, price, xiiij. d. It., a ȝerde and a halfe off tawney to make the seyd Richert Baron a gowne, the price off a ȝerde xviij. d., summa, ij. s. iij. d. It., a ȝerde off russet to make More sone a cote, xvj. d. It., a ȝerde et d. quart. for Harry Bakhall off dorrey, the price off a ȝerde xx. d., ij. s. j. d. It., a payre off hose off russett karyssey for Will. Coke off Northende, ij. s. iiij. d. It., for a payre off hose for Richert Baron, off russett karyssey, the price, xvj. d. It., for a ȝerde off blankked delyvered to John Swayn, the price, v. d. It., to John Blakhall, the yonger, a payre off hosyn off russet karyssey, the price, xviij. d. It., for v. ȝerdes off kendall for master Doley, price off a ȝerde iiij. d., summa xx. d. It., for iij ȝerdes off kendall and an halfe for Morres Escowrte, xiiij. d. It., for v ȝerdes off kendall for Thomas off Wode, xxv. d. It., for Harry Parsone iiij ȝerdes off kendall, and halfe, price off a ȝerde v. d., summa xxij. d. It., to Thomas Mathew a ȝerde off dorrey, h. and quart., price off the ȝerde xx. d.,

Summa, ij. s. j. d.   It., delyvered to Richert Baron a ȝerde and an halfe off brode russett, the price off a ȝerde xx. d., ij. s. vj. d.   It., a cote clothe off Cottohames russet ij. ȝerdes off narrowe clothe, the pris, xij. d.   It., a payre hosen off russet, the price, iij. d.   It., a payre off hose for Chowne off russett karessey delyverd to John Sonte, xvj. d.

148. ALICE, DUCHESS OF SUFFOLK TO WILLIAM STONOR

5 MARCH, [? 1475]

Perhaps the year is 1475 since Alice de la Pole died in May, 1475, and Thomas Stonor is presumably dead ; but No. 113 makes it possible that William Stonor might have been appealed to for help in his father's lifetime. Printed in *Excerpta Historica*, 354.   From *A.C.*, xlvi, 101.

Right trusty and entierly beloved ffrende we grete you well, desiryng and praying yow, all excuses layde apart, that incontinent this lettur seyne ye come to us to Ewelme for certayne grete causes concernyng our wele and pleasir, whiche at your comyng ye shall undrestond more pleynely : and theruppon ye to departe ayen at your pleasir, so that ye fayle not here ynne at this tyme as our parfait trust ys in you : and as in gretter case we woll be gladde to do for you, that knoweth our lorde, who have you ever yn gouvernaunce.   Wreten at Ewelme the v day of Marche · ȝ ·

Alyce Suffolk.

To our Right trusty and entierly beloved ffrende Wyllyam Stoner.

149. TWELVE·MONTH-MIND OF THOMAS STONOR

[APRIL, 1475]

From *Ch. Misc.*, 37, iv, 18.

It., delyveryd to my Cossyn Wyllyam Stonore for the Twelffe monythe ys mynd of my Cossyn, hys ffadyr, at Perton by Harry Kene.

Itm. in prymis j. large wrought Bordeclothe. It., ij schorte Wronge
Towellys.   It., ij longe Playne Towellys.   It., iij Tabyll clothys of
playn clothe that ys to say ij longe and j. shorte.   It., a Blewe clothe
of goold for the hersse.   It., ij Salte Sealers of Sylver, parcell gylt, of the
whyche j. ys coveryd.

150. BOND BY WILLIAM STONOR TO RICHARD FOWLER

9 MAY, 1475

Richard Fowler, besides being Chancellor of the Duchy of Lancaster, was
a prominent man in Oxfordshire.   He was a nephew of Richard Quatermayns
(see Nos. 93 and 116).   Leland states that Quatermayns had " a servant caullid
Thomas Fowler, his clerk, a toward felowe that after was Chauncelor of the
duchy of Lancastre," and was godfather to his son and " namid hym Richard
Quatermains Fowler " ; the second Richard Fowler was Quatermayns' heir,
but proved " a very onthrift and sold al his landes " (*Itinerary*, i, 115).   The
elder Richard Fowler was an arbitrator between William Stonor and his
mother (see No. 156) ; he may be the " Master Fowler " of Nos. 71 and 174,
and " Cousin Fowler " of Nos. 170 and 172.   Quatermayns calls Thomas
Stonor his cousin in No. 92.   Fowler died in Nov., 1477 (Will, P.C.C.,
32 Wattys).   For this Bond, which has been cancelled by cutting, see
Nos. 144 and 145.   From *Ch. Misc.*, 37, iv, 19.

Be it remembred that Willm. Stonore, squier, have borowed of
Richard Fowler, Chaunceller of the Duchie of Lancastre, the day of
making of thies presentes xxxiij. li. vj. s. viij. d. for contentacion and
paiement of part of my ffaders debtes due to Syr Richard Harecourt,
knight, the which xxxiij. li. vj. s. viij. d. I graunte and faithfully promitte
to content and pay ayein to the said Richard Fowler the xxij day of þis
present moneth of Maii.   To the which paiement truely to be made
I hynde me and myn beires by this present bill.   And for the more
seurtie of paiement of the said somme of xxxiij. li. vj. s. viij. d. I wol
and require all personnes being seased in the Manoirs, landes, and
tenementes that late were my said ffaders to his use and behove and
nowe to my use after my said ffaders debtes paied, that thay doo content
and paie to the said Richard Fowler, his execoutours, and assignes the
said xxxiij. li. vj. s. viij. d. afore that thay make eny astate or feoffement

to me or my beires of þe said Manoirs, landes and tenementes, or eny part therof.   In witnesse wherof to þis bill I have set my seall and sub-scribed the same with myn owne hand the ixth day of Maii the xvth yere of the Reign of King Edward the iiijth.   Wyllm. Stonore.

151. THOMAS STAUNTON OR STONOR TO WILLIAM STONOR

[? 1475]

Though the signature to this and to No. 153 is certainly Staunton, it seems clear that the writer was William Stonor's own brother Thomas; in its language it closely resembles No. 142.   Thomas seems to have been of a jocular turn, and there may be some private jest in the use of the name. No. 153 shows that the writer had lately been in trouble, and this letter may perhaps be a little earlier in date.   In both letters " Katermanes " is quoted for a proverbial saying ; possibly it may refer to Richard Quater-mayns—see Nos. 94 and 141.   The letter was printed in *Excerpta His-torica*, 356.   From *A.C.*, xlvi, 124.

If Rygth worchypfull broder and suster, after dew recomendacıon plesse yt you to hunderstonde þat I have a grett mysse of you thys terme. And I lett you whitte I am grette with the Kyng : for I com hoppe be preve sell, and grette nede I hadde now of you and of your counsell for ther ys no more a counsell agynes me but all the juges and serjaunttes and no man dare be with me for displessyng of them : so I am in wars cause then a theffe, for a theff in appell shall have counsell.   I purposse to se my suster or ye com out of Devysshirre, yf I may for the Flete, but sore I fere lest ye shall fynde me in the Flete when ye com out of Devysshyre.   God send never wras tyryngys to Englonde.   Fene I wolde here tell þat I shulde be sende fore to be your gossheppe, but yt hys tolde me ye stryke flatte.   More over suster, remembre my pauntener and my pursse, and þat I have the teune of them sende me shortely, apon pene þat woll fall there on : wat ys þat, trow ye, lossyn my lordesshyppe &c. : quod Katermanes, for the indyngnacion of a prince ys dethe.   No more to you at thys tyme, but Jhesu have you and yours ever in kepyng.   More over I entende to kepe my gresse tyme in þat countre, where fore I woll þat no man huntte tyll I have bene there ⁖

purve not for over many for my comyng, for I woll com but with Willm.,
my man, and my selfe : and se þat my wyne be kowged.

Your fethfull broder Th. Staunton.

To my well beloved broder Willm. ·Stonar thys letter be delyvered in
hast.

152. EDMUND STONOR TO HIS MOTHER AND BROTHER

18 JULY, [1475]

Compare for the date No. 153.   From *A.C.*, xlvi, 233.

Ryght reverent and wurschypfull modyr, y recommaund me unto
yow : desyryng to [here] of yowre welfare, the whyche almy3ty Gode
contynu long to hys plesyr and yowr hertes desyre.   Yef hyt plese yow
to wytt at the makyng off thys letter I was in god hell, and all my men.
No mor to yow at this tyme, but the trinyte have yow in hys kepynge.
And I pray yow let me be recomaundyd to my [sister] yowr wyff.
Wryttyn at Cales the xviij day of July, the day of the departyng of the
Kyng and the duk of Burgayn, my lord and all the oste in to Fraunce-
warde.

Yowr brothyr Edmund Stonor.

153. THOMAS STAUNTON OR STONOR TO WILLIAM STONOR

19 JULY, [1475]

Like the previous letter this is written from France during the expedition
of 1475.   For the curious signature see the note to No. 151.   This letter
shows that William Stonor must have married Elizabeth Ryche in the
summer of 1475 ; her first husband died before 1st July of that year (perhaps
in August, 1474, see No. 168 and p. xxvii above), though his will was not
proved till 4 October, 1475.   From *A.C.*, xlvi, 113.

Ryght reverent and worchypfull broder, with as many hartely re-
comaundacions as may be I recommande me to you, dirsiryng spessially

to here of your wellfare, and of my suster your wyffe also, to whom I pray
you þat I may be recommendet to : and yf hyt woll like you to here of
the wellfare of my broder Edmonde Stonor and of myne, at the makyng
of this letter whe where in good helth and mery, thankyd be Jhesu, and
to say þat Edmonde Stonor parte shall be my parte as and Willm.
Stonor where here.   I putte you out of dowte hyt shall : and more yettes
no man of me in the worde : and I on certen you he shall whante no
thyng þat I on eny forme may do for hym.   My brother Edmonde
tolde me þat my suster, your wyffe, sende a man to Cales, and þat at
your command shulde have speken with me, and a delyvered me a
token : certenly ther cam non suche to me, and þat I was rygth sory
fore.   Evermore, brother, I thankke you for the luffe þat ye sewde to
my sole whan ye harde of my distres, as well as ye have sewde to my
body afore tyme and at all tymes, whiche lise not ne may . . . ¹ esyryng
and quite, but God kennes þat, and my powre, where to my wylle I
shulde as largely quite your kyndenes and gentilnes as ever dud eny
gentlyman to armes : ye gette no thyng of me but my hole harte with
all my powre.   And syr, I thankke you for your good consell, and
certenly I thynkke to do ther after : but ye may thankke my suster,
your wyfe, þat ye be of so gode disposission to avertes and avyse me to
leve all foly, for þat comys of the holy sacrament of wedlokke, wheche
I pray Jhesu sende me sone to after I come home : for I fere me, þat,
tyll þat tyme þat þat youkke of wedlokke ly in my nekke as hyt dose
now in yours, þat youth shall rene in me as hyt has done in you afore
tyme ꞉ I have dispysed þat order afore tyme, and þat repentes me, for
God have ponyssed me sore there fore.   The dewke of Burgon cam to
Cales to the kyng the xiiij day of Julii and departed the xviij day, and
the kyng also, in to France warde.   I suppose the kyng wyll go the
next way to Pares.   The kyng wyll muster all hys host at Fauconbrygge ²
xxx myle out of Cales the morne next after seynt Margarett day : ³ and
yf the frenchemen wyll do us þe day, hyt shall not be longe or whe mete.
They be mony in nomber.   They wryte on there speres : "yf I hytte
the, sheryfe the, yf I mysse the, blysse the " : thesse bene parles wordes.
On of them þat so wrote was stryken to the harte with a narow at Abvyle :
and he nede blyssed hym and yitte shrowffe hym.   I trust mo of them
shall be so sarvedde in hast.   I thankke God I am strynger then ever
I was, for all my coruppud blode hys gonne.   And I have new he hys
now out of preson þat stroke me, and hasse payde for all my costes and

---

¹ The MS. is defective.   ² Fauquembergue.   ³ 21st July.

charges syth I was hurte, and hys bonden to abyde my lordes rewle as
for the offence þat he hasse done me : but I purposse to se England or
I hende with hym.   And, broder, ever as eny comys betwene, ye shall
have worde.   No more at thys tyme, but the holy gost have you yn
kepyng.   Wrytten at Genes [1] the xix[th] day of Julii.   And fare well my
none broder, for be that next letter ye shall here oder tyrynges, Jhesu
be howr goode spede.   And ever fare well my none broder &c., quod
Katermane.

Your broder Th. Staunton.

Thys letter be delyvered to my brother Wyllm. Stonor in haste.

154. WILLIAM STRACCHELEGH TO [? WILLIAM STONOR]

Oct., [? 1475]

In the absence of any endorsement it is impossible to be certain whether
this was addressed to Thomas or to William Stonor.   But the reference to
John Fortescue the younger (Sir John Fortescue of Punsborne, who was a son
of the elder Richard Fortescue, and died in 1500) suggests a late date.
Either 1475, when St. Luke's Day was on a Wednesday, or 1476, when it was
on a Friday, are possible.   These dates fit with the mention of Stracchelegh
in No. 279.   But the letter might be as early as 1469, in which case it would
be addressed to Thomas Stonor.   From *A.C.*, xlvi, 266.[1]

Ryt Worschupful and my speciall gode Master, y recomownde me
unto yowre god masterchyppe : fyrdermore, yf hyt plese yowre masterchyppe, ye grontyd j tenement yn Keyaton wyt the purtenans to Willm.
Mugge for duryng the tender age of John Ley : hyt ys so þat John
Fortescu, the yownger, toke j close of the sayde tenement of the father of
the sayde cylde for ij yere, the wyche ij yere byt past at Michelmas last
was, and layd a downe hys mony affore wytyn pryse of the valu, and
now he wyll hold hyt lengger agaynst the pore man ys wyll, þe wyche
pore man com yn by the grawnte of yowre masterchyp, payyng to yow
myche mony : and yowre masterchyp muste warent hym agaynst al
men.   Y-wryte at Ermyngton te Tuysday next afore the fest of Sci.
Luke þe evangelyst.

Yowre servent Willm. Stracchelegh.

No endorsement.

[1] Guisnes.

155. EDMUND STONOR TO [WILLIAM STONOR]

28 OCTOBER, [c. 1475]

In the official Index it seems to be assumed that this and the next letter were written by Edmund Stonor (d. 1382). But they clearly date from the latter part of the fifteenth century, and the writing resembles that of No. 152. Both were no doubt written to William Stonor by his younger brother Edmund. The date of this letter cannot be fixed, but either 1474 or 1475 are suitable years. On 25 October, 1476, William Stonor was at Stonor (see No. 173); so that year is unlikely. From *A.C.*, xlvi, 7.

Right reverent and wurshypfull Brothyr, I recomawnd me unto yowe, good Brothyrhod, desyryng to here of yowre wellfare, the whych Almyg3ty God contynue long to hys plesyr and yowre bertys desyr : doyng yow to wyt y have spokyn with þe parson of Penyngton of the matyr þat I have spokyn to yow off, and the parson hath told me that hyt was Perkyns dowtter : and Perkyns seythe þat he cowd aweyll me in my lond x. mark a yer.   But I undyrstond nat þat he wull depart fro hony lond with here, but with mony, and what þat ys the parson of Penyngton can not tell.   But, syr, yff hyt wold plesse yow to speke with Perkyns and awys whethyr he wull geve hys dowttyr hys part of Snowys well at Borowyscot to her and to her eyrys, I wold with the glader wyll dele with hym : and in that that he seyth þat he cowd aveyll me in my lond so grett money by yer, I shall beseche yow to speke to hym in what maner of weys : and y beseche yow to be my good Brothyr in any weys, as I have fownd yow herafore tymes.   No more to your good Brothyrhod at thys tyme but the Trinite have yow in hys kepyng.   Wrettyn at Stonor on seynt Symon hys day and Jud.   And I undyrstond Perkyns ys at London.

                                                                        S

By your brothyr, Edmund rot.[1]

                                                                        n

To my ryght worschypfull Brothyr Stonor be thys delyveryd.

[1] In this monogram the lower part of the S forms the o, and Stonor is read by beginning at the top and then to the right, the centre coming in after t and n.

156. EDMUND STONOR TO [WILLIAM STONOR]

[? 1475]

See the note prefixed to the last letter. This letter must be earlier than No. 181, since John Blakall is alive. It is not therefore likely to be much later than No. 155. The right-hand margin of the letter is defaced, and some words have been supplied conjecturally in brackets. Pishill is the next village to Stonor on the north-west. From *A.C.*, xlvi, 8.

My rygth wurschypfull Brothyr, I recommaund me unto yow, desyryng to her off your wellfare, the qwyhych almyghty [Jhesu] contynw doyng yow to wytt that John Blakall browtt to Stonor a dyker for to make yowr dykes in . . . feld betwen the hy way and the ew tre : and John Mathew and I wolde a mad a bargeyn with hym but we [cowd] nott styll there on, necyr we wyst nott how ye wold have hytt, whedyr ye wold have hytt sengyll dycge or [dobyll] dydge, and therffor we mad no bargeyn with hym : but I askyd hym how he wold do a perdge of sempyll dydge, and for . . d. he wold a don hytt a dobyll, sett hym with whit thorn, and a mad the dydge a yerd deppe : and yff hytt wold plesse yow to [send] word to John or to me whedyr ye wold have hytt dobyll dydge or senkyll, and what ye wull geve for a perdge we [wull] send for hym, and yff we can acord off the prys he schall still awayt and begyne. And also brothyr, wher ye speke to B . . es carpenter so to make yowr myll hows, he sayeth he can nott mak hytt but he mak hytt new : but Wyllyam Ale . . wyk [sayeth] that [he] with thyn lytyll space wyll mak ye þat hows to stand ther xx yere, and okapy but lytyll new tymbyre : and we thy[nk] hyt wer þe lestt schardge to yow so, thane to mak a new hows. But I beseche yow brothyr latt not yowr carpenter know þat I send yow thys now. No more to yow brothyr at thys tyme, but the trinyte have yow in hys kepynge. And ye schuld have a Monday next comyng a xl plowys in Pyssyll felde.

S

Your brothyr Edmund rot.

n

No endorsement.

157. AN ARBITRATION BETWEEN WILLIAM STONOR AND HIS MOTHER

28 Nov., 1475

After the death of Thomas Stonor, his executors, Jane Stonor, Thomas Hampden and Thomas Ramsey, by deed indented granted to William Stonor "all thing which to tham shuld apperteigne as executours," and William Stonor took upon him the charge of performing the will "demandyng as well the rentes of diverse landes and tenementes, as diverse goodes, catalles and dueties, which perteigned to his said ffader". Controversies and variances having grown between Jane Stonor and her son, the matters in dispute were submitted to Richard Fowler, Humphrey Forster, and William Danvers, who gave their award on 28 Nov., 1475. The document is much mutilated, and a great part of the statement of claim by William Stonor is missing. After reciting the circumstances under which the dispute had arisen, and stating the claims made by the two parties, the arbitrators gave their award in the terms printed below. This contains all that is of real interest save for those points added in footnotes. From *Ch. Misc.*, 37, vi.

Of all the which controversies variances and demaundes, and of all oþer matieres dependyng betwix the said parties, the same parties have compromitted tham self to abide the arbitrement of and upon þe premisses; the surmises and allegeances of both the said parties by longe and ripe deliberacion herde and understond by thassent and aggreement of bothe the same parties, [we] arbitre, ordeigne, and deme þerupon in maner and forme folowing: that is to wite that the said William shall satisfie to his said Moder of the somme underwritten, that is to sey of þe somme of lxxiiij. li. ij. s. v. d. by her expended for expences and costes had aboute the burieng and enterement of his said ffader: and of þe somme of xl. s. by her paied for þe probate of þe said testament: and of the somme of xxxiij. s. by her paied to Robert Fuller for þe debtes of his said ffader : and of the summe of v marcs by her paied for thexpenses of her said cooexecutours : and that also the said William shall suffre his said Moder to have þe ward and mariage of John Gatton above rehersed,[1] and all oþer landes in þe which the same Johane had jointe astate with her said husbande for terme of her liff, which astate the same William shall conferme to his said Moder for terme of her liff

---

[1] Jane Stonor claimed this wardship "wherof her said husband was possessed".

oonly : [1] and that also the said William shall fynde sufficient seurtie to
his said Moder and her coexecutors to performe the last wille of his
said ffader : and as to thembloyment above rehersed and expenses of
þe said William and his servauntes and also for thexpenses and wages
of servauntes and husbandrie aforesaid, and also all maner of debtes
due to þe said Thomas claymed by the said Johane, We arbitre, ordeyne,
and deme that for asmuche as after the decease of þe said Thomas the
said Johane and her servauntes, and þe said William, his brethren, and
servauntes, and the said servauntes in husbandrie have expended of þe
greynes, catalles, and stuff of houshold of þe said Thomas Stonour to
her not bequested nor yeven, therfore the said William shall have the
said embloyment and debtes towardes the performyng of þe wille of his
said ffader, and þe said William shall also bee discharged ayenst his said
Moder of all þe said expenses : [2] and furthermore we arbitre, ordeigne,
and deme that the said William of þe sommes above rehersed, awarded
to bee paid to his said Moder, shall deducte in his own bandes and
þerof abate þe sommes underwriten, that is to wite the somme of
xlvj. s. viij. d. of þe price cf wolle of cxl. schepe by þe said Johane soo
sold as afore ys seyde,[3] also the somme of vj. li. by her received of thissues
of þe Maner of Ryderfeld Pypperd over C. s. of þe same issues by
her receaved . . . Dorchestre : also the somme of iiij. li. x. s. v. d. by
her received of þissues of þe Manor [of] Boroughescote : also of þe
somme of iiij. li. x. s. by her received of þissues of Burt[on and]
Condycote : also of þe somme of x. li. vj. s. viij. d. by her received
of thissues of P[enyton] Meysy : all the which issues were due to her
said husband and paiable at þe fest [of the] Annunciacion of our lady

---

[1] She also claimed : " to have for terme of her lyfe, by the wylle of her seyd
husband, certain lande purchased by her said husbande in Horton to þe yerely value
of xx. s., also to have seurtie of þe said William for þe full performyng of þe last
wille of his said ffader ".   See Thomas Stonor's Will, No. 137.

[2] Jane Stonor claimed: " to be satisfied for thexpenses of þe said William
Stonore and of his servauntes at diverses tymes coming to þe said Johane, and for
thexpenses and wages of servauntes of husbandrie at Stonor payd by her sethen
the decesse of her seyd husband : also to have the embloyment of þe lande of her
said husband sowen the tyme of his deceasse ".   William's claim included allowance
" for greynes and catalles expended by þe said Johane after þe deceasse of her said
husband ".

[3] William Stonor claimed : " to be satisfied of xlvj. s. viij. d. of þe price of the
wolle of cxl. shepe, late of þe said Thomas Stonor, his ffader, by þe said Johane
sold : also of þe somme of . . . by þe said Johane received of thissues of þe . . .
tenementes underwriten ".   The claim is very imperfect, and only the item " of
þe Manoir of Ryderfeld Pyperd xj. li. " now appears.

last passed before his deceasse out of þe said Manors in þe which the said Jobane had noo jointe astate: also the said William shall deducte in his owne bandes the somme of x. marcs by þe said Jobane received of arrerages due to her said husband at þe ffest of Michelmas last passed before his deceasse : and as to þe somme of xxxviij. li. iij. s. iiij. d. by þe said Johane received of thissues of oþer Manoirs paiable at þe same ffest of Annunciacion the said William shall noo thing therof deducte, but þe same Johane shall have and retaign to her owne use the said somme of xxxviij. li. iij. s. iiij. d. for asmuch as in þe said Manoirs of þe which the said somme was received the said Johane had jointe astate with her said husband: also the same Jobane before the ffest of Cristmas next comyng shall delivere to þe said William the basen, ewer, and two pottes of silver above rehersed : [1] also the said Jobane shall have thoccupacion of þe Sawter [2] above rehersed during her liff, and after deceasse shall leve the same Sawter to þe said William Stonore to thuse of þe Chapell in þe Manoir of Stonore forevermore : also before the said ffest of Ester the said Jobane shall deliver to þe said William the blak boke,[3] and the obligacion of Makeney [4] above rehersed, and fynde sufficient seurtie to þe same William that the said Jobane and her said coexecutours shall mainteigne all maner of accions to bee taken by thadvyse of þe said William for any matere touching the testament of þe said Thomas.[5]   Also we arbitre, ordeigne and deme that eiþer of þe said parties be quite and discharged ayenst other of all oþer matieres dependyng betwene theym before the day of þis present arbitrement. In witnesse wherof as well the said parties as we þe said arbitrours to every part of þis writing endented have set oure seale the xxviij day of Novemb. the xv[th] yere of the regne of Kyng Edward the iiij[th].

[1] This part of William's claim is missing.
[2] William claimed: "a sawter now in þe kepyng of þe said Johane, perteignyng to þe Chapell of Stonore".
[3] "A blak boke conteigning thaccomptes and debtes due to þe said Thomas Stonor."
[4] "An obligacion of Makeney of þe somme of xl. li. made to the said Thomas, wherof xx. li. is yet due." As to this see note on No. 190.
[5] As claimed by William.

158. JANE STONOR TO WILLIAM STONOR

[? 1475]

Probably written soon after William Stonor succeeded his father. As he is married, the date cannot be earlier than the summer of 1475. It may perhaps refer to Penton Mewsey (see Nos. 137 and 301). From *A.C.*, xlvi, 122.

Sone, I send you Goddys blessyng and myne. I understonde by my tenantys and yourys that Maystyr Lewes John desyryth for to haye a letter fro you for to undyrstonde your maystyrschype and youre favor towarde your seyde tenants and myne. Wherefore I pray you to do aftyr hys desyre yn supportyng your ryght, and I woll do to the power that God hath sende un to me my parte wyth the grace of God, whome I beseche to be youre gyde, and that thys sympyll byll may recommaunde me un to my worshupfull and goode dowchtyr your wyfe.

By your pore Moder Jane Stoner.

No endorsement.

ADDENDA

p. xi. Robert de Stonor was canon of Wells from 1343-44 till his death in 1381-82 (*MSS. Dean and Chapter of Wells*, ii, 9, 17, Royal Hist. MSS. Comm.).

p. 88. The Manor of Gusyche, Dorset, was part of the possessions of the Hospital of God's House at Southampton, which was in the patronage of Queen's College, Oxford—not of All Souls College as stated in the Writ (*Monasticon*, vi 675).

END OF VOL. I.

ABERDEEN : THE UNIVERSITY PRESS.

Lightning Source UK Ltd.
Milton Keynes UK
UKOW01f0939180717
305535UK00001B/41/P